Off Belay: A Last Great Adventure

Off Belay: A Last Great Adventure

Jamie Shumway with
Renée K. Nicholson

Acknowledgement

JAMIE ACCOMPLISHED HIS GOAL OF creating this memoir thanks to the many hours that Candice Elliott and Renée Nicholson spent with him capturing and then reworking his stories. He could not have survived as long and as well as he did without the love and support showered upon him by them, and by many others. Family and friends, in Morgantown or far away, frequently checked in to see how all three of us were managing. Help came in many forms – including visits in person or by phone, meals shared with us, and friends who stayed with Jamie when we couldn't be at home. We also know that Jamie's exposure through colleagues and friends to mindfulness meditation, the three principles, and other guides for staying in the present served him well. All of us could take a lesson from him in that regard. We will not even begin to try to list the names of everyone who contributed to our family as Jamie's ALS progressed. The list is surely a long one, and it would be a challenge not to overlook even the slightest contribution because each made a difference to us in its own way. We truly are grateful to everyone who helped us maintain Jamie's life at home throughout his decline while he worked on this memoir; Jamie was grateful, too. A Swedish proverb says that friendship doubles our joy and divides our grief. The community that supported our family demonstrated the truth of that simple statement.

--Betsy Pyle and Wesley Shumway

Table of Contents

Foreword

by Betsy Pyle

WHILE HE MAY NOT HAVE thought of himself as a writer, Jamie was definitely a storyteller. He loved to recount adventures and be the center of attention—not in a negative way, but because he liked to share his experiences and entertain others. Many of the stories in this book are part of my memory, too: river adventures, international adventures, family adventures. So many experiences that we shared in our thirty-one years together might have been lost eventually if Jamie hadn't had the brilliant idea to capture the stories contained in this book. Telling these stories became his primary focus; he wanted to get them down and finish this project before he was finished. He knew that ALS would end his life prematurely and that so many dreams we had for our future would never be fulfilled. There was the trip to Patagonia that we'd never take and the plans to be campground hosts in different national parks during our senior years that we had talked about, half-jokingly, half-seriously. I tried to point out the bright side: he had lived an adventurous and fulfilling life all along, rather than waiting to pack it all into the years following retirement from his professional career. So he devised a plan, which first became an outline, and then eventually this book, in which he looked back over his life and shared stories that stood out in his memory. The memories were spurred on by the simultaneous venture of trying to digitally scan the thousands of two-by-two color transparencies, or "slides," that both of us had been taking for decades. Reviewing those pictures prompted many stories to be told.

They say that it takes a village to raise a child, and, in some cases, we learned, to write a book. When Jamie began to work on the outline, his hands still worked, so he could type on his own. But his ALS progressed to the point where he couldn't continue. He tried dictation software, but his voice was weak and inconsistent, so the software didn't do a good job recognizing and capturing his speech. A longtime friend in town suggested that she could pose questions to him based on his outline, record them on a laptop, and then send the audio files to a transcription service. Candice Elliott came two mornings a week to work with Jamie, and several other friends and family members took their turns at posing questions that related to particular adventures of interest to them. This initial strategy yielded about five hundred pages of transcripts. But in that form, Jamie wondered, who would want to read his tales of adventure? He needed to find someone who could help him craft the transcripts into stories. Luckily for us, one of his doctors, Josh Dower, introduced us to Renée Nicholson. Renée taught at the university and was willing to help. She began to work with Jamie and turn the transcripts into narrative paragraphs. They worked extremely well together, as you will see when you begin to read the following chapters.

I really didn't participate in the work leading to this book until very late in the process, when I offered to both proofread and fact-check. A few times, Renée and Jamie asked me to come and sit with them to make sure they captured a story accurately, but most of the time, I simply excused myself and let them collaborate. I either used the time to accomplish any number of tasks on my to-do list or to collapse in a chair and close my eyes. Let it be said that the work of a caregiver is never really done. I wore so many different hats that I often surprised myself in the ability to keep our life rolling along while constantly adapting to "the new normal" as Jamie's abilities declined with the progression of his ALS. I was simultaneously wife, mother, cook, shopper, laundress, nurse, pharmacist, household financial manager, chief scheduler, and chauffeur, among other things. Our son moved home to be able to help, and we did have some outside caregivers, but I remained the primary caregiver. I simply didn't have time to take on another role – Jamie's chief assistant to help him write this book – even though I tried to help him in every way possible as we navigated the course of his disease together.

This disease challenged Jamie and everyone who knew and loved him. It was hard for all of us to watch his body slowly grinding to a halt. But the determination he mustered to keep going for as long as he could inspired us all. He completed an entire draft of the manuscript and began to plan publication strategies with Renée before his body quit. Along with our son, Wesley, Renée and I had promised Jamie that we would see the book through to completion so that his stories would be shared with his family, friends, and others who also had interests in travel and adventure and in how to live purposefully when challenged with incurable diseases. Jamie was an educator in his professional career and in his personal life as well. He loved to share his knowledge with others—whether the subject was problem-based learning in the School of Medicine or white-water kayaking on a West Virginia river. This book is a lasting gift from Jamie to all of us. His legacy as an educator, an environmental activist, and an inspiring human being shows us that there's a silver lining in every cloud if we look for it with determination.

Prologue

by Renée Nicholson

WHEN I FIRST MET JAMIE, he entered the room in a highly mechanized wheelchair that he operated with a joystick positioned near his chin and manipulated by movements of his head and mouth. He could move forward and backward in the chair, and he could position the seat so that he was tilted, raised, lowered, or moved more upright. Later, as I got to know him, I teased him about his racing driver-like abilities to maneuver his chair. When I first met him, his frame was gaunt and still, and his blue eyes twinkled with life from behind the lenses of his glasses. His voice lacked full breath, and he spoke in a loud whisper.

He wanted to write a memoir.

Although I write, and I've published, I've never done this kind of work before. It was unfamiliar and unknown territory, and I had no idea if I could be successful in helping Jamie. What he gave me was a challenge, and I have to admit, I love a challenge.

First, I read nearly five hundred pages of transcripts that Jamie had previously produced with the help of friends and family, which are integrated with a forty-page outline that Jamie created at the outset of his memoir idea. It's an intense document; the first forty-four pages are mostly ancestry and family history, with just a bit of Jamie's boyhood interspersed. He has captured so much of his life, and his life teems with material for stories.

Some writers come to the page writing about things outside themselves, but I came to writing by pulling from my own experience, rarely stepping outside myself for material. So Jamie's project quickly presented the challenge of getting out of my own head and my own ideas, and jumping headlong into the pages of his transcripts to understand and start to internalize his memories, his stories, and his way of telling them. Even when a writer writes about things outside herself, there's the writing persona that she crafts. But, to help Jamie accomplish what he wanted, my first and ongoing task was to figure out how to get my own ego out of the way. I had to learn things from Jamie's perspective—the words he would use, the sayings that are his, the ways in which he thought—and to scalpel out the voice that is my writing voice.

This is not to say that I didn't use the things I've learned about writing. In fact, I had to use all the things in my bag of writing tricks—but not in the traditional way. So my first task was to start the book with a clear sense of Jamie's voice, which meant that the pages of ancestry and family history would have to be reworked so that we could firmly establish Jamie's persona on the page from the get-go. We talked about this, and Jamie took a chance on my recommendation. And in this way, we started to take all the groundwork he had laid with the help of others and shape it to make the kind of narrative sense that memoir demands.

We started with weekly meetings, but we soon increased that to twice-a-week meetings in order to quickly assemble the working draft of the memoir. One of the hardest things to do in writing from personal experience is to discern what to write about—what to cut and what to keep. His book, in its final draft, is over two hundred pages but less than four hundred, which is a good length for publication. But there were stories that didn't get told in order to keep it at an optimally publishable length. These, of course, were careful negotiations. I made recommendations, but ultimately, the book and all the decisions were Jamie's to make.

Twice a week, I brought material that had been put into rough stories, and we would read these, sentence by sentence, word by word, tweaking, reworking, adding, deleting, researching, addressing, explaining, and doing all the other things that must be done with drafts. Some days,

Jamie would have many edits or even whole new ideas to share. I called these "off script" days, and they produced some of my favorite sections of the book. We explored the idea of an underlying story, and I used an analogy from the novelist Nancy Zafris. She draws a rudimentary fish, with an arc over for the top and an arc under for the belly, crossing the two to make the tail. This represents the top story and bottom story of narrative and how they cross at the writing's end. So we often talked about "the underbelly of the fish," and Jamie added reflective sections that really brought out his philosophic side with quiet, compelling insights.

Occasionally, I would take the notes from our sessions and come back with something really right (usually on a second, third, or fourth try), and Jamie would be visibly moved by what I read to him. It was a satisfaction I'd never experienced before in writing. I think that writers want to move people and be emotionally potent on the page, but we rarely, if ever, know whether our work has genuinely touched someone. In sharing my craft with Jamie, I got the experience of both writer and reader together, and when he would laugh or cry, when he was clearly transported back into his memory, he reminded me how writing can be pure magic. It's easy for a writer to get so concerned with professional ambition that the magical quality that first drew her to writing can get lost. For me, with Jamie, the gift he gave me as we worked included remembering all the possibilities that the written word offers to us as people engaged with the world.

Revision is literally "reseeing," but in our case, it is rehearing, too. We combed through the sentences and passages as we worked to make things accurate and precise. Others helped us to copyedit, always an important aspect, and we continued to polish. Betsy, who has a keen mind for detail and an uncanny ability to draw forth from her memory, was our fact-checker. The draft continued to take shape.

One of the important aspects of our revision was to remember that this book was an act of narrative medicine. The field of narrative medicine was originated by Rita Charon, MD, PhD. An internist and a literary scholar, Dr. Charon has a strong understanding of how stories matter in the clinical setting. One aspect of narrative medicine is receiving the patient's story, and that's how I felt about working with Jamie. I received his many stories and helped him to preserve them in his unique storytelling voice. Sure, I coached him, but in the end, the story was, and always had to be, in his voice and in the way only he could tell it— in his language and expressions. So, committed to this project, he would hone his own storytelling voice as we worked together, yet always, the language and phrases you'll read are in his voice.

In palliative care, there is much literature and discussion about legacy projects, which are ways for patients to review their lives, accomplishments, and heritage. Certainly, Jamie did these things with his memoir. He went beyond those goals, capturing the essence of himself on the page, one that people who knew him will recognize and appreciate. His family, friends, coworkers, and the many others who knew him can "visit" Jamie in these pages he wrote and in the stories he shares. While no one book can capture the entirety of a person, this memoir does evoke Jamie. I believe that there is comfort in returning to his many vibrant stories and in hearing his voice through what we captured on the page. Because we have worked to keep his words, it really is Jamie's work, and my role as his writing coach and friend has been nothing short of life-changing. It truly became a collaborative effort. It wasn't just a privilege to work with him, to get to be his friend, and to befriend his family and circle of friends. Having shared short parts of this book with others who knew Jamie has widened my world, and it has allowed me to meet people that I "met" first on the page—a unique experience for any writer or reader.

As we've been working on the published version of this book, other writers and editors from the publishing world have offered sage advice, book marketing examples and tips, and many other forms of help so that, when this manuscript was ready, we could start the process of publication. I am reminded that books are made from the efforts of many people. There is a lot of satisfaction in this work, in taking the dream of a book and pushing it toward the physical object that others might read and enjoy.

For me, I will always cherish the days I had chances to work with Jamie and how we became friends. I cherish that I've been embraced by his family and his friends. Art creates its own kind of intelligence, and writing gives us the voices we didn't know we had. Often, writers feel alone in their work, but working with Jamie has been all about sharing, about connecting, and about helping him create his book.

The introduction and the epilogue were written last. Jamie and I decided on a technique called "bookends," in which he introduces himself in the present and then finishes with a present-day description of why he chose to write his memoir. It's only fitting to give these sections that present-tense feel, as Jamie has often shared that living in the present was one of the best ways he found to deal with his disease. He leaves us with a good reminder to make the most of our own presents, and to share the present with those we care about. Jamie's book is the blueprint to life well lived and time well spent. His voice and stories will be shared for many years to come.

Introduction: Off Belay

DURING MY LIFE, I'VE ENJOYED the outdoors by learning skills and applying them to activities, and one of those activities has been climbing. Climbing requires a good partner. In climbing, getting to the top is not the only thing that matters. It's also about how you get there. To get up the rock, you need some special gear and skills. One of the methods climbers use is called *belaying*, and it refers to techniques using a rope, so that if a climber falls, he won't fall very far.

When you are *on belay*, you are connected by the rope to your partner. Your partner lets out the rope as you climb up. He is well-secured. As you climb, you place chocks, or devices that help secure you and provide protection, in cracks in the rock. Climbers move up the chocks in what are called pitches, or sections of the climb, and the partners belay each other up the pitch. If you fall, there would be a tremendous jolt on the rope, and your safety, even your life, would be in the hands of your partner and his ability to stop the rope from slipping. Once you climb to a spot where you are secure and can help your partner, you are *off belay*.

I decided to write this book about the stories and adventures of my life. While writing is not exactly the same as climbing, I think I can explain my decision using a climbing analogy. Right now, I'm off belay, in a secure place where I can help my reader through different events and adventures in my life. The stories here are like the various pitches. All the pitches together help create a longer narrative—a climb.

When some people write books, it's something they do alone. But my philosophy and modus operandi has always been to work with others—in pairs or groups. So writing this book has not been something I've done by myself, but I found a partner, just like in climbing.

At this point in my life, I am not able to do the things I was once able to do. When I wake, I cannot move in my bed, so I wait until I hear Betsy, my wife, get up. She sleeps upstairs, and I'm sleeping downstairs, where we converted a space into my bedroom that was once a TV room. It works out well for me, because I cannot climb stairs anymore.

My family and Kim (an aide from a service) help care for me. Like Betsy, Kim is another example of a good-looking woman taking care of my emaciated, skinny, bare body. I have physical therapy three times a week. It is to keep my legs loose so I don't atrophy. We don't want my tendons to shorten up, so the physical therapy keeps things moving and not tightening or shortening, even though my muscular features have deteriorated. I have to admit, I was never very muscular anyhow. I was always a six-foot, 150-pound weakling. However, I am now down to the 120s. No matter what I do, I'm not going to get stronger. I'm only going to get weaker. I have a disease called ALS, or amyotrophic lateral sclerosis, also known as Lou Gehrig's disease.

I've got one last hurrah in me, and it's this book. I don't want to sit and wait for my body to quit. I can tell about my life and the things I've done, not to stroke my ego, but so family, friends, and others can be entertained. These life stories also leave a little more history from my point of view. I've had a great life, done great things, and had a great family. Maybe I didn't get all the awards I could have, but that's really just ego recognition, and someday, I just might get over that. Writing seems like something I should do, to leave something for my family, friends, and future generations. Maybe I've been good at life, finding the right people and forming relationships to have success, produce work, and live well. My mind keeps telling me it's important to do this because who I am is not necessarily who I was. Like in white-water boating, something I've enjoyed doing, I'm spending most of my time looking upstream.

One of the reasons I'm writing this memoir is because it keeps my mind active in the memories of all the very interesting places I've visited. Looking at the pictures of my travels throughout the world has been really good for me. I escape back to these memories when I need them, or when I want to reaffirm that I've done something. I've had the opportunity to do a lot. Now, I'm involved with a disease that prevents me from doing any of the physical things I've filled my life doing. Betsy and I have always said that we were sure glad we took advantage of the opportunities to have adventures, from international travel to canoeing in the Grand Canyon. Weren't we lucky that we did them, rather than put them off until we retired?

Although I didn't know this would happen to me, I took advantage of opportunities when I could, rather than delay them. Now, I feel lucky that I did them as those opportunities arose. It's like a line in one of my favorite movies, *Star Wars*: it's my destiny. By telling my stories, and working with a writer named Renée, who is helping me realize them, I catch the moments again. One of my strengths throughout my life, in both personal and professional contexts, is that I have found good people to work with and to learn from.

For many years, I served as the Associate Dean for Medical Education in the School of Medicine at West Virginia University. I experienced something during my tenure at WVU that plays a huge role in keeping me sane with my disease. It was either the mid- or late 1990s when I got a call from the Dean of the School of Medicine, Bob D'Alessandri, who was my boss. "Jamie," he said, "I've just gotten back from an experience that has transformed the way I think of things. I'd like to discuss it with you."

The experience Bob had was so profound that he gave the chairs and associate deans copies of a book he wanted us to read. This was so our school's leaders could learn about what Bob had just been introduced to as a member of a select, national group. This group came from various walks of life, from deans and college presidents to CEOs of businesses. It was almost like a think tank, and Bob had recently returned from their annual meeting.

One speaker at the think tank meeting was George Pransky. George was a talker, and if you didn't know better, you might think he seemed like a snake oil salesman. George's message was simple but transforming. The book that Bob had us all read was a little unusual, because it was a self-help book aimed at people having marital issues but with principles that could be applied to other things. All of this had to do with a former welder named Sydney Banks and an epiphany that changed his life. George was like a disciple of Syd Banks. It all sounded a little squishy.

Bob asked me to put together a trip for all the chairs and all the associate deans from the WVU School of Medicine to go to the small town of La Conner in Washington State, where George would lead us through a three-day workshop. I arranged for all the chairs, the hospital president and vice presidents—everyone in a leadership role—to make the trip. Even though they thought I was crazy, as the Associate Dean for Medical Education, I was responsible for getting everyone out to La Conner to participate.

The workshop *was* transformational. It was a completely different way to approach the thoughts we have. It wasn't like any professional development I'd been to before. It was low-key, with plenty of time to relax, think, and talk with colleagues. Not everyone in our group allowed themselves to be influenced by the simplicity of the message. Bob received criticism for taking all the leadership across the country to this "snake oil" conference. But Bob was not discouraged. In fact, he asked me to put together another trip out west, and that time, he took the next layer down—section chiefs and the next level of hospital staff. During the second trip to La Conner, the program was more formal, with more interaction with George Pransky's staff. I remember this second time that more people were "getting it." While, initially, they were probably influenced one way or the other by their chairs and bosses who had come before, they eventually got the chances to form their own opinions without the inherent skepticism that many of their bosses had.

I was the point person for planning the trip logistics, and I tried to shield criticism from Bob. It was deflected to me. Bob was convinced that once you understood the main ideas, they could change the way you viewed problems. He was trying to improve our work environment and make it healthier. He believed that the School of Medicine could be more productive if everyone worked stronger together. He wanted to get rid of the idea that the enemy was within the school. The challenges were outside the school. Because Bob believed so strongly in this, we also brought professionals from La Conner to WVU to work with departments and faculty to try to improve the morale, operation, and productivity of the Health Sciences Center. The approach was what I'd call big-time radical.

You may be asking yourself, "What is this transformational message?" It's so simple that it's easy to miss the point or misunderstand. It's been referred to by various names, including the three principles, psychology of mind, health realization, and innate health. I'll use an analogy to explain. Our minds are like rivers, and our thoughts are like leaves or debris that float down the stream. Like anything that flows with water, these thoughts come and go, often return, and sometimes get caught in an eddy where, they go round and round.

It's important to remember that these thoughts, flowing like leaves on the stream, are just thoughts. Stay in the present, and don't get caught in the future with your thoughts. Thoughts can create a psychological experience, but you can also choose not to dwell on them. You don't have to believe all the demons you are thinking of. This can have tremendous application with those who have serious challenges with health or relationships. I guess I can say that I am an example of this philosophy in that I could be overwhelmed by thoughts about what is happening to me because of the progress of my disease. While I can't avoid them, they're just thoughts, and I don't have to pay overattention to those demons, because the thoughts will come and go.

This mind-set gives us choices rather than outcomes, and I've been fortunate to learn how to let my thoughts flow. My mantra is "stay in the present." I developed this understanding over fifteen years ago, never knowing I would have a difficult disease. All diseases are difficult. And I'm not saying mine is worse than others. But I do think this experience of learning that "thoughts are just thoughts, and I create my own thoughts" has helped me all these years later. I'll admit, I'm not elegant talking about it.

Even though my work life was cut short because of my disease, writing is a whole new adventure, and that's why I'm attracted to it. Living life is a kind of therapy, and the things of life keep me growing. I don't know if I would be writing about my life if I didn't have a serious disease, but every cloud's lining has some silver in it. Originally, this was meant as a book about adventures I have had, but I've gone beyond that. In life, I've had the good fortune to experience many unique moments and events, and I have often been in the right place at the right time. So I'm looking at this as an opportunity, a contribution that may be helpful to others. Just like the yin and the yang, there is always a bit of light in the dark.

I began this book with an analogy about climbing, explaining what it means to belay. In belaying, communication is very important. Climbers shout out simple commands to let each other know when they are on belay and off belay. The climbs have variability, and that can include how straight the rope is, how many points of protection or chocks you have, and where the natural places are for you to go off belay, secure yourself, and help your partner up. So, from my place off belay, I hope these stories entertain you and help you as you climb the many pitches in your life.

Family, Friends, and Avoiding Bullies

CHAPTER 1

I GREW UP IN A one-story house, flat-roofed, with three bedrooms, on Maryland Street in Fairfield, California. Behind our lot was a railroad track, with another track fifty yards behind that, the two tracks making a V, which formed a temporary lake because of the January and February California rains. When I was little, I played in the backyard, but when I was old enough to climb the fence, I could play in that lake. My friends and I would build rafts out of scrap railroad ties and other wood we found or liberated from houses that were being constructed in the neighborhood. I had one brother who was five years younger than me, so I didn't play with him much. All I would do is boss him around. He became my gopher, and if I needed anything, all I had to do was ask. We called him Skip, but his formal name was Ralph, after my mother's father.

When I was born, I was named after my father, James McBride Shumway, so I was a junior. For some reason, to distinguish me from my dad when I was growing up, I was called Jamie. When I got to high school, I thought Jamie was too "uncool," so I started going by "Jim," even though my close friends from before high school still knew me as Jamie and still called me that. Jim was what my father went by, so I was Jim Jr. Later, I would go back to Jamie.

I had friends and did local stuff, but because my father worked all the time, we didn't travel much or go on many family vacations.

In the early 1950s, when my family moved to Fairfield, its population was maybe five thousand at most. The Solano County seat, it was a small-but-growing town because of its location. Fairfield is about an hour each way from San Francisco and Sacramento on Highway 40, which is now part of a big interstate system, though it was not back then. It was twenty minutes from Napa Valley; two and a half hours from the Sierras; three and a half hours to Lake Tahoe; and five and a half hours to Yosemite. Fairfield was a central location, and as I got older, it would be a good location for adventures.

One of the many good things about growing up the way I did, and about my parents, was that they had no "plans" for me when I grew up. They wanted me to discover what the right thing was for me and what I wanted to do. They really did not try to make me this or that; they just wanted me to make choices that I could be happy with.

My dad always said, "You can be anything you want, whether it be a ditchdigger, a garbageman, anything. Just, when you decide what that is, go ahead and make the most of it. Take it seriously, and do it." So, because of this outlook, there was no predetermined "Jamie Shumway" who would be this or that. I also didn't think I was better or special. I was just one of the kids in the neighborhood.

My parents would pay me fifty cents to mow the lawn, and I did that as a kid. Then, I got a summer job following my senior year of high school at Pinkerton Hardware, a big store where I was mainly a gopher. In other words, I would clean the floors and clean all the glasses on the glass shelves—the boring part of the job. The good part of the job was when I got to actually cut pipe and help people find things in the large store. It was what I call my first real job.

During World War II, my father was a pilot, nicknamed "Bones" Shumway because he was skinny, like I would turn out to be. Growing up, I learned that he had been approached by executives who wanted to make a TV series or a movie about his exploits during World War II. As it turns out, nothing ever happened with it. There would be times I would get to fly with him, but most of the time, my dad was always working and was not around a lot. My father was an attorney, and he worked as counsel for Solano County, meaning that he handled all the civil cases for the county. My father attended all the night meetings for all the boards and all the county council meetings. He had a good influence on me, but he wasn't around much when I was growing up. My mom made dinner those nights that my dad was home. I don't remember any favorite foods. I was a skinny kid; I probably didn't eat that much. I do remember that, back in those days, we'd eat a lot of fish sticks, whether they were my favorite or not. They were easy to cook, like today's chicken nuggets. Fish sticks were "the thing" back in the late 1950s and early 1960s. I hated brussels sprouts, turnips, and those types of foods, and my grandparents would prepare them on purpose. They also tried to get me to eat beets. Normally, I didn't like beets, but when I was with my grandparents, I would eat what was in front of me, or I would be in big trouble. If I didn't eat my vegetables, my mom would let me know that I was disappointing my grandparents, and that was not good. It wasn't until I was older that I tried more adventurous foods.

CHAPTER 2

MY MOTHER'S PARENTS WERE YOUNG and were married when Ralph Edwin Scovel, her father, was in medical school in San Francisco. My mother's mother, Victoria Alden, was primarily a homemaker and had married several different men during her life. My mother was the only child she had with my grandfather. My grandfather, either prior to or after World War II, worked with a famous French scientist and surgeon, Dr. Alexis Carrel, and Charles Lindbergh. Lindbergh, of course, was an engineer, and my grandfather allegedly worked on two projects with him. One was a method to sustain human cells to live outside the body. The other was a very, very early idea of an artificial heart. Now, no one can be sure if these are real or fiction, but what I do know is that Lindbergh was friends with my grandfather. Not only do I have letters from Lindbergh to my grandfather but Lindbergh would also stay at my grandfather's place in Marin County when he would visit the Bay Area. After the loss of his child, and after the war, Lindbergh became a very private person, and he would stay with my grandfather to maintain his privacy. The house was down in a ravine on a private drive and couldn't be seen from the road, so it was a good sanctuary. It also had a gate, but if my grandparents were expecting company (like when they knew my mom was coming) the gate was left open. You couldn't see the house from the gate, because the hill blocked it. I used to play on that hill.

There was a downside to playing on the hill, which was the risk of poison oak that grew all over the place. There was another way I could get the poison oak, and that was by petting the dogs. The poison oak oil would gather on the dogs' fur. My grandparents always had dogs, ranging from dachshunds to Labrador retrievers.

More than once, I would go to Marin to see my grandparents and came back home, three days later, breaking out in a poison oak rash all over my body, which caused swelling. The pustulant rash itched like Hades. Obviously, as a kid, some circumstances repeated themselves more than once, and sometimes I would be at my grandparents', pet the dogs, and then have to go in to pee. A few days later, I would have that poison oak rash all over my "not-so-private" parts.

Later, my grandfather would move to a ranch, where we would occasionally visit. My mom always hoped that we were on our best behavior when we were at her father's house. My grandparents were more international. They were cultured and lived a different lifestyle than we did. During the time I was growing up, my grandparents lived in two different places. First they lived in Marin, and later they moved.

The place in Marin was a couple of acres and was very hilly. It had a swimming pool and a target range to shoot with bows and arrows. The house was basically a mansion. My grandfather was a surgeon in San Francisco, and, though they didn't live a lifestyle of decadence, they had enough money to buy good things.

It was in the early 1960s, around the time I started high school, when my grandparents moved from Marin to a small ranch near Shingle Springs, in the foothills of the Sierras. It was a gentleman's farm. They had horses and had about one or two dozen cattle. I got to ride English saddle on a Tennessee walking horse, and I got to herd cattle on horseback. It was really just moving the cattle. I got to fish in a pond that supplied water for all the acres through irrigation that had been set up. It was really a cool place to be, this little pond they had. It was about an acre or two. I had a raft. I got to make things like that raft. When I would go spend a couple of weeks with my grandparents on the ranch, one of my jobs was to muck the horse stalls. In other words, every morning, I had to shovel the poop out of the stalls.

My horse, Old Red, was actually a circus horse that had lost the tips of its ears from winter frostbite. He was a very gentle, old horse.

CHAPTER 3

WHEN I WAS GROWING UP, my neighborhood had lots of open lots, because it was still being developed. My friends and I would play in them. We would have dirt-clod fights, playing war, where an eight-to-ten-inch piece of grass was tossed like a dirt bomb. We dug holes for forts, topping them with liberated pieces of plywood that we covered with dirt. As kids, only we knew they were there.

When I was kid, I remember playing with boys and girls and not having any problem making friends. Of course, like any kid, I had to watch out for bullies and try to avoid them. I did, for the most part. I was nice-natured. There were enough kids in the neighborhood whom I could play with. Tommy Balmer was my best friend, and there were several girls my age who were also good friends. We would play with them. There was one girl named Mary Tomasini. Mary was a tomboy, so she would play with all of us boys. Those are the kids whom I remember playing with the most. We mainly played cowboys and Indians, good guys and bad guys.

These were early signs of my adventures to come.

I also remember one toy at Christmastime. My grandparents and my family made me a cardboard rocket. It wasn't fancy, but I climbed in it, sat down, pulled the bars back, and made believe I was in a rocket ship.

Mostly, I played outside. Playing outdoors was everything back then, and most of my early adventures started in the backyard or in the neighborhood. In California, in the winter, the temperature only goes down into the forties at the coldest. Otherwise, it'll be in the fifties—warm enough to play outside. Fairfield is in the split in the Coastal Range, which means that, except for the constant winds from the west, we had moderate weather. Fairfield sits right at the point where the pressure differential from the Central Valley and the Coastal Range tries to equalize itself, causing the winds. Still, even with wind, it was warm enough that I could play outside, and the only time I wouldn't play outside was when it rained.

We had a pup tent that we put in our backyard, and the neighborhood kids and I would stay in it on special occasions, having sleepovers with friends. I don't remember who thought it would be a good idea, but on one birthday, I got a bow and arrows. Maybe someone remembered how excited I got shooting at targets at my grandparents' house in Marin, California. They had a section of the property set up with bull's-eye targets for shooting arrows. However, I shot my birthday bow and arrow in the pup tent. I don't know why, because I knew better. There'd been a kid in there. We got very lucky that the arrow wasn't real sharp and that it didn't hit the kid, but I was in big trouble.

Even as a kid, if I did something bad, I would feel guilty, and I would tell my parents. When I shot the bow and arrow in the pup tent, I told my mother. Her reaction was the general reaction during the 1950s: "You're in trouble; wait until your father gets home." I cannot remember what they did to me, but I remember feeling guilty that I'd acted in a reckless and irresponsible way. I had a sense of right and wrong, but my actions didn't always fit with what I knew was the right or wrong thing to do.

So, I punished myself. I took my bow and arrows, and I broke them, snapping them on the ground, standing on them with my feet and bending them until they broke.

CHAPTER 4

BRANSFORD ELEMENTARY SCHOOL, WHICH I attended, was about three or four blocks away from our house on Maryland Street. My sixth-grade teacher at Bransford Elementary, Mr. Park (not his real name), was a big man, about two hundred pounds and well built. He was strong and had a good sense of humor. I remember specifically that he could draw caricatures. In the 1950s, Disney had put out a movie version of *The Legend of Sleepy Hollow*, so he used to describe me as Ichabod Crane, and in my caricature, he drew me with an overwhelmingly protruding Adam's apple.

Mr. Park had a low boiling point, and my best friend, Tommy Balmer, had a talent for driving people nuts. Tommy was one of those overactive kids who did crazy things that would often just bug the heck out of people. I remember that Mr. Park once got so frustrated that he picked up Tommy, held him in the air, and shook him. Mr. Park had lost his temper, and, picking up Tommy by the shoulders, he jammed him up against the wall and shook him to make him calm down. By today's standards, a teacher behaving like that would not be tolerated, though I'm not saying Tommy didn't deserve it. His behavior could drive an adult crazy.

I also remember an embarrassing moment with Mr. Park in either the sixth or the eighth grade. It was my turn to get up and give a presentation. I needed orthodontics, so I wore braces to straighten my crooked teeth. Before I gave my presentation, I stood up in front of the class, and I tried to open my mouth.

"Wait a minute," I said. "I can't give this presentation. I can't speak with rubbers in my mouth."

The whole class cracked up. Even Mr. Park cracked up. "What did I say?" I asked.

All I was trying to say was that I had these dang rubber bands that held my teeth together, causing some pressure when they moved. I had to get them out of my mouth before I spoke, but of course, the word "rubber" meant something else, as I found out later. At the time, I wasn't embarrassed, but I wondered why the class and the teacher cracked up. After it was explained to me later, I thought, *Oh, I said something amusing.*

Unfortunately, many, many years later, I read that Mr. Park was convicted of sexual crimes with kids. As an older man, he was arrested and convicted of improper behavior, and that was very sad for me to hear, because he was by far my favorite teacher when I was young. I'd had him for both sixth grade and for eighth grade, and he'd made an impression on me.

I had known Tommy Balmer since the second grade or even earlier, and we were friends throughout high school. There are things that I remember specifically about Tommy. Once, while sitting together in the lunch room, he reached over and tried to grab one of my French fries. Before it got to his mouth, I pinned his hand on the table with my fork. I'm not saying that was my best behavior, but Tommy could really annoy me and other people because of his insistence—what one might call "ADD" behavior today. So, sometimes it wasn't just the adults who got frustrated with him. Tommy was good-natured but overactive and would just do dumb things to get you going. He was a year older than me but was in the same grade. Where I was a skinny kid, he was a more regular size, with more weight than me but not chubby. He had dark hair—black or dark brown. Tommy was of medium height, and I would grow taller than him later, nearly six-feet to his five-feet, nine-inches. He lived across the street, a house or two down from me, and he was my best friend, along with Kerry Myers. We'd all play together.

Sometimes, Tommy and I had an intense relationship, kind of like sibling rivals. Back then, *Zorro* was our favorite TV show. For Halloween, I wanted to be Zorro, and my mom made a costume. At school, there was a dress-up day, and Tommy also showed up as Zorro. While we were good friends, we could also get jealous, and even though nothing happened with the Zorro costumes, I was disappointed that Tommy was also Zorro.

CHAPTER 5

WHILE I HAD MANY FRIENDS and liked most of the kids in the neighborhood, there were always a few bullies. My worst childhood enemy lived down the street. His name was Billy Johnson. Billy was maybe a year younger than I was. We all had bicycles and would ride up and down the street, just like little kids do.

One day, I was on my bicycle, and Billy Johnson could see that I was riding down the street. Upon seeing me, he came running out of his house with a broom handle. Just as I got to the front of his house, he ran out and stuck the broom handle in my front spokes. The bike flipped up, and I went flying across the concrete-and-asphalt street, crashing my bike and scraping my face and my arms. My bike was damaged, because the spokes were bent and broken in my front wheel—all because Billy Johnson, the mean kid, had chosen to pick on me. I don't think I ever did anything to him. He'd done it simply because he didn't like me. He was just a mean kid who saw the opportunity to make me crash.

CHAPTER 6

SOME OF THE THINGS THAT I made when I was growing up, from about fourth grade to high school, were wooden go-carts. A go-cart is just four wheels on plywood. You sit on the piece of plywood, and you control the direction by placing your feet on a two-by-four that has a bolt in the middle and wheels on the end. If you push one way or the other, the go-cart turns. To power the go-cart, one could mount an engine, like a Briggs & Stratton four-cylinder, lawn mower engine, on the back of it.

Now, all the kids did this, and there were some big kids down the street who also made these go-carts. Kids tend to attract each other when there's some energy and action or something fun going on. So the big kids were showing everybody their go-carts, and, of course, these kids were at least fifty, sixty, seventy pounds heavier than I was. We all got chances, in turn, to ride the go-cart. A bigger kid, who was a little overweight, rode the go-cart first, and he did fine going up and down the street.

When it was finally my turn to ride the go-cart, we forgot to loosen up the gears, so when I got on it (and I was really light), the go-cart took off at full speed. I went around a corner on two wheels, leaning in to keep it from flipping over.

"Oh my God," I said. "I'm going to die."

I saw an open field in front of me that was a city lot with no house. There was a sidewalk around it, showing an intention to build. That open lot was my opportunity. My only chance to live was to go up into the field, where the go-cart would stop, because it wouldn't be able to go in the dirt.

Trying to get to the field, I hit this sidewalk straight on. Then, I went airborne. I was boosted up in the air, and I ended up in the field, upside down. I felt a big, big swelling on my temple. I had hit the ground and had gotten a knot.

I went home. "Look, Mom," I said. "Look what happened. Stuff always happens to me, doesn't it?"

My mom turned, looked at me, and she agreed.

CHAPTER 7

SINCE MY FATHER WAS AN attorney in town, he and my mom felt it was important for us to be seen in the "right places." One of the right places was called the Green Valley Country Club. It was only about four or five miles from where we lived, and the club included an eighteen-hole golf course and a swimming pool.

I didn't play golf as a boy, but I did enjoy going to the swimming pool. However, the pool presented a problem, too. I was a very skinny kid, and I was embarrassed to go swimming with my shirt off. I didn't want people to see my body. If I did take my shirt off, I usually hid behind a tree around the swimming pool and then ran and jumped in the water quickly. That's a good example of my inferiority complex when I was a kid.

Later, there would be another event that included the country club. I was either sixteen or seventeen years old. My father, being one of the attorneys in town, liked good cars, and consequently, all the car dealers liked to try to sell him fancy-wancy models. One weekend, he came home in a convertible Corvette. It had a big, V8 engine in it.

"Here, Jamie," my father said. "You want to try driving it?"

Of course, I said yes. We lived out in the country a little bit, about four or five miles from Green Valley Country Club. That drive had the curviest, windiest roads to it, so of course, I figured that driving to the country club on the windy roads was a great test of this big, V8, high-powered Corvette. It had all the bells and whistles—the gear shift and the clutch—and it ran really, really well.

I drove up to the country club, and I saw some friends, and, of course, they came by and said, "Wow, Shumway. What sort of car is this?" They knew, of course, what it was, and they didn't expect to see a kid like me drive up in a Corvette. They were all oohing and aahing. Some of the bigger bullies came by, and they thought that was pretty cool. They talked me into opening the hood so they could look at the engine.

One idiot had a broom with him, and he started sweeping inside the Corvette engine. I was so afraid that it was going to get broken, or that they were going to damage it. I would be stuck there, or they would scratch it or wreck the paint, and I would have to call my dad and explain what happened. Fortunately, I managed to get them to stop, and I closed the hood on the engine, and I drove home as fast as I could. Of course, the car went very fast, and I undoubtedly left a little bit of rubber when I left the country club, just to impress my friends and the big kids.

My first car was an Austin A40, an English sedan that was very small. It belonged to my grandmother Isobel and was given to my mom. It was a great car for a kid, because it wouldn't go much more than forty-five miles per hour, since it had a four-cylinder engine. Of course, I tried to make as many improvements on that car as I could. For example, I added a tachometer, and I added some driving headlights on it.

One incident with the car was a fender bender. I had been trying to flee from the site of a student fight. In high school, during those days, the kids would threaten each other and basically duke it out. The fights were usually at a set time after school in a park, classic *Grease*-type stuff. One day, I parked in the parking lot, went out and watched a fight, and then, all of a sudden, we heard that the police were coming. We all ran back to our cars, and unfortunately, I had the bad sense of trying to flee the site of this crime. I hit another car that was also pulling out of the parking lot. Boy, did I get in big trouble. My parents put me on restriction, and I couldn't drive for a couple of weeks.

One of the things I did with that car in the later high school years was going on road rallies. I went with one of my best friends, Kerry Myers, who was a year older than I was. He would navigate, and I would drive. Since I was the driver and had a British car, he called me Sterling, after the British race driver, Sterling Moss.

Another friend of ours, Pete Underwood, owned one of the early 1965 Ford Mustangs when they just came out. It was a really cool car. We wanted to go to a Sports Car Club of America (SCCA) race at the Laguna Seca racetrack, which was down by Monterey, California. It was a two- or three-hour drive from Fairfield, and it was fun for the three of us, driving down in Pete's Mustang. One thing we got to do was to get into the inner circle of the racetrack, where we parked our car and watched the sports car races. We also got to drive on the racetrack itself to get to that parking area. It was really cool.

CHAPTER 8

THERE WAS ONE GIRL ON whom I had a crush. Her name was Priscilla Toon, a pretty blonde and a friend in elementary and high school. Even though I had a crush on her, I never did anything with her, because I didn't know what dating was about. I didn't date until I got to college. I was too embarrassed to hold her hand or do anything like that. I could call her my girlfriend, but she was more a girl who was also my friend.

There's one time with Priscilla that I remember, when we were at the elementary school, playing around in the back as kids would do. I wanted to show off a little for her. Some kid was hitting pop flies with a regular, standard hardball. I'd brought my mitt, because I wanted to be a cool kid, even though athletically, I was a total dud. This kid hit a pop fly and said, "Jamie, can you catch that?"

"Watch this," I told Priscilla. "I'll catch it."

I held my mitt up in front of my face, and the pop fly went way up in the air and started to come down. I held my mitt in just the right position, out in front of my face, to catch the ball. Unfortunately, the ball missed my mitt, because I was off just a little. Instead, the ball hit my nose, and it started bleeding. The ball hit me hard enough to break my nose.

Priscilla gave me her scarf to put over my bloody nose. I got on my bike and rode home. When I got there, I said, "Hey, Mom, look at this." I took the scarf off my nose, and it was all bent and crooked.

My mother took me to the doctor. The doctor looked at my nose and said, "Oh, we can fix this." He put his thumb on one side of my nose and pushed, which popped the nose back into where it should have been, because it's cartilage at that young age. It's something I remember specifically happening with Priscilla Toon.

CHAPTER 9

SOMEONE TALKED MY PARENTS INTO sending me to dance lessons. They said, "Wouldn't it be a good idea if your kids could learn to dance?" There was someone offering ballroom dancing lessons for kids. This was probably right before high school. I remember dancing with a friend of mine, who was another girl that I knew. Her name was Kathy Keeler. She became my dance partner.

We had a little recital. We did a swing-type dancing routine to Glenn Miller's music. The actual dancing went something like this:

Step-touch-one-two-three;
two-step-touch;
one-two-three, one-two.

That was what I did with my feet. It was cool, and I enjoyed it.

CHAPTER 10

I TOOK PIANO LESSONS FOR three or four years, starting in elementary school. I enjoyed playing, but I didn't like to practice. I stopped taking piano lessons, and I regret my decision to this day. We'd moved into the country, so it wasn't as easy to continue piano lessons. Also, I started high school, and the whole nature of what my time was about—studying and sports—got in the way of piano. Also, the good piano teacher, my favorite piano teacher, moved away. I took lessons for about six months with an old guy who really didn't know what he was doing, so that didn't work. For those reasons, I made a mistake and stopped taking piano lessons. It wasn't until I was an adult that I said, "Wait a minute. I'm an accomplished, successful person." I started taking piano lessons again and think that has been very good for me. Unfortunately, today, I am no longer able to play the piano, because my hands don't work anymore.

CHAPTER 11

BACK IN THE 1960S, IN high school, I was just your typical, skinny, gangly type of kid. One advantage to this was not being overweight, so I could do many things some kids got winded doing. In my high school gym classes, there were differently colored shorts that you got to wear based upon your physical ability to do certain things. As a freshman, I came in with white shorts, just like the others in my grade. We were immediately suspect, because we'd been tagged (especially by the jocks) as being freshmen. After the physical fitness exercises and tests, I could move up in the color of shorts. I think that the ranking went from white to purple, green, red, and then gold. It was something like that. For the super athletic kids, there was a gold satin and a blue satin.

I remember that I had a distinct advantage with this system. Remember, I was a gangly kid, and because of my light weight yet tall height—I was approaching five-feet, eleven-inches or six-feet—I had an advantage when doing the required number of pull-ups to make red shorts. The test included sit-ups, squats, push-ups, and chin-ups. I could do all of those, but my talent was running the mile. I had to run the mile in under eight minutes. Running was my least favorite thing to do, not because I couldn't stride, but because I got exhausted. It used every ounce of my physical presence. Eventually, I got red shorts, which was pretty good, and it gave me some distinction when I went out for the PE classes.

As a young kid, I didn't think about my physical stature. But as a teenager, a beginning teen, I was aware of my skinniness. Later in life, as a young man, from college and beyond, I took advantage of my light weight and worked on muscle development that gave me advantage with sports and activities—namely mountaineering, rock climbing, and all sorts of winter-skiing activities. But this was later.

If you look at how adolescence is viewed today and then compare it to back then, I would say that, at the time, I went through normal development through puberty. It was part of the change that happens between girls and boys as they become women and men. So, I don't think my puberty was any more different or traumatic from anybody else's. But part of it was being more sensitive to my body. There's a phrase, the "great equalizer," (even though it should be the "unequalizer") that sums it up. People develop their secondary sexual characteristics at different rates. I think that high school is a tumultuous period for anyone, because of hormonal peaks that occur while the teenage mind is trying to develop some stability. It's like an oscilloscope, where one looks at a slow incline in one particular area, then it's a spiked-up/spiked-down association of experiences.

In high school, I wasn't a slave to fashion, just white T-shirts and blue jeans. I didn't get into big trouble. I was probably a Goody-Two-Shoes type of kid and was popular, but I hung around with the nerds. Even when I found a girl whom I liked, I really was too shy to ask her to go out to a movie or anything like that. I was a pretty good tennis player, and I played on the high school team. I was probably the third or fourth player ranked on the team, so I was always competing in high-end doubles matches, at least. In the early 1960s, tennis was not as popular as it is today. In fact, it was considered, for lack of a better term at that time, a "faggy" thing for guys to do. I was playing something that the cool kids in high school really didn't respect at all.

CHAPTER 12

IN THE LATE OR MID-1960s, when I had just started in high school, my grandfather died. There's a bit of mystery around his death, and I actually have three different stories about it. My grandfather, at this time, was a retired physician, and though he wasn't practicing medicine anymore, he wanted to be involved with something unique in the community. He had a history with interesting people, like Dr. Carrel and Charles Lindbergh. He got interested in a Swedish firm called DANO, one of the very early recycling companies, which looked at turning used food and food waste into fertilizer. DANO had a way to put the recycled waste back on the land to grow more food. My grandfather was ahead of his time, but he was complicated, too.

My grandfather had married three times. The first was my mother's mother, and I know that the marriage was annulled, or they got a divorce not long after my mother was born. I don't know the story. After that, he married another woman, Edwina. She had lupus, and they had a daughter, Maxine, who would die of complications from lupus as a young woman. Edwina died during World War II. Then he met Isobel, the grandmother I knew, who was a New Zealander, while he was serving on a naval ship in the South Pacific. My grandfather was able to get Isobel on a ship to come to the United States, and, once here, he married her. Shortly after this happened, Maxine died, young, in her twenties. The exact dates, however, are sketchy to me.

When I was a little kid, my mother reestablished a relationship with her father, after Maxine died. At that time, it was Isobel and my grandfather, and he was much older than she was. So I never knew Maxine; I just knew of her. She had been in private schools and college, doing well, except for her disease. But, as a young kid, I remember going with my mom and brother to visit my grandfather and Isobel in Marin County. When they moved to the ranch in the foothills, I was told that it was for my grandfather's health. But that made little sense, and it sets up the three stories and the mystery around his death. I can't recall what's true.

First, I was told that my grandfather had died because he had inhaled fumes from formaldehyde. He'd had some snake eggs preserved and dropped one of the bottles, and the fumes overtook him. They burned his throat and caused breathing problems because he was an older man. This is the story I heard first.

Then (I think it was my dad who told me this), my grandfather had gotten mixed up with some bad men. He had been duped into believing in what these bad men were doing. The problem was that these men were going to be convicted and sent to jail, and my grandfather was, too, as an unknowing accomplice. Going to jail as an older man was not a good choice, so he took his own life.

But there is another story that my grandfather had cancer, and being a physician, he knew it was a cancer that could not be dealt with. His life would be painful and unpleasant until the cancer took him, so he took his own life. He didn't want to go through it. That was fifty years ago, and there wasn't hospice and the ability to care for the dying that we have today.

The only thing that's for sure is that he did take his own life, for whatever reason. When I was a kid, how could my family explain it? But what he left was a real mystery.

CHAPTER 13

I ALWAYS RELATED WELL IN groups, and being editor of my high school yearbook was no exception. As a junior, I was the advertising editor. This was a boring job, because I had to go around town and convince people, vendors, salespeople, and company owners to buy advertising space in our yearbook. I got along well with adults, so it was easy for me to go into a business and ask them if they would contribute. First, I had to convince them. Once they agreed, all the popular girls—the pretty girls—in school would come in and demonstrate or stand for pictures in their store. It was quite the thing. Being the ad editor, I got to know all the cool people in school, because the jock guys and the gorgeous girls wanted to have their pictures taken at all these businesses in town. It gave me access to what I refer to as "the beautiful people."

When I was a senior, I was chosen as editor-in-chief of the yearbook, which was called *La Mezcla*. I was in charge of the whole thing. One of my innovations to the yearbook came from a workshop I attended. There, I learned about how to lay out the pictures across two pages, in what was referred to as Mondrian design. It gave the yearbook a more artistic flow. It worked well, since a yearbook is a story in pictures, and it was innovative and different. I had a staff that worked with me, and I gave direction to help them lay out the pages. So, where there were multiple pictures, my staff and I would lay them out, allowing the pictures to tell the story and having the natural eye flow from left to right. It was harder than you might think. This was 1966; we didn't have computers. This is one of the early times I remember being successful working in groups.

The Magic of the High Sierras

As an undergraduate at the University of the Pacific, a five-thousand-student private college in Stockton about an hour and a half from Fairfield where I grew up, I earned a bachelor's degree in sociology. But that's not how I started college. I started college as a science major, thinking that I wanted to be a dentist because I'd had all this dental work growing up. I said, "Hmm, these guys make lots of money by putting rubbers in people's mouths to straighten their teeth."

I also had a good biology teacher in high school, and even though it wasn't my best subject, I had fun. Plus, I had been told in the second or third grade that I had a lower reading ability, and it had affected my confidence. So, I was not an avid reader, since I was told I didn't have the skills.

At this point, I was very much interested in dentistry as a future. Of course, you had to take the heavy-duty science classes in college, and, in my first semester, I had twelve hours of science and four or five or six hours of the basic requirements (like Western civilization and English), so I worked my butt off to pass the science classes and blew off my English and history classes. My first GPA was a 1.75.

Let's just say that I was not mature enough to continue with science, but I didn't learn that immediately, so in my second semester, I said, "Science is still important, and I think I'll try again." It was a second semester of chemistry and biology with all the labs. Again, I had another semester of history and English. Lo and behold, it was still a struggle. In the second semester, I talked to the biology advisor, since that was my major, and he helped me learn some study habits. I didn't exactly know how to study for science. I discovered that I hadn't worked very hard academically in high school. All throughout my first year, I would study hard during the week and party on the weekends, and by the second semester, I was doing better, but I had a deficit from the previous semester. I needed an average of a 2.0 to advance as a sophomore.

Then, there was an event that served as a catalyst for me to think about school differently. Unfortunately, or fortunately—it depends on how you view life events—around Easter of the spring semester, I was in a very serious car accident. I was returning Kathy Keeler's parents' big Ford Galaxy station wagon. Kathy had been my dance partner when I took lessons as a kid, and I was returning it to Fairfield from college. I was on a two-lane road, which was the best way to get from Stockton to Fairfield, and I was about twenty minutes outside of Fairfield coming back, when there was this big semi truck sitting at a stop sign. I entered the intersection at fifty miles per hour, and the truck pulled out. The semi truck made a half-circle around both lanes of the road, turning, and I slammed into him, going from fifty or sixty miles per hour to zero. I remember people coming to get me out of the car. I did have a seatbelt on, and the seatbelt broke my hip.

I remember that people came rushing around me, and I was trying to stand up, even though I had a broken hip. "Just relax, we're here, and we'll take care of you," the people at the scene said to me. I passed out and woke up in the hospital.

I was broken up, in little pieces. I didn't die, obviously, but I was in the hospital for weeks to repair my broken bones, and as a result, I was out of school. I would have been able to get back in college to finish the year, but I had lost all that time because of my accident. So, I withdrew that semester.

By the start of the new school year in 1967, I was ready to go. Everything was fine. And I was good to go back in another way. I had completely changed my major. I became interested in the social sciences.

When I returned in the fall, now a semester behind, I was continuing as a freshman again. This time, I took courses that I was interested in. In the long run, it was a difficult way to realize that maybe I wasn't born to be a science major. I took more liberal arts, psychology, and more of the required English and history, and all of a sudden, I did better academically. Some people need to be hit over the head before they figure things out, and I was one of those people.

After four years, I was still in such a hole GPA-wise, but I earned mostly B's, and maybe an A here and a C there. I graduated with a 2.99, close to an overall GPA of B. I excelled in sociology courses, psychology courses, and anything not related to science. They made more sense to me and seemed to be more consistent with what I was interested in. Of course, college wasn't just about all the courses.

CHAPTER 15

ON THE FIRST DAY AT college, I was walking on a sidewalk underneath the windows of a big dorm, which happened to be a girls' dorm. There were girls hanging out the windows, yelling down to people below.

I remember walking by the dorm, and this girl hung out the window and said, "Hey, you." I looked around and couldn't see anybody else that she was yelling at.

I looked up. "You mean me?" I said.

"Yeah, you," she said. "Wait right there. I'll be right down. I want to meet you."

That is where my shell broke, and I realized that I was attractive to the opposite sex. I attended college during the rock 'n' roll, hippie era, but I had been a shy kid. When I was in high school, sure I liked girls, but I never went out with any.

CHAPTER 16

DURING THE FALL SEMESTER OF my freshman year of college at University of the Pacific, we had a freshman camp so that we could all get to know the other students coming into the freshman class. Of course, this appealed to me. A couple of weeks into the semester, the faculty who were involved in the freshman camp said that we could take a trip to Yosemite. A faculty member, a young hippie professor, said, "Anybody who wants to come backpacking with us...come on." So we packed into his VW Microbus.

At college in Stockton, we were less than a four-hour car drive to Yosemite, a place I'd never been. So I went, but I didn't know what I was doing. I was eighteen years old, and I really didn't know much about the great outdoors. I had never been camping or backpacking. My family didn't have time for that. For the trip, I only had tennis shoes, not the boots needed for the trail. I had an old army rucksack that I got from the army/navy store, and I did my first backpacking trip in Yosemite carrying this rucksack, which left sores and bruises on my shoulders. My feet hurt, and I slept overnight in a borrowed sleeping bag in a tube tent. A tube tent is a plastic tube that you crawl into and run a line into the upper part so that it makes a V. Despite my lack of equipment, I really, really enjoyed the Yosemite trip.

The faculty member who took us (I think he was one of my psychology professors) got loaded on the way there, smoking dope. He said, "Jamie, would you like to drive the VW Microbus?"

"Sure, I can do that," I said.

If you don't know much about Volkswagen Microbuses, there was a lot of play in the steering wheel. The steering wheel's not parallel with your body, and it's kind of flat. When driving, you're kind of moving it, because there's so much play in it.

Also, the professor had forgotten to fill it up with gas. To get to Yosemite, we traveled through the back hills, and there weren't many gas stations around. So I had to only use gas going up the hills and coast the whole way coming down the hills, to conserve the gas we had, all the way back to Yosemite Valley. The good news was that gravity was on our side, as we lost altitude coming down the mountain. We would coast downhill and power uphill.

The Yosemite trip was the beginning of hippie times for me, because I learned from a college professor who had a hippie lifestyle in his VW Microbus.

Overall, it was a great opportunity, because I met other students who were interested in exploring, and we made a few trips to Yosemite. There were others at the university involved in these adventures. In essence, this was like an "outings" club, but it was mostly just individuals who would get together. We'd phone each other and ask, "Are you going to be able to go backpacking this weekend?" It wasn't an organized-club event.

One of the things that I learned to do in college, as I was being introduced to the great outdoors, was how to backpack. I purchased a backpack. I bought the top-of-the-line without even being certain if I was going to stick with it or not, because that's kind of the way I do things. Back then, I bought a classic Kelty Storm frame backpack, and I still have it today. It's been a long time since I've used it, but it's downstairs in my basement. I'd have a sleeping bag that I tied to the bottom of it. In the pack part, I'd put what I needed, primarily food and any extra clothing. Obviously, you were trying to limit what you needed. I could get my backpack weight down to between thirty and forty pounds—more than forty, and it was really difficult to handle. I always believed in going light. Plus, there was the tent, which usually has a lot of weight. I had a plastic tube tent. I'd put a line between two trees and set the plastic over it. I'd raise it up and then put rocks in all four corners, which basically created a triangular-shaped pup tent. Some people had real tents, but I didn't yet. I believed in a minimalist approach.

On one of the trips, we went out on a classic hike to Tuolumne Meadows in Yosemite National Park, and we hiked up to about nine thousand feet to a lake. This hike kind of got me hooked on doing these things. Our hike from Tuolumne Meadows down to the valley floor was a three-day backpack, and we covered about twelve to fifteen miles a day. The good news was that it was all downhill. In actuality, you're going up and down, and up and down, but in the big picture, it was all downhill.

I remember that we started up at Tuolumne Meadows and went into the high country, and we then headed west. We headed back down, and there were several passes that we had to go over and basically work our way down. We were in bear country, so we really needed to be careful with our food—something I learned early on. One of my first experiences in Yosemite was with some friends who had their backpacks dragged away because they had their food in them. We found the packs about one hundred yards away, all torn up, with all the food gone.

From this experience, I learned that if I wanted to protect my food when I was backpacking, I had to put it in a sack and then string it high in a tree, out of reach of the bears. If you're doing a three-day backpacking trip, if you leave your pack on the ground, the bears will eat all your food on the first day. Then, you're going to be really hungry, and you'll have to eat nuts or berries or something for the remaining days.

During these hikes, we were in the middle of nowhere, but it was absolutely beautiful. I went other places in the Sierras, but Yosemite was such a beautiful area.

In the early days, we would make fires, and we ate canned food that we could heat in aluminum bowls. In the later days, once I got more sophisticated with my backpacking equipment, I would carry a lightweight gas stove. We drank water from what people reported would be safe water, and, to protect ourselves against harmful micro-organisms (primarily Giardia), we would drink the water with iodine. Now, iodine did the job of killing anything you didn't want to swallow as far as micro-organisms, but it didn't make the water taste very good. As time went on with the backpacking, we would get more sophisticated systems, and we could actually filter the water against waterborne micro-organisms.

I backpacked from 1967 through 1972 in California. During the time I backpacked, I was between nineteen and twenty-four years old; I could take on the world.

CHAPTER 17

I REMEMBER, AS A KID, going on a trip with a church youth group and being taught how to ski with rental skis. I also remember spending the night in a church and sleeping under the pews. We skied the next day, got on the bus, and came home. When I got home, I convinced my parents that skiing was the best thing since sliced bread. That Christmas (I guess it was the Christmas of my senior year in high school), my parents gave me skis as my big present. They knew that I had another group ski trip planned, where we would go up into the Sierras, only about three hours away from where I grew up in Fairfield. I can't remember many of these early ski trips on my wooden skis. I do know that from that point on, I was really hooked on it. I tried to go skiing as much as I could.

When I got to college, the University of the Pacific was only two hours away from a ski resort in the mountains. It was called Bear Valley Ski Resort. I remember many trips to Bear Valley on the weekends. We used to go up only for the day because we did not have a place to stay up there. We would leave at six and get there at eight in the morning. Then, we got on the slopes and skied all day. Around four thirty in the afternoon, when Bear Valley closed, we got in the car and arrived home early in the evening. Of course, it was dark and was always a tough drive home because we were so tired, but I remember doing that sort of thing many times.

I fell in love with skiing. In fact, if I were to rank all the activities I have done throughout my life, I would have to say that Alpine skiing is highest on my list of things that I could do well. Even up to the days of when I knew something was wrong with my balance and legs, and I was feeling the weakness from my disease before I knew I had it, I was still skiing as best I could. Bear Valley is where I really developed a lot of my lifelong skiing techniques. And when I came to West Virginia, I learned how to cross-country ski. Finally, I learned how to combine cross-country and Alpine skiing into a particular technique that is called Telemark skiing. Mostly, I wanted to be a graceful parallel skier and to be able to do that on just about any terrain. I quickly developed the ability to be a parallel skier on the most difficult runs. That was my goal. Speed was not a goal. My goal was to have the ability to ski anywhere, on any slope, in an artistic form.

Sex, Drugs, and Rock 'n' Roll

CHAPTER 18

I MET MY FIRST GIRLFRIEND in class the spring semester of my freshman year. This was before the car accident, and her name was Karen Greatbody (not her real name). And, yes, she had a great, beautiful body. She was shorter than I was, probably about five-feet, three-inches; I was nearly six-feet tall. She was blond, she was cute, and she liked me. Karen had grown up in Oakland and was much more experienced than I was about dating, because she'd had a boyfriend in high school. Still, Karen and I started going out. I must admit that it was with Karen that I learned what girls were made of. I guess I'd say that, because she helped me understand how to make a girl feel good, but she basically got frustrated with me because I wouldn't do anything sexually with her; I didn't know what to do. Actually, I was afraid to make those moves. She had helped break me of my naïveté when it came to sex.

We dated for about a year, and after about a year, that relationship ended, like young-love relationships do. I do not know if I loved Karen or not, but she's my first potential, true-love girlfriend.

Later, a friend of mine was going out with Karen long after I had stopped going out with her. I remember going skiing with him. He gave me a pair of skis. They were a new, metal set of skis, and I really liked using them. I wanted a pair just like his. I got over the fact that he was dating Karen, even though I had dated her first.

After that, I saw Karen a couple of years later, and she had turned into a little more of a hippie. Remember, those were kind of the days of free love.

Back then, I had long hair down to my shoulders, I listened to rock 'n' roll music, and I was involved in the antiwar movement. I had always kind of believed in moderation, and sure, I smoked pot, but I never tried any other drug. Drinking was another thing we all experimented with. When I hit college in the late 1960s, marijuana was becoming more available, but when I was in high school in the early 1960s (from 1962 to 1966), it was really not part of the scene like it is today.

CHAPTER 19

ONE OF THE THINGS YOU do as a college student (if you ever watch the movies, you know this) is have a classic road trip. When I was a junior, I developed a friendship with a guy—the one who actually ended up dating Karen Greatbody, my first girlfriend. He was a friend; he was not a real close one, but he talked me into a road trip.

"Jamie," he said, "let's get in the car and go to Los Angeles."

It was a six- to eight-hour drive down the Central Valley on Highway 99. This was a good start to our classic road trip. When we got to LA, we said we would like to listen to some music. We kind of looked around in the newspaper to figure out what bands were playing at what places.

We were told by friends that the Hollywood Palladium often had good groups playing. I agreed to go there, and when we arrived, we found that there was this little-known group performing. It happened that, later, this particular group would become famous, but this was well before that happened. On the day we had gone to the Hollywood Palladium, it wasn't that crowded, so we managed to get up front, not in a seat but kind of in a ground area, like a mosh pit today.

We had heard about the band playing, but they weren't big time. Not yet. At this point, they weren't really popular, and they said when they got on the stage they were going to play one of their new sets of songs. And then they said, "We're going to play a rock opera." A rock opera? We'd never heard of that. And, lo and behold, it was The Who, and they played from beginning to end *Tommy, the Rock Opera*.

CHAPTER 20

It was either later in my sophomore year or in my junior year that I met another girl. Her name was Mary (not her real name), and she was a good-looking, small, blond girl. Mary had actually grown up in Stockton, where the University of the Pacific was located. The only issue with Mary was that she was sixteen years old. She was a child prodigy, smart as hell, and she'd entered college as a freshman when she was only sixteen. I met her in freshman camp, where I was a counselor. Mary was an amazing young woman who was very confident, very bright, very full of herself, and very beautiful.

Mary came from a family where she was intellectually out of the rest of her family's league, so she was a handful. I was afraid to go see her at her house, because her stepdad didn't trust young men who were dating Mary. Her mother was also a beautiful woman, so I knew where Mary got her looks from. One thing I remember in particular about Mary is that she ran away from home. This happened after she had been seeing me for about six months. She came to visit me and spent the night.

Then her parents called me to ask, "Have you seen Mary?"

I said no, because I had gotten advice from my dad, who was an attorney, about this sort of thing. He had warned, "Be careful, or you will end up in jail for having sex with a minor. It'll be statutory rape."

I didn't see Mary for a while during her emotionally difficult time. I must admit that it probably did affect our relationship, because I was not there to help her during her difficult struggles with her parents.

Mary and I were boyfriend-girlfriend during her freshman year and into her junior year, but she transferred to UC Berkeley. Even after I wasn't really dating her anymore, I wanted to go visit her. I was still in puppy love with her. When I asked to come see her she said, "Sure, I'd love that." So, I went to visit her for a weekend in Berkeley and spent the night with her.

Mary had this gorgeous apartment with a piano in it. She played the piano, as she had been a child prodigy, and was brilliant. We made what I thought was love that night. After, I asked, "How was that?"

"It was okay," Mary said.

I didn't really understand, because she was giving me different vibes. "What do you mean? Do you still like me?" I asked.

"Yeah, I like you as a friend," she said.

"Then why did we make love together?" I said.

"Because that's what I do," she said.

I really didn't understand what she was saying. I looked around her house. "What do you mean, 'That is what you do'?"

"I'm a call girl here in Berkeley, and I have these ongoing clients that like to go out with me, and I go home to do what I do in sexual situations," she said.

That took me by surprise. A girlfriend I had started to like had turned into a high-priced call girl.

Not unexpectedly, I found out that, later in her life, Mary had gone to law school and is now an attorney. I would really love to find her and see what else she did with her life. My relationship with her was the first time I ever admitted to being in love. After being with her a year, I was convinced that I did love her, but it was an immature love.

CHAPTER 21

In 1968 and 1969, there would be rock concerts in the Pacific football stadium. It was an old stadium and could hold maybe thirty-five or forty thousand people. It was a wooden stadium that had been built down into the ground, so it wasn't in use much anymore. The student government decided that we would have rock concerts in the stadium, and we brought in two different bands in two years.

When the student government put on the concerts, they needed volunteers to be medics. Being a medic was being one of the safety people helping others in trouble. One of the things that I enjoyed doing was volunteering as a medic, since I wasn't in student government, but I was part of the student leadership at the local YMCA.

Also, my girlfriend, Mary, gave me a dog, a golden retriever named Guinevere, who would also be part of the medic team.

The first concert that we had where I was working as an on-site medic featured the band Chicago. It was a great concert, and everybody was in a good mood. The crowd was mellow, and we would walk around and find people who were dehydrated from having too many drinks or who had perhaps been cut by broken glass and other minor things. The atmosphere was not like it is at stadiums today. There weren't restrictions on what you could bring in.

The volunteer medics, like me, went around and took care of people. I had my dog, Guinevere, and she had a bandana. As we roamed the stadium, she knew where I was, and I knew where she was, because she checked in with me. Guinevere would help people feel better, because she had this big, lovely, wagging tail.

At the time I volunteered as a medic at the concerts, I had an interest in helping people, but little did I know that, later in life, I would have a career that included medicine.

The following year, we had another concert, and the headlining band was Tower of Power. The crowd that came to this concert wasn't like the one the previous year to see Chicago. The Tower of Power fans were not a mellow crowd. People came looking for trouble, and the whole crowd was different. Rather than smoking marijuana, people were taking drugs like barbiturates, the real downer types of drugs. It made things very difficult.

During the Tower of Power concert, there were many fights, and I recall that someone got shot in the stadium. There were the medics, like me, and we needed to go to the site and see if we could help. We managed to remove the victim, the person who was shot, and stop his bleeding. We took him to the medic tent, where a real doctor and ambulance services were available.

So, I saw both sides of the concert scenes as a volunteer medic.

There was one other concert that I attended but not as a medic. This was a concert at Altamont, which was about an hour south of Stockton. For the concert, a farmer had lent out his land, which was a natural bowl, with hills rising in the back.

We were about a quarter-mile back from the stage, which was a rough estimate. It was a free concert, and there were hundreds of thousands of people there because it featured The Rolling Stones.

As I said, there were hundreds of thousands of people, and when the Stones came on, everybody got up and moved forward. If you can imagine it, the people up front were getting compressed, and they had no way to escape or any way to get out. Many of them were being pushed up onto the stage, and the Stones had hired The Hells Angels to be their security. The Hells Angels violently removed people, shooting, stabbing, and hitting them. People were getting beaten up, shot, and killed. I was far enough back to be safe, but I was there. It became a famous historical rock concert, documented in a 1970 film called *Gimme Shelter*. Like seeing The Who at the Hollywood Palladium, I had a knack for being in the right place at the right time.

CHAPTER 22

WHEN I WAS IN COLLEGE, or maybe right after I graduated, in December of 1970, I went sailing with my two old friends from Fairfield, Tommy Balmer and Kerry Myers. Tommy had been my best friend, but as I grew older, I had more in common with Kerry. Tommy was working as a photographer and had a sailboat, a twenty-one-foot Santana, which was a single-masted, overnight boat.

Even though Tommy owned the boat, Kerry was the experienced sailor. Kerry had crewed on big sailboats that raced in San Francisco Bay. We trailered Tommy's twenty-one-foot boat down to Southern California. We decided that we wanted to sail out to Santa Catalina Island, as the song and story goes, "twenty-one miles across at sea." We sailed from Long Beach Harbor to Santa Catalina Island, through the twenty-one miles of ocean out to the island. The problem was that, through those twenty-one miles, there were huge swells and waves.

As we were sailing, Tommy got seasick, really seasick. Kerry Myers, who was an experienced sailor, did not.

"Jamie," Kerry said, "you're not gonna get seasick, because you'll just do what I'm telling you to do. Keep looking at the horizon; don't even think about the boat going up and down, up and down." Luckily, we made it to Santa Catalina under Kerry's wise leadership. Tommy eventually recovered on the trip, and we spent the night at Catalina Island. There was room for four downstairs, and there were only three of us, so we were fine sleeping on the boat. We hoped to go out on Catalina Island and see the sights.

This is not the only sailing adventure during my college years that Kerry and I would have. Before Catalina Island, Kerry talked me into getting a small, single-person racing sailboat. It was called a Laser. Although it was really designed as a one-person boat, both of us could sit in the Laser. We decided to take the Laser out into San Francisco Bay.

"We should leave from Tiburon," Kerry said. Tiburon was just north of San Francisco, across the Golden Gate Bridge. So, we decided to sail out and see how it went.

The area we chose to sail was called Raccoon Straits, and there was a reason for that, which we learned when we got out into them. We started our sailing adventure about two o'clock and were out a couple of hours on this little, fourteen-foot Laser sailboat. And then, the wind picked up. In fact, it considerably picked up. We were a couple of miles off the shore. I said, "Well, maybe we should turn around and head back in."

Like two young men who were fearless, we turned around. And that meant the wind was coming from our back. So we had to basically have the sails out as far as we could get them. The wind speed picked up to about thirty knots, and we had our hands full. We were sitting on the back of the boat as much as we could, to basically prevent the nose from diving into the waves. We were going very fast, and there's a phenomenon that we experienced. We exceeded hull speed, which means that we were going faster than the boat could handle. So when we exceeded our hull speed, basically, our nose dove into the water, and we did a three-sixty flip—as in *flipped over*. We landed on the side of the boat, and we had to flip the boat up and get back in. And there we were, in San Francisco Bay, crashed. We broke our tiller, which is what you hold onto to control the direction of the boat. We had to bend over and have our arms on the broken part to maintain any sort of directional control. Nothing else broke, and we managed to eventually limp back to shore.

What Am I Doing?

CHAPTER 23

⎯⎯᧑

I STARTED COLLEGE IN 1966, and a year later, I must admit, I was liberalized. This happened from the people I met, from the professors I had, and, I had realized that, in the world, all things weren't necessarily as my parents thought they were. My father was a Republican. He wasn't necessarily a conservative Republican; nonetheless, he was much more conservative than I was.

In college, I adopted a liberal view, and one of the reasons that this happened to me is because there was a local organization on campus called the Anderson Y center. It originally was a YMCA/YWCA center for students, but the minister who ran it was very liberal and political, and he had a strong antiwar sentiment. I kind of fell right into the antiwar movement because of the minister who ran the YMCA. He and I became pretty close friends. I painted his house and did work for him, and he taught me a lot about what was wrong in America and why things like the military industrial complex were not necessarily good things.

One of the things that happened to me in my first antiwar meeting at the Anderson Y center was that I went back to being called Jamie. Someone whom I knew and grew up with, another student from the same area as me, referred to me as Jamie. Now, before that time, I was going by Jim. During my freshman year, everybody whom I met always referred to me as Jim, because that's how I introduced myself. I was Jim among many Jims and among many Jameses. So, when this friend who grew up with me as a little kid, who happened to go to the same college, referred to me as Jamie, I thought, *Wait a minute, that's a very unique name. Not everybody has the name Jamie—especially boys.* You hear of girls being called Jamie, but boys less so; so from that point on, I realized my identity and who I was. I started to introduce myself to new people as Jamie. From that point on, it stuck, and through my whole career and my retirement, I've always been known as Jamie Shumway.

Through the Anderson Y center, we'd wind up with opportunities to talk about the war in various churches in the community. I was a student speaker, part of the leadership of the antiwar movement on our particular campus. I got to go to these churches and talk about peace and why war is not the best solution—certainly not the Vietnam War.

I believed in civil disobedience, but such that it was legal, as part of free speech. I did not believe in the more radical, uncivil, or destructive and illegal disobedience. My beliefs included working within the system, under the laws that we have, to work out our differences. About that same time, in 1969, there was a big change, because the lottery draft system was reinstituted. Every young man over the age of eighteen was assigned a number, based on the day and month of his birth. Lower numbers were not good. My number was ninety-six.

So I was going to be drafted, whether I was in college or not. The day came when I had to show up at the Oakland Induction Center and experience the lunacy that the center put young men through, trying to see if they were physically fit enough to be in the military.

I did not want to go into the military, nor did I believe that Vietnam was a just war. So I found out what the rules were for medical qualification and disqualification. Through my research, I found that there was a weight-and-height rule: if you weighed under a certain amount at a certain height, you were not qualified to serve. I don't understand why that rule existed, but I'm glad it did, because I was a skinny kid. I realized that my normal weight was within five pounds of the disqualification point. I had found a way that would disqualify me to serve. The rule regarding the weight may have been adopted for something stupid, having to do with having the uniform falling off or something like that. Or maybe it had something to do with not being strong enough. I'm not sure exactly why they had the weight rule, but it was part of the legal code of being qualified for military service.

The rule for my particular height and weight range was that if you measured six-feet, you had to weigh more than 131 pounds, and if you measured at five-feet, eleven-inches, then you had to weigh more than 127 pounds. I was right around 130. I said to myself, "Wait a minute. I'm right there at the border."

Six months prior to going to the Oakland Induction Center, I managed to go on a diet to get myself down to 122 pounds. But when it was my turn in the line to get weighed and measured, I went in, they measured me at five eleven even though I was close to six-feet, and they weighed me in at 122 pounds. They said, "You pass."

"Wait a minute," I said. "I'm sorry, but the rule is 130, 131 for six-feet, and 127 for five eleven. This is not right. I protest. I am medically ineligible."

"No, no," I was told. "We'll pass you on, and you'll gain a few pounds once you get in the military. We'll fatten you up, no problem."

"Excuse me; that's not the case here," I said.

"Okay, go see the psychiatrist down the hall in that office."

I went down and saw the psychiatrist. Basically, he tried to give me the same story. "You're just a little underweight right now," he said. "We'll fatten you up, and everything will work out."

"I'm sorry," I said. "They make the rules, and these are legal rules. I don't qualify."

"Okay, we'll give you an H1 status, which means that, at the present time, you're temporarily ineligible to be drafted, for height and weight qualifications," the psychiatrist said. "But in six months, we need to have you come here again and see if your weight improves."

"Okay, no problem," I said. I knew this was my normal weight and that I wouldn't qualify. "I'll come back in six months."

What I had to do was go on what I called "the crash." It was a long-term dieting process, designed to both keep me healthy but at the border at 121 pounds.

Six months later, I went through the same routine. I was weighed and measured. Once again, I was told, "You qualify. Next."

"Wait a minute, that's not true," I said. "Your rule is—" Et cetera, et cetera, et cetera.

Again, I went in and saw the psychiatrist. "You're just a little underweight right now. We'll fatten you up, and you'll be fine," he said.

"Excuse me; I don't qualify," I said. "You make the rules. I don't qualify here because this is my normal weight."

Of course, there was the record of the previous visit, and the psychiatrist looked at it and thought it over. Then, he looked at me, and he saw that I was underweight, the same number of pounds from six months earlier. He wrote "4F" on my form, which meant that I was medically disqualified from being drafted.

CHAPTER 24

ONE OF THE THINGS I did to keep from being drafted as long as I could was to get a teaching credential. I got my degree in sociology, and I was a classic general bachelor's grad with no particular skills and no particular job future. Since I really liked working with people, I decided that I would get a high school social science teaching credential, and that I did.

I was a student teacher after I completed my course work around 1970. I was still living in the northern part of Stockton, and I had three part-time jobs. There was a children's orphanage in town, where I volunteered to tutor the children in their primary and secondary school studies, and I may have gotten paid a little bit, too. It was fun to do that. I also was a student teacher and a teaching assistant at Pacific.

When I was a student teacher, I was assigned to Lincoln High School, on the north side of Stockton, and I was assigned to a supervising teacher who was a big, burly guy. He was also the football coach. Normally, this was not the kind of guy I would associate with, but I soon found that he knew what he was doing and was a good judge of character, and I learned from him.

One day, I came to school to work with the class as a student teacher, and my supervising teacher came to me and said, "Jamie, we have a problem." He then explained that a young, sixteen-year-old student was out in the athletic field, yelling my name, and from what he knew, she was intoxicated.

"We feel that you should go talk to her, calm her down," my supervising teacher said.

At this time, I was twenty-one years old, with long hair, and I looked more like the students than the teachers. The girl in the field was a very attractive young lady and very hippie-like. So this was an awkward situation. But, since she wouldn't talk to anyone else, I went to talk with her. In the field, I explained to her that there was a significant age difference between us and that I was her teacher. So, regardless of what she wanted, it wasn't going to happen. I finally did calm her down, and the counselor was able to come and get her.

Once I got back to the social studies department, after the carrying on, I was asked what I did to cause this scene. "I didn't do anything," I said. "I talked with her and calmed her down, and she'll be okay."

This wasn't the only awkward situation I encountered as a student teacher. One evening, I went to the college because there was a band giving a concert in the dining hall. I went with a friend, Jack (not his real name), who didn't always use the best judgment, and he had no scruples when it came to girls and doing the right or wrong thing. We were at the concert, and two attractive girls from the high school where I was a student teacher came in. I knew these girls, because they were in my social studies class. So these girls were only seventeen or eighteen years old, not college girls. They'd come to the concert stoned or drinking.

My friend Jack, who had a reputation when it came to girls, immediately offered the girls a ride home—not *home* as in their homes, but a ride to his home. So now I had to step in and fend off Jack. There's a big difference between a high school senior and a college senior, and I knew that letting them go with Jack would be a mistake. Still, it's not easy to fend off a friend when he's interested in two attractive girls. His personality really was below his belt.

I did manage to get the girls home to their parents, but it's not the kind of thing I thought I'd have to do as a student teacher.

Later, I would find myself in another, rather uncomfortable situation that included Jack. In college, I had dated Karen and Mary, and later I met a woman named Melinda who went by Lindy (not her real name). I went to a party at Lindy's because I was interested in her roommate. At the party, where they were serving vodka and orange juice, I drank a lot—in fact, I drank too much. As a result, I must have passed out.

I remember waking up the next morning with both Lindy and her roommate next to me. Of course, this doesn't mean anything happened, but it was a bit of a shock to wake up like that.

While Lindy's roommate wasn't interested in dating me, Lindy was interested, and I went out with her. Lindy was popular and talented as a singer. She was popular with bands, and at concerts and parties she would sing. She wasn't a rock and roll singer, but more like Barbra Streisand. We were going out, and sleeping together. But one morning I came over to see her and she wouldn't let me in her apartment. She made excuses and didn't let me in. I knew Lindy had a boyfriend before she met me, and thought maybe they were back together, or she was seeing both of us. I didn't know. Anyway, my relationship with Lindy didn't last very long. This was a time when many young people experimented with relationships and sex. There was a sense of rebellion from the war and from traditional ways. So, it was not so strange that Lindy and I didn't last.

What was strange, however, happened two weeks after I had gone to see Lindy. I'd broken out in a skin rash, which was very sore and all over my genitals. I didn't know what it was, so I went to see a doctor.

Because I'd had unprotected sex, the doctor explained to me that I'd contracted genital herpes. I didn't know anything about this, so I had questions, like how I got it and would it go away? The doctor explained that if I had unprotected sex—meaning without a condom—that I could pick it up from a partner. I also learned I would live with it, that it comes and goes.

A couple of months later, I was telling Jack about what happened. "Oh," he said, "I've had that for a while." It turns out Jack, whose judgment was not always the best, had sex with a prostitute in San Francisco.

I put two and two together: Lindy had been seeing Jack at the same time as me. I was scared, because Lindy had been with Jack while she was also having a relationship with me. But I was also concerned and worried because her previous boyfriend had had bisexual relationships, and later, I worried that I had been at risk for AIDS.

At the time, I'd been acting like most of the young people my age, but of course, our actions can sometimes have unintended consequences. I knew that I would have to be a lot more careful in the future to protect myself and others.

CHAPTER 25

IN ADDITION TO STUDENT TEACHING at Lincoln High, once a week or a couple of times a week, I worked as a teaching assistant at Pacific. In other words, I worked as a seminar leader for the University of Pacific's freshman cultural-events course, which dealt with many social and political issues. I considered myself part of that, being an antiwar activist, and I fit right into this particular role. It gave me a little bit of financial support to keep things going, too.

The real money for me after graduation came from working as a substitute high school teacher at Lincoln High School. I subbed in social studies, since this is where I did my student teaching. They knew me, so I was a good bet for substitute teaching. I got regular work. When a teacher called in sick, I'd be there for three or four days. That's really what supported me in Stockton after I graduated. I had the same apartment I had in college, and I shared it with a roommate. I think the apartment cost us about $300 a month. We split that in half, so I needed $150. Food was relatively inexpensive, too. I wasn't getting rich, but I was surviving.

I completed my degree in 1970, got my teaching certificate, and worked my three part-time jobs until the end of 1971. So, in 1972, I was looking for a steady job.

At this time, the University of Pacific came up with a new program that was gaining some popularity across the private college campuses. It was called "University Without Walls." They needed a staff position to help develop this program. Fortunately, I was hired. Little did I know that this type of program would follow me throughout the rest of my life. It was very innovative. It fit in with my style of trying to be creative and going outside the normal bounds of education.

I was hired in the fall, and then there was a national meeting in Miami of other small private colleges who had the University Without Walls program. I went to Miami to attend that conference.

I had never been to the eastern United States. I got on the plane in San Francisco and flew all day. I got off the plane in Miami, in the evening, and walked outside the door. It was December and was cold in San Francisco. I walked outside in Miami, and the humidity and the heat just hit me. I said, "Wow."

I was young, and there were many pretty women (girls, if you like) in Miami at this conference. Of course, I hooked up with some of them, and they showed me around Miami. They took me to Miami Beach. We went to a few night spots, and they also took me to the Everglades. I saw alligators up close and personal. At the actual the conference, I took my notes.

When I came back, I developed the University Without Walls program at the University of the Pacific. The program was for nontraditional students who wanted to come back and earn college degrees. These were students who had jobs and were primarily adults. For the program, we could come up with a curriculum and a delivery system that these students were able to work on. They could earn degrees and maintain the jobs that they needed to support themselves. This was, of course, all before the age of the Internet. One might say that I was an early innovator. It led me into what I've done for most of the rest of my life.

You Can't Always Get What You Want

CHAPTER 26

⤚ formspace

HAVING JUST GRADUATED FROM COLLEGE, being out for about a year, I met people. At that time, I wasn't dating anybody in particular, but I did have a friend who had a roommate whom I was interested in going out with. She wasn't available to go out, but she said, "My roommate might be interested in going out with you."

That was Judy.

It was the fall of 1972 when I asked Judy to go out. She was cute, bright, and about a year younger than I was. She was in a college-degree program, just finishing up, and all the attractive pieces were there. Again, I wasn't seeing anybody else. It felt like time for me to develop a relationship. I was about a year or two out of college, and I didn't know what I was going to do. However, it just made sense for me to go out with Judy, and we'd been dating a bit when she said, "I have this job offer in North Carolina, in Chapel Hill." Then, she asked me if I wanted to move to North Carolina with her.

I really didn't feel like I was in love with her, but I was looking for a change, an opportunity. Now, I didn't know about Chapel Hill at all.

"Would you consider going with me?" she asked. "My dad, who's a physician, is now a dean of the public health school at East Carolina University. He's been there about a year, and I would like to go out and be closer to him."

It was a whimsical decision. I was ready to go on an adventure. Staying in Stockton, my career would eventually become the so-called big fish in a small pond. I could have taught high school, and I had many friends in California, but I was young and full of myself and saw going east with a woman to a place I didn't know to be a great adventure and an unknown opportunity.

We flew to North Carolina with two large cargo trunks. She had one, and I had one. We carried everything that we thought was important to take with us. We arrived in the winter of 1973. We flew to the Raleigh-Durham airport, got a taxi ride into Chapel Hill, and stayed in the Carolina Inn, while we looked for an apartment. We found a basement apartment for the two of us just south of town, and that's where we lived for six months.

Judy had a job, and within the month, I found a job. My position was as a financial aid counselor at the University of North Carolina, where I was hired to be the program director in the financial aid office for the federally insured student-loan program. The gentleman who ran the office was a southern gentleman. He kind of looked like Colonel Sanders. He hired me because I just made a good impression.

Judy and I settled in, playing house. She had a job; I had a job. We'd come home, tell each other our ups and the downs of the day, and were very supportive of each other. Over time, though, the relationship faltered. It didn't sour, but the magic wasn't there anymore. After about six months, we'd come home, but we weren't talking to each other.

Finally, I asked her, "What is wrong? Why are we not talking?"

"Well, I don't feel that we made a commitment to each other. Here we are, living together, and things aren't getting any better," she said.

"What do you mean?" I asked.

"I think for things to get better we need more of a commitment to each other," she said.

This was the early 1970s, so I guess I still had that traditional idea about relationships and marriage. We were both living independently, and we both had jobs, so we weren't dependent on our parents. Judy convinced me that our strong, emotional attachment would resume if we were married.

We wanted to have a wedding back in California, where our relatives and friends were, because we had only been gone about six months or so. Our wedding was in a town where her grandparents lived; it was held outside, in the wine country just north of Napa.

We went back to North Carolina, and for a while, things went back to where I was more comfortable. I guess, to be honest, that I wanted more physical intimacy in our relationship, and after we got married, Judy felt more comfortable doing that.

Judy and I never talked about starting a family. We knew we were young. We were beginning our careers, but, really, they were just jobs. We really didn't know what we wanted to do in the future. Maybe Judy was thinking about going back to school, and I thought that was always a possibility for me.

After about four months of being married, the same old problems returned. We wouldn't talk to each other. There was no sex, and it just wasn't working. She seemed very distant, and it was done, but I didn't want it to be done. I wanted to fix it. I don't think that she, in her mind, was interested in fixing it. Judy and I were married for a year, so we went on with this for a good, long while before I figured out it wasn't going to work.

My philosophy was that you can fix problems if you are willing to talk to each other, but I couldn't get Judy to ever talk to me about the problem. She kept saying, "No, nothing's wrong" or "I don't want to talk about it."

We slept in the same room, in the same bed, but never the twain would meet in bed. One night, I woke up and asked her, "What's wrong? What do you want?"

"You make me sick," she said. "I don't want to be with you. I want a divorce."

I was shocked. I wanted to fix the problem. I wanted us to see a counselor, but she was not interested. She kept saying, "No, no, no. It's over; leave."

"No," I said. "I built this house." We were, in fact, living in a house that we had built at the time we were having problems. We had moved out of the basement apartment. We built a contemporary house in Chapel Hill, just about a mile outside of downtown. It was a simple, single-story, Western, modern-style home. I had built a deck in the back.

So, I said, "No. You need to get out."

"Okay," she said. Little did I know that she had a boyfriend with whom she could live. It wasn't until a couple of months later that I did find out about this boyfriend, after we'd separated. A divorce takes six months, but after a couple of months of us being separated, I found out the truth. I sold the house. Then, we split the money, and I went back to financial ground zero. I thought there was something wrong with me, because I'd failed in a relationship. I thought I was doing everything right. I was a faithful, loving, caring husband, yet that wasn't enough.

Because of the split, I felt that there was something wrong with me. I was working at the university and got a recommendation for a psychiatrist. She was an older woman, the psychiatrist, and she was very Freudian. Her philosophy of life was to "follow Freud." It was interesting to talk to her for a session, but it cost me money. "There's nothing wrong with you," she said. "You were just in a failed relationship. You didn't do anything wrong. It just wasn't meant to be for the two of you."

CHAPTER 27

I FOUND A BASEMENT APARTMENT I could rent from a woman whose husband was a professor, but they had been divorced for a while. It was a long walk into town, but I could ride my bike. I still worked in the financial aid office. Since I had found out that there was nothing wrong with me, I also realized that other women were attracted to me, and I was attracted to them. But I wasn't ready for any long-term commitments with other women. I needed to find out that I was sexually attractive to other women; I needed to not jump into a long-term relationship.

I think, over six months, I had seven or eight different women whom I developed relationships with. It kind of worked like this: I'd meet somebody, then I'd go out with her. Fine, if we were attracted to each other, we'd kiss; we'd go away, and a week later, we'd go do something else. Soon, it developed to the point where I was sexually active with these women, and this was a pattern. Once I went to bed with a woman, after about a month or so, I became dissatisfied, because I'd reached my goal.

I say this in a straightforward way. Obviously, it's not as simple as that; nonetheless, being sexually intimate was something I didn't do much with Judy, and I wanted to know that I was okay and that other women were attracted to me. It took experimentation to convince myself that I was okay. Over time, I would slow down and develop more meaningful relationships, and those were relationships where I saw women as friends, realizing that not all women were potential sexual partners.

At this point, I had met some women who were my age, and they became good friends. I can't remember exactly how I met one of my good friends, but she has remained a friend throughout my life, and I still stay in touch with her. Her name is Liz Bryan, and shortly after I met her, she invited me to join a club.

"Jamie, you may be interested in joining this club that I just joined," Liz said. "It's the UNC-Chapel Hill Outings Club. They have great weekend trips planned in the Appalachians, the Smokies, all around the area. I know you're an outdoors person and would really, really enjoy doing these sorts of things."

Because of her suggestion, I went to an Outings Club meeting. The Outings Club was a student club at Chapel Hill, so it had mainly undergraduates in it. I was several years out of college, and I'd begun taking a graduate class during this period.

The great thing about the Outings Club is that it gave me something to do on the weekends, and here was a group of individuals that really enjoyed going out and doing different things. I went on a few hikes with them, but what really struck me was when someone expressed an interest in the Outings Club getting into rock climbing.

When asked, I said, "I know nothing about rock climbing."

"That's not a problem," I was told.

There was a first-year medical student at UNC-Chapel Hill named Mohammad, who had experience as a climber. "Mo" was his nickname, and he would teach us how to climb. I also met another individual in the Outings Club who was interested in climbing, and his name was Wesley Byerly.

For a month or two, we practiced skills on some boulders at UNC-Chapel Hill. Also, to prepare, I read three or four books about rock climbing. We purchased equipment as a group, and Mo gave us climbing lessons, including how to stretch before the climb and different techniques. I must admit that, in the early days, we were not very skilled, but we were willing to learn.

With Mo's leadership and the potential of another individual who was strong and young as well as interested in climbing, we went on our first outing. I kept a log of all the climbs that I did over a period of years. According to that logbook, this climb was in 1977. I was divorced in 1976, and this was one of my first climbs.

The good news about Wesley Byerly, an undergraduate, was that he was about ten years younger than me. When I met him, he said, "I'm from Hickory, North Carolina. That's where I grew up, and my parents are there." Hickory was not too far from Linville Gorge, where we learned that there were many places to climb. One of those places that Wes suggested we try was a place called Table Rock.

Table Rock was this big outcropping of rocks on one side of Linville Gorge, and it was basically a rock-column type of flat-top rock, rising up on the top of a hill. It was beautiful. The first climb I ever did with Wesley Byerly was on Table Rock. Wesley had done it as a kid but didn't have much experience. One of the good things about Table Rock was that there were recognized routes to climb, because someone way back when had put bolts up the routes, so you kind of knew where to go.

Wes and I did our first two-pitch climb on Table Rock, which was rated a 5.3. This was on August 6, 1977. That day we did another climb called Jim Dandy, another one-pitch climb, rated a 5.4. In climbing, anything that is rated a four-point-something is a good, steep, stiff walk, but when you get into a five rating, it means you have to have some skills because of ledges. As you get up into 5.10, and above, that's when the verticality of the climb changes to more of an overhanging rock and you have to learn how to handle this. These are all classifications of free climbing; in other words, you're just using rope and your attachments as protection.

CHAPTER 28

AT STONE MOUNTAIN, NORTH CAROLINA, there was a classic climb called the Arch, and it was a 5.6. Stone Mountain was different from other rocks I'd climbed, because the other rocks were quartzite, a metamorphic rock that got pressed together under heat and pressure making it very solid. It wasn't crumbly like sandstone, but it was a good rock. Quartzite rock is really good to climb on.

At Stone Mountain the rock was granite, a very strong rock that, when you climbed it, wasn't smooth. It had a small roughness to it. If you know what granite is, you'll have a feeling as to what Stone Mountain's about. The Arch (again, the lowest-rated climb on Stone Mountain) was 5.6 and had five pitches. The pitch is basically a rope length, where you have the lead climber who brings up the second climber, and then you're both on the rock. You anchor yourself as a seconder, and you lead out the lead climber, until the lead climber gets up to the next pitch.

Stone Mountain required a different technique. On other climbs, where you're going up vertical rock, there are handholds and footholds. At Stone Mountain, there are no handholds or footholds, yet the surface of the granite is sticky enough to climb if you have the proper, rubber-soled shoes. No regular tennis shoe would work; you needed to invest in rubberized climbing shoes to go up Stone Mountain.

The whole technique of Stone Mountain is this: if you're on the lead, you keep going. If you were to stay still on any one of the friction points, you would eventually start to slide. You had to keep going before you started to slide.

The Arch was a great climb, because it also had one other feature. There was a crack to the left of the route, and you could actually hook your fingers underneath it as you were going up, to give you a little more stability. All of the other climbs on the Arch were rated 5.8. They were open, meaning that there was no crag. To climb those, we had to go up from bolt to bolt, which was maybe a hundred feet farther up than our last piece of protection. What this meant was that once the leader got going, the leader needed to keep going. If the leader fell, the seconder would bring in as much rope as possible, so the leader's fall wouldn't hit the ground. We usually climbed the Arch in teams, a team consisting of two people, and the first team would need to go up a couple of pitches, which would be a couple of hundred feet, before another team would start the same climb. I was usually paired with Wes. He was a very strong young man with good upper body strength, so he would be fine. I was more skilled with the footwork, and I was good at the friction type of climbing. We would share leads, but if it was a steeper friction part, then I would usually go first.

CHAPTER 29

I WAS IN GRADUATE SCHOOL during the period that Wesley Byerly and I were doing a lot of our climbing. Once I had lived in North Carolina a year, I was considered a resident and could pay in-state tuition for graduate school. I took a course while I was working full-time at UNC-Chapel Hill. The course I decided to take was called College Teaching, since it was clear to me that I liked teaching. This course was taught by two individuals who held doctoral degrees in education and ran the Office of Medical Education on campus, which worked to help medical faculty be better teachers of medical students. When I took their course, things fell together in terms of where my interests were. I liked teaching but not kids. I preferred to teach adults, bright people with specific career paths.

A year later, still working in the financial aid office, I entered the program as a full-time graduate student, and my position in the financial aid office provided me with support from special funds that the director had reserved for deserving students. I entered a master's program and, after a year and a half, I received my master's in adult education. As I worked in this program, I saw that there were opportunities and jobs in medicine. Medical schools needed people like those two faculty members I'd taken the first College Teaching class with, and so I did an internship/fellowship with the UNC-Chapel Hill Office of Medical Education. While I was still figuring out my personal life, my professional life perhaps gave me more stability.

Wes and I were trying to be the climbing division leadership of the Outings Club, so we offered weekend climbing trips and rock climbing clinics. We took anybody who could walk. People would come out to climb, and we'd try to get them up easy climbs. Usually, we did the clinics at Moore's Wall. At one of the clinics, we basically had three or four people up on the wall. Wesley and I and a few other experienced climbers were present, so we'd always have at least one experienced climber to two new people.

At Moore's Wall, there was a little ledge that led to a very smooth part in the rock. Now, if there's a smooth part in the rock and there aren't any hand- or footholds, you have to approach the climb differently. We used different approaches, so we managed to get everybody up on a ledge. It was only twenty or thirty feet off the ground. It was fine. We made sure that everybody was properly tied in, because we were using straps around their waists, properly clicked in with carabiners, and we'd make sure that the carabiners got clicked into a safety.

I was going down the line, checking the three people in my group, and I noticed this one big, strong guy. He was clicked into the rope, so I thought that everything was fine until I saw where he had his carabiner clipped. The idiot had his carabiner clicked into his belt loop, not into the rope that was around his waist. If he fell, he would have fallen all the way to the ground, because his belt loop certainly would have torn. So I gave him hell.

"Where's your climbing partner who should've checked out your proper safety clicking-in?" I asked.

Basically, I prevented a potential climbing disaster by getting him to move the carabiner to the rope that was around his waist. The moral of this story is that we were taking a risk by having inexperienced people in these climbing clinics. I have to say that I think we were just lucky that we had no disasters.

Testing One's Bravado

CHAPTER 30

WHEN I WAS IN GRADUATE school, Wesley Byerly and I were doing a lot of our climbing together, and we needed to find a source for outdoor gear. Wesley ran into a shop called Appalachian Outfitters, a popular retail backpacking store throughout the East Coast. There was one on the way to Durham, North Carolina, about twenty miles away. Wesley told me about this store and about the person who ran the store, who was, of course, a young woman about our age named Freedom.

Wesley became friends with Freedom. Of course, it was an outdoor store run by a cute woman and, as things worked out, Freedom offered both of us part-time jobs working at the store. Here was an opportunity to get our outdoors gear at the reduced price for employees. As well, it turned out that both Wesley and I started dating Freedom. This didn't really cause any problems for the three of us, because we were all good friends, regardless of our relationships with each other. We were just having fun. And Freedom, as you can imagine, was a free spirit and a very attractive young woman. Wesley and I would work at different times in the store to help her out. Of course, we got paid minimum wage, and, more importantly, we got our 20 percent (or more) reduction on any equipment we needed, so it was a good deal all around. This was during the time that Wesley and I were in the Outings Club, so we had many requests for equipment that we bought for our friends.

Our relationships with Freedom and the store only lasted a couple of months. It was the summer of either 1977 or 1978, and it was just a part-time summer job. I have to admit, I enjoyed selling boots and outdoor equipment. Most of the customers had not had much outdoor experience like Wesley and I had.

Something I specifically remember about the job was that we would bicycle to work. It was about fifteen miles on a country road between Durham and Chapel Hill, so it was quite a bicycle ride. At least we were staying in shape. However, one day, Freedom let us know that the store had closed. Apparently, she had gone into work one Saturday and opened the doors to the store, and everything was gone.

"I mean, were we a part of a big robbery?" she'd said. "What's going on?"

The whole Appalachian Outfitters chain was going into bankruptcy, and so all the stores—not just ours—closed. We speculated that what happened was that the bosses, the powers above, basically came in and cleared out all of their stuff as if it were a theft, trying to lessen the amount of new inventory that they had. Then, they could indicate this false theft of all the retail goods as part of the settlement. The bankruptcy case was currently happening in the New York and the New England areas. To us, it was the strangest thing. Obviously, Freedom was out of a job, and there was no more stuff for us to sell. It was not a big deal, as far as the job was concerned. It had been fun to do. In the fall, I was going back to my graduate school classes, so I wouldn't have worked past the summer anyway.

Summers allowed time for climbing. Early in July, the summer after I first started to climb, I returned to Moore's Wall. It was about an hour and a half from Chapel Hill, so on the weekends, we would just do day trips, leaving early in the morning and coming back late at night. There was a route on Moore's Wall called Baby's Butt. The reason it was called Baby's Butt was because the rock was so smooth. Also, there weren't many handholds on quartzite rock. It was rated a 5.7+ and required four pitches to get up the rock.

What made "smooth as a baby's butt" climbing interesting is that there was a vertical crack up about seventy-five feet of the climb. The only way you could get up that area was to do a classic, layback approach. The layback is when your feet are up against the wall, and your hands are in the cracks. It worked when the wall that your feet were up against was at ninety degrees. In this ninety-degree angle, against the wall where your shoulders were touching, your hands were in the crack, going up. It was a classic climbing move, and I was skilled at laybacks. In fact, they were my forte, and my skill was increased because of my light weight. I only weighed about 135 pounds, so it was easy to manipulate my body. While this was a type of technique that I was skilled at, I was not skilled at doing overhangs, where I had to lift or pull myself up by my arms. I could, but I felt less comfortable.

CHAPTER 31

IN JULY OF 1979, WESLEY and I climbed the Pulpit at Stone Mountain, North Carolina, which was rated a 5.8, and was about fifty to seventy-five feet from bolt to bolt. It's a seven-pitch climb. The more significant climb at Stone Mountain was called Mercury's Lead. It was a four-pitch climb that rated 5.10. This was the most significant climb that I'd done or, at least, the highest-rated one I'd done. I had the ability to keep going during the vast, wide-open, granite pitches of Mercury's Lead, until I got to the next bolt to lock in. Completing Mercury's Lead was significant to me, and I mainly accomplished it because of my light weight and my technique and foot skills.

While I was not an upper-arm strength climber, I was a good strategic climber, and I understood what worked well for me. So I would excel on the friction climbs. My climbing partner, Wesley, had great upper-body strength and would excel on any climb that required his upper body to pull him up. We both had our strengths and weaknesses, and, together, we made a good team.

My climbing days in North Carolina pretty much lasted from 1977 through the summer of 1979 and a little bit into the spring of 1980. Most of the climbs that I did were at Moore's Wall, Stone Mountain, or Linville Gorge. I kept a log, and if you look at it, you can see a list of all the climbs that I accomplished. In the fall of 1980, I moved to Kentucky, and, for a brief period of time—the fall of 1980 and the spring and summer of 1981—I did a few climbs at the Red River Gorge, which was a couple of hours from Lexington. These were not significant climbs and only ranged from 5.4 to 5.8. By those days, I'd already accepted my first professional job, and my climbing time became limited. I had other things in mind, rather than spending my weekends climbing.

One of the great things about being in the UNC-Chapel Hill Outings Club was that I quickly developed many, many friends with similar interests to mine. Not surprisingly, many of those friends were women, but not all of them were. A few of these women were people that I dated, and most became my good friends.

As a group, sometimes, we would all do crazy things. One of the popular things happening in the mid-1970s was streaking, which became a big event on college campuses. Large groups of people would run naked across campus. Although the participants were naked, it was basically harmless. The streakers would run and hide, so the campus police wouldn't catch them. My first encounter with streaking happened while backpacking. I was with a close group of friends in Great Smoky Mountains National Park. It was an afternoon that was very, very hot, and up ahead of us, there was a stream. Considering how popular streaking had become on the college campuses, our small group of backpackers—maybe five or six—asked, "Why not backpack naked?" We were all friends. None of us had dated each other, so it's not like there were any boyfriend-and-girlfriend issues. And it was hot, so we all decided to take off our clothes and finish the last couple of miles before we got to our proposed campsite by the stream. We wore only our hiking boots and packs.

When we got back to campus, we realized that there were groups of undergrads streaking. Although we were graduate students and older (we were close to thirty years old, while the undergrads were eighteen to twenty-one), we figured, *Well, heck. We can streak, too.* However, we had a variation. Not too far from Chapel Hill was an old quarry, where rock was cut out to use on the side of stone buildings and various things. It was full of water. It had a wonderful little cliff to jump off into that water. We decided to go there, take off all of our clothes, and go skinny-dipping in the quarry pond.

When we got out of the water, we didn't get dressed. Instead, we got into our cars naked to see if we could drive back to town without making too much of a big fuss. As it happened, we did get back to town, and even got back to our apartments. My introduction to skinny-dipping and the whole streaking craze allowed me to not worry about what my body looked like. Remember, I was this skinny kid, so I didn't feel that I had the greatest body in the world. In our group, there were all kinds of people. On the opposite spectrum from me, there were the fat kids, and they did it, so what was the difference?

CHAPTER 32

DURING MY TIME IN CHAPEL Hill, I earned two graduate degrees. The first was an MEd in adult education, and the second was a PhD in medical education. So I was progressing in my studies and profession as I was finding adventures with the Outings Club and with friends. One of the dreams I had from reading many mountaineering books was to go out to an area with a much higher altitude and try mountaineering. Most of my adventures at this time were climbing the local rock or cliff bases, where I developed skills in climbing. Mountaineering required a whole different skill set that I had only had the opportunity to read about in books. I read about the many significant mountaineering feats that others had performed in Europe and the Himalayas. I wanted that kind of challenge.

In August of 1978, my adventures would take me across the country. With Wesley Byerly, I had the opportunity to go out to the Rockies and do some classic mountaineering. Wesley had a VW Microbus, and we it drove across the country to Wyoming to the Wind River Range. We went to one of the larger mountains, Gannett Peak, in that section of Wyoming. Our goal was to climb Gannett Peak—a rock, snow, and ice climb. It appealed to us, because there were actually a few glaciers left on Gannett. It was about a two-and-a-half to a three-day hike just to get to the base, so this really was a big trip for us.

Wesley and I arrived at the head of the trails, and from there, it was classic backpacking for a couple of days. Once we got to Gannett, we were above ten thousand feet, and we had another three thousand to four thousand feet to go up to climb Gannett. When we arrived, we needed to prepare ourselves. For a whole day before the summiting day, we would go up the surrounding snow fields and practice falling and doing self-arrest with our ice axes. If we were to fall on Gannett, we would have to stop ourselves by self-arresting with our ice ax blades, which would drag into the snow and ice to slow us down, stopping us from falling to the bottom.

Then, summiting day came. Wesley and I woke up at three o'clock in the morning. We ate something and drank as much as we could. First, we had a caldera, basically a rock field, to go over. It was quite an unusually long entrance before we got to the mountain itself.

We left our backpacking gear at our camp, but we were certainly carrying a lot of climbing equipment in our day packs, including some water and something to eat if needed. The reason we started to climb so early in the morning, as the sun was starting to come up, was because we wanted to hit the ice and snow before it got too soft from the sunshine. Also, out west in the late afternoons, because of thermal convection, there were mountain thunderstorms, so we needed to get off the mountain before the time the storms came. We needed as many daylight hours as we could get.

In classic mountaineering two-person team form, we got through lower rock fields, and eventually started up the slope. As we started up, we needed to protect ourselves, so we put on our crampons to provide some grip in the snow fields. Regular hiking boots would slip. We also had a rope attached to each of us, as well as our trusty ice axes in our hands, secured with a little nylon strap around our wrists. These straps ensured we wouldn't lose our ice axes if we dropped them. We were very well prepared.

Starting up the lower snow fields of Gannett, we ran into our first obstacle. We came to a crack in the rock we needed to cross, and what we eventually did was find a snow bridge we could take across the crevasse. We set up a belay on one end that allowed one person to cross.

First I crossed and then I belayed Wesley, and he went across. Luckily, we did everything right, and we got through that crevasse, which was also called a bergschrund, a mountaineering term for a crevasse that splits the snow field from the beginning of the glacier.

Then, we were actually on the glacier. We had to be careful, because snow opened the future cracks in the glacier, and these were places where we could fall in. So we always sent one person first, while the other person held back to protect the first, since we were on the rope together. Those are the types of things we did, and eventually, we got to the final summit run. We only had a couple of hundred feet to go, and we'd be on the top. There, it was primarily snow and ice, but there was some mixture of rock. It was very interesting to climb on rock with our crampons on, but we managed.

Then, we had a problem. Wesley was getting sick. He had a headache, and we were thirteen thousand feet up (or something in that range). While his head ached, his stomach was also hurting, and he said he just didn't feel well at all.

"Jamie, I can't continue," he said. "You go ahead, and I'll wait here, and you can come back."

Well, I knew that wasn't good judgment. "No, Wesley," I said, "it's more important that we stay together, and if you're feeling mountain sickness, we need to go down. We need to drop a couple of thousand feet and go back to camp."

So Wesley and I made the decision to head back, even though we could see the summit, and we were only a couple of hundred feet below it. With just a steep snowfield to go to get to the top, we decided not to go for safety reasons. However, this often happens in mountaineering; we were very close, but we had to use our judgment. The right thing in this case was to come again another day. As it turned out, on this climb, Wesley had not eaten properly. He also hadn't had enough fluids. This resulted in him needing to get back down out of the altitude. The next day, we packed up our backpacks and headed back down, having come so close to the summit but not truly reaching it.

After Wesley and I came down from the peak area and hiked back to our vehicle, we decided that, since we were on summer vacation, we were going to go to Estes Park, Colorado. At the base of the Rockies, Estes Park is the gateway to a beautiful national park, Rocky Mountain National Park, but there was another reason that I wanted to go there. My current girlfriend, Carol Delaney, had a sister who worked in Estes Park. We had a free place to stay, and Carol was on her way, too. She was working for a moving company, and she had hitched a ride on a moving van and was going to be dropped off.

The only problem with our plan was that I knew Carol's sister's name, but I didn't know exactly where she lived. I also didn't have a phone number for her. But, I had confidence that we would run into each other in Estes Park somewhere. When Wesley and I arrived, the first place we went to was a nearby mountaineering store, where we stopped to look at all the gear. While we were in the store, I asked whether anybody knew Susan Delaney. And everybody became very quiet.

"We're friends from North Carolina," I explained. "We want to see her, and we're trying to catch up with her." Then, we walked outside. A few minutes later, a woman walked out of the store. Inside, she hadn't told us that she was Susan. Outside, Susan introduced herself, and we made the connection purely by luck and by chance. Susan knew from her sister Carol that we would show up some time, but she had no idea when. These are the sorts of things that happened in the 1970s, when I was young and traveling openly and freely.

We stayed with Susan, because she had an apartment close to her summer job at Estes Park. I thought that was perfect. Eventually, Carol came, and when she did, we went climbing in the park, which was part of the Rockies. It was going well until one day, when we were on a little, granite cliff. Carol was leader, and I was belaying her. She took a leader's fall, missing a handhold. It might have broken off or something. I caught her on the rope before she hit the ground, which was quite amazing. Because her protection held, it didn't pop out like a zip line. The fall was scary, but she didn't fall on the ground. She was a little bruised, as she was swinging out and hitting the rock. Somehow, though, everything was okay.

There were some other climbs we did in the park: Lumpy Ridge, Twin Owl, and Northern Pipes. We also did the Spearhead climb. These all were in the 5.6 to 5.7 range. It was near summer's end, and although we had a great time staying in the park, our vacation came to a close because of the start of school. I had about a month before I would resume grad school. We ended the trip with the Delaney sisters and got to go to the Nitty Gritty Dirt Band concert at Red Rocks, an amphitheater just outside of the Denver area. Then, Wesley and I drove the VW Microbus home.

Humble Beginnings from Religious Persecution

࿊

WHEN I TALK ABOUT MY experiences, I often focus on my adventures, the things I did outdoors, and the way I explored. But I have explored in another way, and that's through learning about my family's history. We all come from somewhere, and like many people in this country, my family's beginning in America was comprised of people migrating from Europe. My migrating ancestors happened to come to America at the beginning of the exploration of this country, and I find it interesting being part of that lineage.

An oral history is something that one generation passes on to another, and I've tried to write down things that I heard from my father or my mother to get some sense of our background. Of course, there are stories I was told by various relatives, as well. To help me fill in the gaps, I actually have a book from around the turn of the twentieth century, published in 1909. It's a Shumway family genealogy book that Dad had. It included the stories of the French Huguenots in my family and beyond. So the Shumway side of the family is well documented.

Of course, there is also the maternal side. I think it was when I was in my teens that I asked questions to my mother about her past and her family. She talked about her father, and one thing kind of led to another. So I got little snippets of oral history. Every year, we would visit my mother's father for events like Thanksgiving. He was the grandparent that I knew, and stories were told at those family gatherings.

My father's side of the family has an interesting story. His ancestor was one of seven sons of a French Huguenot family that came over to the New World in 1696. In the 1600s, the French Huguenots were expelled from France. As proof of these claims, I quote the following from pages seven and eight in the beginning of the book *Genealogy of the Shumway Family in the United States of America*, complied by Asahel Adams Shumway:

CIRCULAR

Dear Sir:

Is it desirable to have a meeting of the Shumway family? Is it not well to erect a Monument of some kind to the memory of Peter Shumway, 1st, a French Huguenot, who left his home and country on account of religious persecution, about the year 1695, came to Boston, Mass., in the same vessel with Peter Faneuil (Faneuil Hall) and the Sigourneys; married there an English lady, Miss Smith, and settled with a colony of his own people at Oxford. The place, or farm, where he lived and died is known, and the place or very near the spot in the old Churchyard where he was buried. Portions of a fort they built for protection from Indians are still standing.

The names of his sons were Oliver, Jeremiah, David, John, Jacob, Samuel and Amos.

All the Shumways in America are unquestionably descendants of the said Peter.

It is the earnest desire of my father, Peter Shumway, now at the age of 94 years, grandson of Jeremiah and son of Peter, that I invite your attention to this matter, and ask your interest and co-operation.

Have not the persecutions of the French Protestants in years past an important bearing upon the present condition of that people?

A very interesting sketch of the Huguenots in France and America may be found in Harper's Magazine for November, 1870.

The writer will be pleased to receive any items of special interests with reference to the family. Please to circulate this note to persons of the same name and if you wish for more I will send them to you.

An answer at your earliest convenience will oblige,

Yours, Very truly,
F. Peter Shumway.
Leominster, Mass., May 1, 1871

It is reported that there was a Shumway, a blacksmith by trade, who made guns during the American Revolutionary War during the bitter cold and difficult winter at Valley Forge in Pennsylvania. Shumways were also in the Mexican, Civil, and Spanish Wars. The Shumways, it can be said, had a strong sense of independence, a hard belief in a particular religious order, for lack of a better word, and a sense of adventure. They left the country that they knew to come to a new world and start again. They were forced to leave their country, but they did it and thrived. So, this may be a stretch, but maybe all of my outdoor-oriented adventures made me believe there is some genetic contribution through my ancestry. Maybe the pilgrims, the French Huguenots exploring a new world, contributed in some way to many of the outdoor-oriented adventures I've had.

Coming of Age

CHAPTER 34

I WAS FINISHING MY PhD at UNC-Chapel Hill. I had written the dissertation and pretty much was in the revision process, meeting with my committee and doing revisions, putting on final touches. In the meantime, I knew I needed to find a professional job.

There were many jobs available in medical education, but all of them seemed to be in Chicago, and I wasn't at all interested in moving to Chicago. I never saw myself as a big-city person. I always thought, academically, I would do better if I were in a smaller city, for example, one of the state capitals or one of the smaller Appalachian towns.

I looked at a position in Texas and one in Illinois, but then I saw an interesting position in Lexington, Kentucky. It was at the University of Kentucky, and they were looking for a director of faculty development in the Office of Medical Education. I applied, and within a month or so, I was notified that they wanted me to go to Kentucky for an interview. I showed up at the interview, and I must admit, I was a little nervous, and I'd forgotten to bring a tie. I called the director of the office, who had lined up all these interviews with faculty and staff and administrators at the medical school in Kentucky.

"Whoops!" I said. "I forgot to bring a tie."

The director was a young man, and he laughed. He brought me a tie, and the interviews went fine. Within a week, they offered me a job in the Office of Medical Education as the director of faculty development. I had really no other places I wanted to go, so I accepted the position to start in September of 1980. I moved to Kentucky. I didn't know anything about Kentucky, but I had heard it was a pretty place. It's not too far from rivers and mountains.

There was one issue. The problem was that I still had my girlfriend at UNC-Chapel Hill. Carol was ten years younger than I was. She was in nursing school, and she was finishing her senior year that year. Of course, I was young and in love, and I tried to talk her into coming to Kentucky with me when she finished.

She didn't come along.

That December, I wanted to come back and visit her. I'd been gone since starting my new job in September. However, she wrote me the classic "Dear John" letter: "Our relationship is over; I found someone else that I'm going out with. I'm sorry. Have a good day." It was the beginning of a lonely period for me.

Already heartbroken and sad, I knew I had to make plans to see someone. However, I had my dog with me in Kentucky, so I boarded her. Guinevere, my golden retriever, was now about ten years old. She was the same dog who had assisted as part of the medic team at the stadium concerts at University of the Pacific, years before.

Saddened that I got a "Dear John" letter, I went to the mountains to visit friends in North Carolina. While there, I got a terrible call. It was from my veterinarian. My dog had died. Now, I would return to Kentucky and really be all alone. I went back to the University of Kentucky to resume my position in January of 1981 without much. It was cold. I had very few friendships in Kentucky other than my work relationships. No dog, no girlfriend—my life was changing.

CHAPTER 35

IN MY FIRST JOB, I was hired to be the director of faculty development for the School of Medicine, in the Office of Medical Education at the University of Kentucky. The nature of my job was to help improve the teaching quality of the faculty in the medical school. This was not an unusual job, as there were other professionals at other medical schools who did this. But it was my first professional job doing this, and one of my strengths was working with people; in particular, I was good at working with faculty who were physicians to help them be better teachers. I was working with very brilliant people, and they were eager to learn, and I think it was a natural role for me.

However, one of the downsides or traps that may occur in working with bright, young physicians is that you wake up one day and say to yourself, "Wait a minute. Here I am, working with physicians and teaching them to be better teachers. But what physicians do is take care of people and teach their patients how to take care of themselves. I'm young. Maybe I want to be a physician, too." I did not make this decision just because physicians were getting paid a lot more than us educators. I was pretty much in the same environment, working with them to help them do better jobs in teaching their patients to care for themselves, and their students about what it took to be physicians. However, I went through an identity crisis, thinking about what it would take if I were to become a physician, too.

Ironically, when I had first entered college, I'd wanted to be a dentist. Now, I was considering medical training. I was working full-time when I enrolled and took a biology course and another science class at the University of Kentucky. I did this for two semesters; both were two-semester science courses. Basically, I got a high B in one and an A in the other. It showed that I had the ability to do something like that.

After taking these classes for two semesters, I rethought my decision. *Do I really want to become a physician? I'm working with physicians; I'm in their environment.* Many of my friends were physicians. I got to thinking that I didn't necessarily have to be a physician to be successful and do things with that particular peer group. In effect, what I did was kind of modify my thinking and say, "Well, I can learn the science that I need to be like them, to help them do a better job teaching the students." That's where my interest really was, at least professionally.

CHAPTER 36

IN THE SPRING, I HEARD about a club. Since I had similar success with the Outings Club at Chapel Hill, I became interested in this group, which did a lot of white-water canoeing and kayaking. It was called the Bluegrass Wildwater Association. I went to some of their meetings and went on trips for beginners in the spring. I started to make connections and became more social. This time, the outdoor adventures were white-water-based, not necessarily hiking-based, as I had done in North Carolina. One of the things that I learned about myself was that, when I looked back on my patterns, when I moved to a new place or I had a change in relationships, I tended to gravitate toward clubs and outdoor activities. Unlike in North Carolina, this was not a campus thing. It was a community club with people in it who had similar interests. Many of the people were just like me age-wise (early thirties and older). I fit in well.

First, I went to roll sessions in the local pool in Lexington, which were sponsored by the association. There are skills and techniques to learn if you want to roll a kayak. It's best to learn in a pool in the winter, rather than getting right on the river, where you might test it out and sometimes not do very well. I got to know some people that winter in the Bluegrass Wildwater Association. It was in January, February, and March of 1981. At the pool sessions, everybody was prepared to start paddling on the rivers, which ran best in the spring because of the spring rain and things like that.

This was a natural for me. It was very active. It was an outdoor activity. I needed to learn the skills of white-water canoeing and kayaking, just like I learned the skills to do rock climbing back in North Carolina. In both white-water boating and in climbing, one has a passion for the environment, and it requires a certain skill set to be successful. It's true of climbing up a rock or going down a river with rapids. In either activity, mistakes can lead to injury or death. We who wanted to do these activities and develop the skill sets did so because they allowed us to be in control of our own destinies.

One of the important things to know about white-water boating is that it is not the same as white-water rafting. Rafting usually includes paying customers who are guided down rivers. Very few people own their own rafts. Boaters learn the skills to kayak or canoe. To call a "boater" a "rafter" is a faux pas that novices often make.

Since I was a new member and had been to the pool sessions, I was invited out on the rivers with the group. "You should come on some boating trips with us," an instructor said to me. "We would loan you a kayak. I think you will have fun."

CHAPTER 37

I BOUGHT MY FIRST KAYAK, which was fiberglass and had a cut-down deck. In other words, it was a little bit thinner than regular-sized kayaks and flattened a little bit. It was designed by a gentleman by the name of Vladimir Vanha. Now, Vladimir Vanha lived outside of the NOC (Nantahala Outdoor Center) in North Carolina. He lived in the western mountains of North Carolina, and he was an excellent boat maker and had quite a reputation. I bought one of his old, used boats.

I went on one trip to the NOC, where we kayaked. I was using a borrowed boat that time down the Nantahala River, which was not terribly difficult, but it was a beautiful setting. At the beginning of the easier kayaking, I got hooked, because I liked being with people and camping out with them, and I liked boating. The Bluegrass Wildwater Association has the philosophy of learning by living or dying, and they would have beginner trips on big rivers. For example, I had a beginners' trip on the New River Gorge in West Virginia. It was a beginning kayak trip, and I swam five times going down the New River Gorge, which means I tipped over and couldn't roll myself upright, so I had to get out of the kayak. My roll skills were not developed at the time. On the New River, I dealt with holes and big water. I knew it was a big-water river that had a history of being one of the premier white-water runs, and here I was, a beginner, going down the New River Gorge. I loved it. I thought I was going to drown and die several times, but I didn't. Of course, I went back to do it many more times.

Every spring, the Bluegrass Wildwater Association would have a long, three-day trip over Memorial Day weekend, like the trip we took on sections of the Emory and Obed Rivers. They would call it the Emory-Obed clinic, and they would run you down the local, free-flowing streams in the Emory-Obed watersheds. This, I recall, was south of Lexington and on the Tennessee border area.

One of the trips that they took beginners on was on the Cumberland River. It was the section called the Big South Fork of the Cumberland River. Little did we beginners know that on this particular one, there were three huge rapids; basically, we had to make it over three separate five to six feet drops on the river without dying.

On the first drop, I did fine. I stayed upright. My kayak nose went over. I hit the water right. When under the water, I bounced right back up, and I didn't swim. I stayed in my boat, and I managed to get myself up. Then, on the next drop, it was the same routine. I got really tired from working really hard. Finally, on the third drop (which, again, was a five feet drop), I made it fine. It was memorable. Really, this was the beginning of my white-water boating days.

Each year, we would go on trips. One of the trips that we did the following year, where I really gained more white-water skills, was when we went to the Ocoee River in Tennessee. The Ocoee River was a dam-controlled, Class III to IV river, a high and very fast river. I was kayaking down it for the first time, and I flipped when I went over a small drop at the beginning of the river. The water was shallow, and I could feel my helmet bouncing off rocks under the water. However, I was able to roll up. Then the big waves started, downriver a little bit, and still, I did fine. I negotiated and successfully navigated my first world-class rapid. My kayaking skills were developing. I became a regular club member, and I was completely hooked.

CHAPTER 38

IN LEXINGTON, I LIVED IN an old, historic building. It was what some people call a shotgun house. Built in the mid-1800s and restored—it actually had a historic building marker—it was a two-story building split into a lower-story apartment and an upper-story apartment. "Shotgun" means that it was long and not very wide. The apartment was very close to the university, so I could walk or bike to the medical school.

I met a woman who had the same name as an old girlfriend, but she spelled it differently. I don't know exactly how I met her. I may have seen her from a distance, as she was a research assistant in the School of Medicine. She was working with a surgeon who did a special type of microsurgery. He reconnected small vessels, and Carole assisted him. Carole had graduated from the sciences as an undergraduate, and was a little older, closer to my age than the younger women I had gone out with. I don't know what it was about her, why I was attracted to her. It took me a long time to court her. She wouldn't allow me at first. I saw something in her that I liked, and eventually, she agreed to go out with me.

Carole had a certain amount of aggressiveness in her. She wanted to be in control of any sort of relationship. I didn't know what her other relationships were like. She may have had a boyfriend she was breaking up with. She kept it very secret. Initially, she would have kept our relationship from not developing very fast at all. After a while, it was clear that we were destined to be boyfriend and girlfriend. Later, I saw some faults in Carole, and I found out that she was manipulative.

I met Carole in 1982. We probably saw each other for over a year, then, during the last six months of '82 or the first six months of '83, she became more possessive of me and wanted a more serious commitment on my part. Carole had a temper and would break in and out of relationships for short periods of time. Something in my mind said, "Wait a minute; you've been through this before. Don't make the same mistake when you're in a relationship that has been rocky with a woman."

When I tried to tell her that I wanted to break up, she couldn't handle it. At these times, she would have migraine headaches, and she would seek the help of a physician friend of hers who gave her drugs to control and reduce her headaches. Now, I didn't understand that, and I questioned our relationship's stability. Is this really the person whom I want to be with for a longer period of time? I tried to break up with her twice. When she had these headaches, I felt sorry for her and would go back to her and try to help her through the difficulties she was having.

In the end, which I think was in May of 1983, I finally broke up with her for the last time, and it was a good thing. I didn't worry about what she was going to do. It was one of those classic, relationship break-ups. We went in our own directions. I think Carole also came to the conclusion that we were not meant to be. In the last six months, she was talking about marriage. I wasn't at all interested in making that mistake again.

But something else important happened during this time. During the time I was seeing Carole, I received a phone call from California. It was from Heddy, the woman that my father had married after my mom. She was crying, incoherent, and very frantic. Heddy told me that my father had died.

"How did he die?" I asked her, because he was in his early sixties.

"He committed suicide," Heddy said. She explained that she arrived home and went in the house and found him with a gunshot wound in his head and blood everywhere. She didn't know what to do.

I'd had a difficult relationship with my father.

His death was a big shock to me—one that I thought I could handle, but a month later, I had kind of this itching on the side of my torso, under my armpit, on my ribcage. *What's going on now?* I thought. The itching broke out into a rash, and then the rash intensified and covered half of my upper torso. What had happened to me was a classic case of stress-induced shingles. I had attributed it to the passing of my father and to not really mourning or dealing with that very well.

My father was an alcoholic. I knew he had a drinking problem. I didn't know the extent of mental discomfort and anguish that this caused him. It's not to be predicted, but it's also not to be misunderstood.

When I was younger, I remember that my parents would yell at each other all the time, and it bothered me. In high school, I would hear them fighting, disagreeing, and it was not a good relationship when I was growing up. I remembered the bickering, and part of the reason was because my father would drink and then get angry or lose his senses—not in a violent, physical way, but in a disruptive, verbal way. My father would swear and cuss all the time. I had a harmonious childhood in some respects, but there was also this background tension, and it impacted me, too. As a kid in the 1950s, I felt that it was common for all the parents to have a drink or two in the evening. So it was hard to tell it was a problem.

My father was born in Illinois. His father and mother had been bankers, and during the 1920s, and when the Great Depression hit, they lost everything they had. My father grew up on a farm, and he helped my grandfather, his father, take care of a school. I remember that my father would tell me stories of how he would walk through the snow in central Illinois to get the stove running at the school on winter mornings.

My father didn't love farming. He got flying lessons when he was a teenager. At some point, he signed up to be in the Royal Canadian Air Force when World War II was heating up. When the Japanese attacked Pearl Harbor, he was released to go into the navy. In California, before leaving for the Pacific, he met my mother on a blind date. My father and a buddy were young naval officers, and they were stationed in San Francisco, getting ready to be deployed in the South Pacific. They were pilots. My mother and father got to know each other. Before he was to go on his deployment, they got married.

During the war, my father was called "Bones" Shumway, because he was so skinny, much like me. When I was growing up, I learned that he was approached by TV or movie executives who wanted to make a movie or a series about his exploits during World War II. As it turns out, nothing ever happened with it. But my information is sketchy at best, because he never talked about what he did and what he experienced in World War II.

My father flew a dive bomber. If you understand what dive bombers do, they come in and drop their bombs at the enemy's ship. He was involved in the second battle of the Philippines. This was General MacArthur's retaking of the Philippines, an intense air battle with the Japanese, and that's primarily where he flew his dive bombers. My father was stationed on the USS *Intrepid*, one of the aircraft carriers in the South Pacific at that time. He undertook many flights against the entire Japanese fleet. For a period of time, his buddies were getting shot down, but he kept going out on missions continuously to drop bombs on the Japanese fleet. He earned many medals, such as the Navy Cross and the Distinguished Flying Cross.

My father didn't talk much about the war.

I always looked up to my father for his work helping people in Solano County. And I think I was the more fortunate between my brother, Ralph, and me, because a lot of the heavy-duty arguing between our parents started when I was away at college. My brother was at home, having to deal with it. I'd come home to visit, but it wasn't frequent—because why would I want to come home and hear arguing and see my father drinking every night? So I avoided coming home. When I did come home for a holiday or something, I would go around the house and try to find hidden liquor bottles and pour the liquor down the drain.

Upon hearing about my father's death and getting shingles, I went to a doctor, who diagnosed me. I had not had closure about his alcoholism and his mental anguish. I don't know if his anguish was war-related. I was still with Carole at this time, and she was always supportive. But she would also say not to tell anybody that my father had committed suicide. Carole would tell people that he died of a broken heart. I never really understood this, but she wanted to avoid the stigma.

Love Stories

CHAPTER 39

ABOUT A MONTH AFTER BREAKING up with Carole, I went to a Sierra Club meeting, and then a bit later, I began to offer a community education class. The class that I offered was about canoeing rivers in Kentucky. It was four weeks of community education for one hour on Monday nights. During the last week of the class, I arranged for the students to go on a canoe trip down one of Kentucky's scenic rivers.

At the first class, I was talking about the various parts of the canoe. I had drawn a canoe on the board, and I talked about the gunwales. I spelled it "gunnels" on the board. There was a woman in the back of the class who raised her hand and said, "Excuse me. Are you sure that's how 'gunwales' is spelled?"

I was immediately struck, taken by her.

I didn't know what to say to her, frankly. "That's a very good question," I said. "Why don't you look it up and come back and tell the class and me next time how it's spelled?"

When class ended, I said to myself, "Wow. Who was that who asked me that question in class? Boy, I hope she comes back to class, even though she knows that I'm a jerk." I was struck by her beauty, her presence. I really wanted to see this woman again.

"If she comes back to class, be cool," I told myself. "Don't be over-anxious. Just go on as usual, and see how things go."

At the next class, I arrived a bit early to set up, to draw some things on the board, and refresh my memory of what I was going to talk about that week. She came into class early, too.

I said to myself, "This is great, but don't be overeager. Don't ask her out." I really wanted to, because I wasn't dating anybody at that time. And I couldn't contain myself. I thought, *What the heck? Before class starts, let me ask her to do something.*

So I asked her if she would like to go out and have a cup of tea after class. And we did go. It was Betsy. She was a brand-new college professor at Kentucky, and she'd decided to take my class, rather than one about symphonies or one about wine tasting. If I were her, I would have taken the wine-tasting course.

And she did tell me how to spell "gunwales" correctly.

During the early days of going out with Betsy, I invited her to go backpacking overnight in the Red River Gorge, which has some beautiful arches and some table-like rocks that you would normally find out West. One of the things we did is hike up one of the rock arches. It wasn't climbing. We could hike up and overlook the gorge and the river below. We decided to camp on top of the large, stone arch.

Betsy had brought her little coffeepot, which had a top on it. We were sitting there on the edge when I said, "What?" Something had happened. The top of the coffeepot fell off and rolled down the rock. And fortunately, we weren't dumb enough to try to grab it. It forever disappeared. And we always remembered that. It was one of the experiences that pretty much solidified my feelings toward Betsy.

She also liked the outdoors. She liked to go backpacking and camping. I thoroughly did, too. She was a PhD in geography, and I had my PhD in medical education. Betsy had just turned thirty, and I was in my mid-thirties. We were healthy, we were financially independent, and we had good jobs. I knew that she was different and special, but I wasn't ready for a commitment just yet.

CHAPTER 40

ON MY MOTHER'S SIDE, I am descended from John Alden, the carpenter on the *Mayflower*. The Shumways, the French Huguenots who came to the New World, are not well-known. Both the Pilgrims and John Alden are very well-known. Like the French Huguenots, the Pilgrims came to the New World to freely practice their religion. On both sides, I have a family history of adventurers who came to this country to start new lives, despite the unknowns. They must have had a strong sense of being in control of their destinies.

John Alden received his fame by asking Priscilla Mullins, another Pilgrim, to marry him. The famous Miles Standish was also a potential suitor for Priscilla, and a fictional account of John and Priscilla Alden's courtship and their entanglement with Miles Standish was the subject of a Henry Wadsworth Longfellow poem. The fervor of their courtship is captured in the following lines toward the end of section III in the poem "The Courtship of Miles Standish":

"Has he no time for such things, as you call it, before he is
    married,
Would he be likely to find it, or make it, after the wedding?
That is the way with you men; you don't understand us, you
    cannot.
When you have made up your minds, after thinking of this one
    and that one,

Choosing, selecting, rejecting, comparing one with another,
Then you make known your desire, with abrupt and sudden
    avowal,
And are offended and hurt, and indignant perhaps, that a woman
Does not respond at once to a love that she never suspected,
Does not attain at a bound the height to which you have been
    climbing.
This is not right nor just: for surely a woman's affection

Is not a thing to be asked for, and had for only the asking.
When one is truly in love, one not only says it, but shows it.
Had he but waited awhile, had he only showed that he loved me,
Even this Captain of yours—who knows?—at last might have
Old and rough as he is; but now it never can happen."

Still John Alden went on, unheeding the words of Priscilla,
Urging the suit of his friend, explaining, persuading, expanding;
Spoke of his courage and skill, and of all his battles in Flanders,
How with the people of God he had chosen to suffer affliction,
How, in return for his zeal, they had made him Captain of
    Plymouth;
He was a gentleman born, could trace his pedigree plainly
Back to Hugh Standish of Duxbury Hall, in Lancashire,
    England,
Who was the son of Ralph, and the grandson of Thurston de
    Standish;
Heir unto vast estates, of which he was basely defrauded,
Still bore the family arms, and had for his crest a cock argent
Combed and wattled gules, and all the rest of the blazon.
He was a man of honor, of noble and generous nature;
Thought he was rough, he was kindly; She knew how during the
    winter
He had attended the sick, with a hand as gentle as a woman's;

Somewhat hasty and hot, he could not deny it, and headstrong,
Stern as a soldier might be, but hearty, and placable always,
Not to be laughed at and scorned, because he was little of stature;
For he was great of heart, magnanimous, courtly, courageous;
Any woman in Plymouth, nay, any woman in England,
Might be happy and proud to be called the wife of Miles
    Standish!

But as he warmed and glowed, in his simple and eloquent
language,
Quite forgetful of self, and full of the praise of his rival,
Archly the maiden smiled, and, with eyes overrunning with
    laughter,
Said, in a tremulous voice, "Why don't you speak for yourself,
John?"

So I'm connected through my ancestry to one of the earliest romances in the American colonies. John Alden is directly related to my mother, and her maiden name was Berte Alden Scovel. Although John and Priscilla were in love, they were worried about offending Standish, but after hearing that Standish had been killed by Indians, they agreed to get married. However, Standish wasn't killed by Indians. Still, he blessed their marriage, which produced eleven children, and the Aldens helped found the town of Duxbury, Massachusetts.

CHAPTER 41

BACK IN LEXINGTON, KENTUCKY, IN the fall of 1983 when I met Betsy, I had a job working as a consultant on a project in Saudi Arabia. The project included preparing curriculum and evaluation materials for training dental assistants and dental hygienists in Saudi Arabia at the oil company known as Aramco, so they could provide dental care to the Saudis that were working there. I learned that I would need to travel to Saudi Arabia.

This wasn't the first time I'd done this kind of travel; I'd traveled there a year before. This time, the consulting trip was in January of 1984, right after Christmas. While I was in Saudi Arabia, I had lots of downtime to think about Betsy and my future with her. What I figured out was that I was very much in love with her and that she would be a wonderful woman to spend the rest of my life with.

Of course, before I went to Saudi Arabia, I didn't have the nerve to tell her, and I hadn't really solidified how I felt. In Saudi Arabia, I had lots of what I call "nighttime downtime." I worked hard during the day, and in the evening, I just slept. Then, I'd wake up and work hard the following day. With the free evenings, I really thought about it. When I got back from Saudi Arabia, I had pretty much solidified in my mind what I wanted to do.

I got back in late January. I invited Betsy over to my house for dinner. And I remember that it was a special dinner that I'd made her: trout almondine, as fancy as I could make it. And we had wine with dinner, special wine. And after dinner, I remember getting on my knees and asking her to marry me.

The good news is that she said yes.

Now, however, we had to figure out a wedding. We were both older, and we'd both been married before. She was a college professor, and I was a middle-management consultant. We thought we could get married during the University of Kentucky spring break, which that year was in March. So we got married on March 24, 1984, in the Hunt-Morgan House in Lexington. The Hunt-Morgan House was an old, historic, Federal-style house built in 1814. We had a very informal wedding. The university hospital's chaplain married us. Friends and family came in from all over the country, and there may have been forty or fifty people there, at the most. It wasn't very religious, and the only things said were the basic wedding vows. We all stood around in front of a fireplace and had the wedding. So it worked out very well, because both of us knew what we wanted.

Then, of course, Betsy moved in with me.

CHAPTER 42

As a newly married couple, Betsy and I were both interested in doing things on the water. I had already been a kayaker, and Betsy did some kayaking after we first met, but she decided she was more comfortable canoeing with me. Betsy had a very close friend up in Minnesota who had a cabin on one of the northern lakes, and we went up there in August of 1985 to visit. We also decided that we were going to do an extended canoe trip in the Boundary Waters Canoe Area in Northern Minnesota. I actually have a slide collection from the Boundary Waters canoe trip that we did. As we all know, a picture is worth a thousand words.

Betsy and I arrived in Northern Minnesota after driving up, and the first thing we needed was to get Betsy's good friend Renee's aluminum canoe, because, at that point, we didn't have a canoe that was light enough for us to take up in the Boundary Waters. We knew that we would have to portage the canoe frequently from one lake to another.

"Portage" is a French word, and it refers to moving the canoe from one body of water to the next. There are things you need to consider when you have to portage your canoe. First, you have to have a canoe that you can pick up, flip over, and balance on your shoulders. Weight is an issue, but so is distance. In the Boundary Waters, where we canoed this trip, there were special trees with crosspieces, where you could lean your canoe. There were also signs to let you know how far it was to the next lake. The distance terminology on these signs is not in miles, not in feet, not in yards, and not in meters. They're in measurements called "rods." A rod is about the length of a canoe, sixteen-and-a-half feet. If there are seventy-five rods to the next lake, that's a fair distance—almost a quarter-mile.

There's a trail to get from lake to lake. Unfortunately, you can't portage everything all at once. Remember, it's a quarter-mile each way. On the first portage, one person takes the canoe, and the other takes the stuff in the canoe, like the paddles, life jackets, and stuff like that. Left behind for the second trip are the "bills" bags. These are like duffle bags and are waterproof, with shoulder straps to carry them on your back. Each bills bag is thirty to fifty pounds when filled with all the camping equipment—stove, food, sleeping bag, tent, and all that kind of stuff. One person can't carry both bags, so both have to walk back to get them. They are like giant duffle bags. They span from the top of your head to your knees, about four feet tall and two feet wide. You put the two straps over your shoulders to carry the bills bags on your back.

Hopefully, with two people, there are only three walks, but all in all, the distance adds up when you're carrying your stuff from lake to lake. Luckily, you only do a couple of these portages a day, because most of the time, you're on the water.

Renee loaned us her aluminum canoe, and it was about fifty-five pounds or so. I could handle that on my shoulders, portaging it between the lakes in the Boundary Waters region. After a few days of visiting Renee at the cabin, which was on one of the bigger lakes in Northern Minnesota, Lake Vermillion, we left with the canoe on top of our car to the Boundary Waters. It was a great, beautiful August that summer. We had about ten days or so before we had to get back. This was probably one of the earlier trips that we did in extended canoeing. We had Betsy's car from graduate school, a Toyota Corolla station wagon, and with Renee's Grumman canoe, we really had everything we needed to start this trip.

We picked a route consisting primarily of small lakes, where we would make a big circle for the eight or so days that we were out. We knew that there would be some challenges, and the major challenge would be heavy winds on big lakes. We avoided a route that had really big lakes, because we were more interested in just going from one little lake to another. Because we always approached canoeing together, whether on white-water or in the Boundary Waters, it was no-fault canoeing; if we messed up, it was no one's fault. As a team, we thought of ourselves as one, and it worked very well. We were able to maintain that approach throughout all of our canoeing adventures. We had our act together as a new couple, doing the outdoor adventures together, so we were good partners.

The Boundary Waters area was beautiful. It was in August, and, of course, we had to deal with bugs and mosquitoes. If we stayed in the wind, we could pretty much avoid those mosquitoes and the bugs, although the little, black flies would normally give us a hard time. We tried to always camp in windy areas.

Betsy and I were tired at the end of each day. The trip was basically like a backpacking trip, yet we were in a canoe. Now, at several points in these lakes, we ran into lots of beaver activity, and some of the portages we had to make were to go around beaver dams, lifting our canoe over these beaver dams and then hopping back in. The water was easy, so it wasn't like we had to deal with rapids, but we had to deal with these obstructions that would come from the beaver areas. However, we ran across very few people.

We did a little bit of fishing, but we also had brought our food. We weren't dependent upon catching fish. The fish up there are good, but they're very bony, so you had to be careful about what you caught. But we were not there primarily to fish. We were just there to see the sights and enjoy being out. And it was beautiful. The temperature wasn't very warm, nor was it cold. It was in the sixties and seventies—very comfortable. We had some views, and we were hoping to see the northern lights, but we never really got a true view of them. In the middle of the summer, it was the wrong season, and maybe we weren't far enough north to see that sort of spectacular natural beauty. Everything was so peaceful. It was so quiet. All we could hear was our own boat and the sound of birds.

We heard many loons. They have very distinctive calls, which we thoroughly enjoyed. When we heard a loon, we would stop and listen to its call and try to figure out what the loon was saying.

It was the first long vacation I took with Betsy. I remember that the sunsets at the end of the days were absolutely spectacular.

CHAPTER 43

AROUND THE TIME WE GOT married, Betsy was teaching, and I had my job working with the dental auxiliary training project. But this was not the job that I wanted. It was a limited, grant-funded position. And I was looking for something else that would involve campus-based medical education, rather than dental education (or another health profession).

That fall, Betsy found an advertisement in the *Chronicle of Higher Education*. After she read it, Betsy said, "Jamie, this is you. It basically has your name on it."

It was a position at West Virginia University, in the School of Medicine. The position was to develop the educational programing of two residency programs. The first was a combined internal medicine and pediatrics residency, called medicine-pediatrics. The second was an internal medicine residency that was community-based. So there was primary care internal medicine and the combined "med-peds" residency. When I saw this ad, I said, "Well, that's interesting. I'm going to the Association of American Medical Colleges' annual meeting in a month, and maybe I'll talk to someone there about it."

However, Betsy said, "No. Apply now. This really sounds like what you want to do and have been trained to do."

I agreed, so I wrote to the guy at West Virginia University, a physician, who was the chair of the search committee. I wrote a letter that said, "Here's my CV, outlining the experiences I've had. I would be glad to talk to you about this position in a month at the Association of

American Medical Colleges' (AAMC's) annual meeting. I hope you'll be there, too."

Within a week of sending the letter, I got a phone call. It was the chair of the search committee. "Jamie," he said, "we would like you to come to West Virginia University School of Medicine and talk to you about this position."

"Fine," I said. But I then realized I was being asked to go interview for this job. I couldn't go for an interview without talking it over with Betsy.

"Go," she said. "Don't worry about me."

"I do worry about you," I said. "I want to be with you. You're in a tenure-track position here at UK. And I'm now talking to these people in Morgantown. There's considerable distance." It was about a six-hour drive between the two places.

Betsy was firm. "Don't worry about this," she said. "This really sounds like something you would be interested in doing."

So I went to the job interview and immediately liked the people I talked to. It must have gone well, because I was actually told by one of the people I talked to that I shouldn't be surprised if I got a phone call at the beginning of the week. I kind of knew what that meant: a potential job offer. As it turns out, I did get a job offer at the beginning of the week, and it sounded exactly like what I wanted to do. It was what I'd been trained to do at North Carolina. Everything was good from my perspective. What I had to tell the individual on the phone was that I was married, and that my wife was a tenure-track professor at the University of Kentucky. I said that I didn't know if I could leave, because Betsy also needed to decide what she wanted to do.

Obviously, Betsy and I had a lot of talking to do. But I told the individual on the phone from West Virginia who was offering me the job that, before I could consider accepting this position, I wanted Betsy to come back with me and look at the possibilities for her. We needed to explore it there to see if there would be something that she would be interested in, to see if she could make a change, too.

As it happened, Betsy was interested in changing. For a long time, she had talked to me about the work she was doing at Kentucky. Betsy enjoyed the teaching, but the research expectations and other things were grinding on her. What was important, we both agreed, was that we stay together.

We both went back to Morgantown, and explored WVU's opportunities for Betsy in geography. And it looked as if there were going to be openings for her particular skills in geography for the following spring, if not the end of the summer. Also, I kind of got my feeling for Morgantown and what outdoor activities were available in the region. I hung out at Pathfinder and various other outdoor stores. Together, Betsy and I made the decision to go to Morgantown, West Virginia. We were able to find a home, and we moved on December 20, 1984, to start our new life.

More good news was that Betsy was from Ambridge, Pennsylvania, on the Ohio River, just outside of Pittsburgh. So it was less than a two-hour drive to her mother's house. We chose a very small house in the northern part of Morgantown, a couple of miles from the Health Sciences Center, so it would be easy for me to commute to my job. Betsy had a little bit of a longer drive to downtown, but Morgantown is small. We put the house in Lexington up for sale, and it quickly sold.

I started my new job at WVU on January 2, 1985. We were in the dead of winter in West Virginia. The snow was falling, and we said, "This is great. What a wonderful area." But we didn't know anybody, so we decided to kind of look around and see if we could meet people who enjoyed doing things in the outdoors, as we did. That first winter in West Virginia for Betsy and me, as I recall, was a great one, because we got to go cross-country skiing a lot. I remember that it snowed quite a bit, and we had local hills, mountains, whatever you want to call them, around us. We would soon make day trips to various places to go cross-country skiing.

We were new in town, and I was brand-new in the School of Medicine, so I had an opportunity to meet people socially. Our first few months in Morgantown, Betsy and I did various things with medically oriented folks and went to social events, primarily around the School of Medicine. Then, Betsy started looking in the newspaper, and she saw that there was a local Sierra Club that had just formed a West Virginia chapter. We thought this was great, because both of us had been involved in Sierra Club activities. I started mine back in college in the 1960s. Since both of us enjoyed the outdoors, which we realized during our courtship days in Kentucky, this made a whole lot of sense. We met people with similar interests and an enjoyment of the outdoors. They shared our passion about the political appropriateness of trying to save the natural spaces that we have around us for our generation and future generations. Also, we found people our age who, like us, did not have children yet. Many had been married for a year or two, and we were all kind of in the same place at the same time. We were young adults, and it was a natural coming-together. Now, we had connections to people who would go on outings, or lead outings to the areas that we didn't yet know about, in West Virginia.

Our involvement in the Sierra Club was a good thing for Betsy and me because, unknowingly at the time, it provided access to some future opportunities. Here I was, a new member of the School of Medicine and newly married. We didn't have any children, so I was looking for an opportunity to make a contribution to something, and since West Virginia was such a beautiful state, it only seemed natural that I would have gotten involved with the local group and chapter of the Sierra Club. For us, it really opened a whole network of people to become our close friends. They remain so to this day, thirty years later.

I was actually a founding member of the group in Morgantown with my new friends. One person in particular, who actually had a leadership role, was Greg Good. Greg was asked to drum up interest in Morgantown and form a group that would be one of the early focal points of the new chapter for the state of West Virginia. Some of the more memorable trips were later on, but Greg Good was a great outing organizer, and he started showing us some of the beautiful settings in

West Virginia where we could hike and camp. Little did I know at the time that it would pretty much set the tone for my future involvement in outdoor opportunities and conservation issues in the state.

Another person whom I met early on, who also worked in the Health Sciences Center and also had a strong environmental ethic and interest, was Mary Wimmer. Mary was a biochemist, researcher, and teacher in the Health Sciences Center. There was also a new couple who shared a strong environmental interest: Candice Elliott and Jim Kotcon. This was the beginning of a circle of friends that we had gotten to know shortly after we moved to West Virginia.

Getting Established

I WAS RECRUITED TO WEST Virginia University by Bob D'Alessandri to plan and create a curriculum for the new, primary-care residency programs, both in internal medicine and combined medicine-pediatrics. My job was to work with the faculty and help them develop some of the areas that were complementary to being primary care internists or pediatricians. So what did that mean? It meant looking at what they were being taught, not just in terms of how to be a doctor, but looking at the other areas of interest and help that they needed. One particular area was, for lack of a better word, the psychology of helping patients understand what good, healthy behaviors were.

We had a colleague named Melinda who was a faculty member in internal medicine, and she was double-boarded in internal medicine and psychiatry. One of the things that she was able to do was help the residents make good choices concerning the psychological needs of their patients. She had this ability to determine who got it and who didn't, and with those who didn't, she identified how we could help them with extra curricula. The curricula varied: it might have included reading cases in journals or might have included discussion groups. However, we were looking for a broader sense of what it was to be a primary care physician.

During that time, when I first came to WVU, I got to know several of the residents in medicine-pediatrics and internal medicine. At this time, I was in my thirties, and the residents were in their mid- to late twenties, so it was a good combination. I related very well to the young physicians. In fact, that was a pattern of mine (making friends who were physicians), and it happened at West Virginia University, just as it had at the University of Kentucky. These new people were, perhaps, seven to ten years younger than I was, but I've always related to and done things with younger people. Of course, in my thirties, I didn't think of them as being younger. I just thought of them as good people with whom I wanted to become friends.

My career progressed at WVU. After two years, the then-current dean saw that I had skills at developing curriculum, and he appointed me to the school-wide curriculum committee as a consultant. In this role, I would work with the leadership to think through changes that were needed. As I continued in this work, I established myself as the educational curriculum guru. While I knew what needed to be taught, I was not in a position to significantly change what we were teaching.

In either late 1989 or 1990, Bob D'Alessandri, the physician who recruited me to WVU, was asked to be dean. Within a month or two of Bob's appointment, he asked me if I would join his administrative staff and be the associate dean (or, at that time, assistant dean) for curriculum. Of course, I said yes, because I liked Bob and saw him as a visionary individual who could lead the school through the type of changes that he wanted. Plus, he and I got along very well.

At that point, I became an assistant dean. However, I explained to Bob that for me to have credibility as one of his staff at the dean level, I needed to advance my academic credentials. "That makes sense," Bob said. "You should be considered for promotion."

"I would also like to be considered as any other regular faculty member," I said. I had become eligible for tenure, and it was an interesting process. I had a reasonable publication record, and I had given many presentations at national meetings. The first year of Bob's appointment, I was promoted to an associate professor, but I needed to wait another year before they considered me for a tenured position. I went through the academic stress of preparing my files and making sure I was doing what I was supposed to do. This process included getting recommendations from outside reviewers who would understand my role as a non-physician, a PhD-level educator in the promotion and tenure (P&T) process. My publications weren't scientific discoveries; they were basically technical papers on how best to change curriculum or how to teach people to do things that were better educationally.

It took me two years to get established as a regular, full-time, tenured faculty member in the Department of Medicine, which was my home base. I had a joint appointment in the Department of Pediatrics because of my involvement in the medicine-pediatrics residency program. All of that took a couple of years of me busting my butt, for lack of a better phrase, making sure that everything was proper and that I had done all the right things. As it turned out, I didn't have any problem, at least to my knowledge, but I certainly worked hard those years to make sure I had all my P&T ducks in order. Even after I got tenure, I didn't slack off, because I knew that, someday, I wanted to be promoted to be a full professor. My activity toward getting publications in peer-reviewed journals continued.

If I were to philosophically describe my role at this time at WVU, I would say that I was a change agent. That doesn't mean I had a plan and forced the faculty to follow it because I was the education dean—no. I knew in my heart and in my mind that the faculty would do the right thing, given time and the ability to think things out. My role, as a change agent, was to provide opportunities and an atmosphere for change. I remember holding workshops for faculty on different occasions, bringing people from the outside to come in and expose our faculty to new things or new ways of thinking. I truly believed that the faculty wanted to improve and really cared about the education of our students. My job was to provide them with source material so that they could work through that.

I think that problem-based learning, or PBL, is an important example. PBL was pretty new, even though it had been around a long time, and not all that many medical schools used it and did it right. At WVU, we adopted PBL pretty early on.

I didn't feel that it was my role to say, "Faculty must do this." Rather, my role was to have the faculty discuss and learn about these things and then find the right fit for them. PBL, for example, still benefits students to this day. WVU implemented the first-year curriculum changes in 1997 and 1998, and then implemented the second-year changes a year or two later. By managing the change this way, we stayed in cycle, and no student class would get dropped out of cycle. To my knowledge, the curriculum that we developed in the mid- to late 1990s is still pretty much in use.

Howard Barrows was the father of PBL. He started it in Canada, in the 1970s, and then went to Illinois and worked in the medical school at Southern Illinois University. That's when PBL became a major part of South Illinois University's curriculum. Barrows wrote several books and many articles about PBL. I got to know Barrows in the early to mid-1980s. He knew that I was an educator, and I had the opportunity to do a presentation and a workshop about problem-based learning with him at a national meeting. Eventually, the faculty at WVU adopted PBL as an instructional approach.

The pedagogy behind PBL is that students will learn material better through the experiences of problem solving. Not only do students have to know the subject but they must also develop thinking skills as they solve problems. The benefits for students of PBL include working in groups, identifying what they already know, identifying what they need to know, and learning how and where to access new information that may lead to a resolution of the problem. PBL is also a shift away from traditional classroom lectures to more active learning.

In addition to PBL, we wanted to increase other instructional activities to move away from lectures to increase more student-oriented or student-involved learning. We designed other parts of the curriculum to have faculty work with students in small groups. One of the things that the basic science faculty did was to have problem-solving activities every week, and they, again, worked with smaller groups of students to actively involve the groups in the learning process.

Another activity that I helped initiate and also instructed was the ethics class. I typically cosponsored a group of about fifteen students every other week, after these students received lectures in ethics. That was, again, a case-based, small-group activity, where the students presented ethical cases that were assigned to them. The students interacted through a series of questions following their brief case presentations.

Since I was a facilitator of some of the small groups, we would add in critical questions to get the students to think about the ethical implications of how they approached these complex cases. The whole purpose of the course was not to teach them what to do in all ethical situations, but to give them a background and a scientific approach to analyzing difficult patient cases by bringing out the ethical implications. It also gave them a basis for further research into the types of ethical dilemmas physicians face when making various decisions about patients. The scenarios were not uncommon, as most medical decision making involves ethics to some degree.

Even with my disease, I was able to co-facilitate some ethics groups for two more years following my resignation of my position as an associate dean. It was fun, because it kept me involved with medical students. Issues arose as my voice became weaker, caused by lower capacity in my lungs. I would also get fatigued easier, and after the two-hour group discussion, I would be worn out.

My skill in the ethics small-group facilitation was not content-based but process-based. I helped groups become more communicative and learn from each other. This experience can be traced back to my master's degree and the professors at Chapel Hill who influenced me. The way I viewed my work was to help others to bring out the maximum potential of groups. From these groups, the students got a much more integrated, synergistic understanding of what it is to be a doctor.

CHAPTER 45

As my career progressed, so did my outdoor activities, even during winter. One time, on our way to New Germany State Park in Maryland, Betsy and I were driving a new car to go out cross-country skiing. It was a van-like car that was pretty ugly-looking, but it worked for us. We were on our way, probably about a mile out on the small, country road to New Germany. We crested the hill, and then the road went down and dipped at the bottom before coming up the other side. There was ice on the road. We crested the hill and looked out over the bottom, and there were two cars stopped, one in each lane. They were just talking to each other. Because of the ice, we were not able to stop. The two cars at the bottom in the dip were blocking both sides of the road. We had no choice but to slide into them. We did everything we could, but there was no way that we were going to be able to stop on the hill going down toward the dip in the icy road. Now, the guys in the road were local buddies just shooting the bull, and that's fine; but given the conditions, we were doomed to run into them. It was a slow run-in. It wasn't anything that was horrible, just a fender-bender type of situation.

Unfortunately, the first couple of winters, that wasn't the only time the driving was bad. I remember once, at Blackwater Falls State Park, a group of us in a car together did a 360-degree spin around a corner, coming down the mountain, because of ice. I also remember a weekend outing when we had to get out of our cars to push them over a hill while leaving Helvetia, West Virginia. But we never turned around. The cross-country skiing was worth it.

On Rivers

CHAPTER 46

Throughout my life, I have always been a group person. When I was young, I hung out with the neighborhood kids, and in high school, I was editor of the yearbook, which had many people involved. I was also part of the antiwar groups in college. In both the UNC Outings Club and the Bluegrass Wildwater Association, I did things in groups and took on leadership roles in them. This would continue through my professional life.

I've talked about some of the similarities between the Outings Club and the Bluegrass Wildwater Association, but there were some differences between climbing and boating. In climbing, you always needed another partner. Wesley Byerly was my main partner. Because you work in twos, you form a tight bond.

Boating is done in groups of three or more. This is because, if there were an accident, one boat could go seek help, and the other could stay. In some ways, this made the boating more social.

In both cases, we were weekend-warrior adventurers.

There was an incident I heard about on the Upper Gauley River in West Virginia, involving a person who served as a guide. For whatever reason, his canoe went over a major rapid at Sweet Falls, and the front of the canoe hit the rock bottom. It was stuck, with water from the falls rushing over him. The boater was in the middle, but there was an air eddy in front of him, so he could breathe. The US Army Corps of Engineers was asked to stop releasing water from a dam, so, eventually, the boater was rescued when the water level went down. This happened to be videotaped, and I was asked to show the video at a national white-water film festival in Lexington, Kentucky.

The activities, like boating, did have a sense of destiny to them. I like to think of it like one of my favorite movies, *Star Wars*. It's a classic, like *The Wizard of Oz* and *Gone with the Wind*. In *Star Wars*, Darth Vader tells Luke Skywalker his destiny is with him, but Luke chooses another destiny. I think it's like that—I wanted to be in control of my own destiny.

Although I didn't know the boater from the Gauley River incident very well, we did go kayaking together on the James River, in Richmond, Virginia. There, the white-water went right through the middle of the city.

CHAPTER 47

⎯⟆

IN JUNE OF 1987, I took an extended river trip in Canada on the Missinaibi River, and paddled about one hundred miles of it. Betsy and I were invited by some friends from the Bluegrass Wildwater Association in Lexington. So we were off to another adventure. The Missinaibi River is beautiful, and it eventually flows into James Bay. The part that we explored was more at its headwaters and not the big part that went into the bay. We were pretty far north, and it was very isolated—a wilderness area according to Canadian standards, although there were some small houses along the way. In the United States, wilderness areas try to keep human impact more minimal.

Our friends on the Missinaibi River trip included Beuren Garten and his wife, Patty, as well as the person we called "Dandy Don," or Don Spangler. Beuren and Don were regular white-water boaters. So there were five of us on this trip and three canoes. Dandy Don had the solo canoe. I took my Mad River canoe, which, I should note, weighs about seventy-five to eighty pounds, whereas, when Betsy and I were in the Boundary Waters in Minnesota, we portaged a fifty-five-pound canoe. So, this time, I was portaging a white-water canoe that weighed at least twenty pounds more.

We all rendezvoused in Michigan, drove to Canada, and put on the river. It was very similar to the BWCA trip, yet we were definitely on a river and not portaging that much until we got to major waterfalls.

Of course, being white-water boaters, we considered running them. So there was a little bit of portaging, but not a whole lot.

Some of the things that we had to watch out for in the evenings were the bugs. In Canada, in the northern part of the hemisphere, the black flies and the mosquitoes are vicious. They will go for you. I remember the black flies biting me wherever they could. We tucked all of our long pants into our socks, but you would see the bites at the edges, where the pants met the socks, if skin showed. Also, on your wrists, you would see bites, which would often be in the area between your long-sleeved shirt and the gloves you were wearing.

Because we had three boats on the trip, sometimes we would tie the boats together and raft down the big, wide sections of the river. When there was a tailwind, we would raise a tarp to make a sail. It pushed us for a mile or two.

The wildlife and the birds were incredible. On numerous occasions, we saw big animals. One night, Betsy woke me up.

"Jamie!" she said. "I hear something." She claimed that it sounded like a crunch and whoosh of water and that it seemed to be getting closer.

"You're just having a dream," I said.

"No, it's real," Betsy said.

And then, all of a sudden, I heard this chomping. I said, "Betsy, maybe we better look outside the tent and see what is happening."

When we looked outside the tent, in the river that we were camping next to, there was a huge moose with a full rack. It would dip its head into the water to eat the grasses and the water plants. When it lifted its head, its rack of horns would be full of wet grass, and the water poured off the rack, back into the river.

Since we were white-water boaters, one of the challenges of our trip was scouting the small waterfalls that occurred every twenty-five miles or so. We were prepared for the four to five feet drops and would often run them after scouting them, if we didn't face any serious challenges. If there was a waterfall with a much greater drop, then we would obviously carry our canoes around it. Some of the times, we saw remnants of other boats that had not been so lucky. I still remember a particular, crunched-up aluminum canoe on the side of the river.

One of the cool things that happened on the trip was that Dandy Don was a great cook. He knew how to cook wonderful meals. So if we would catch fish, he would cook it. He would fix us baked beans one night, and then he'd smash them up, and we'd have refried beans the next night.

After a while, we got to a point where we were nearing the end of the river trip, and it was time to meet Dandy Don's wife, Chris. She really helped us by acting as our shuttle driver, managing to get the vehicle from the put-in to our take-out. After we got off the river and met Dandy Don's wife, we put our boats on the trailer and got back in their van.

We said, "Wow, we're in a beautiful part of Northern Canada. What else is there to do?"

We had heard about a railroad that ran north, and we said, "Let's get on the railroad and make a trip." The trip was up to a town called Moosonee, primarily a village founded by trading companies like Hudson Bay Company. Moosonee is very far north, at the bottom of James Bay, which flows into Hudson Bay. We found that it was a pretty desolate place, but we had made a reservation to spend the night in a hotel. Not too far from Moosonee, you could actually go out on the big bay and see polar bears, so we were pretty far north.

I remember that, in Moosonee, I ordered orange juice at breakfast, and I recall that the waitress brought in this glass with some orange liquid in it. I took a sip, and I said, "Wait a minute; this is not orange juice. This is Tang."

I said to her, "I'm sorry; I thought, on the menu, it said orange juice."

"No, no, this is orange juice," I was told. Well, at that point I realized that we were very far north, and available goods and services were few and far between.

In Moosonee, they don't have paved roads. Everything is dirt. The town was built by the Hudson Bay Company, and you can look at the various buildings and see that they're primarily wood with steep roofs, because of the snow in the winter. Moosonee has often been called the gateway to the arctic. So anything north of Moosonee, which is one of the most northern towns in central Canada, is really arctic in nature. It was quite an adventure going up to Moosonee. After we looked around, we got on the *Polar Express* train and returned. When we got back to our vehicle, so ended our adventure in Canada.

CHAPTER 48

WITHIN THE FIRST COUPLE OF years in West Virginia, Betsy and I befriended our outdoor group. Somehow, in a lack of good judgment, I got elected group chair. I don't know why they elected me, but back in college, I had gotten involved with the Sierra Club in Northern California. I don't remember much about my involvement, but I do remember joining and being part of the Sierra Club, probably in letter or name only. I was involved from that period in the 1960s up through the mid-1980s, when I became more active. Many people we met in the Sierra Club became part of our main social circle, although we did care about the mission, too.

I kept up with boating, too, and one of the people that I went boating with a lot on day trips during the weekend was Ann Chester. Ann was a colleague of mine at the Health Sciences Center, and she had learned to boat when she was in college. Ann is about five years younger than I am, but we got along very well, and we would often go to the Youghiogheny for our day trips. The lower Youghiogheny River is a Class III-plus river, depending on water level. Higher water levels make it a little more challenging. It usually runs around two feet or so.

Well, one particular day on the Youghiogheny River, we were about two-thirds of the way down, where there is really only one more rapid to speak of, one we had done a hundred times. I'm really not exaggerating. I have probably boated the Youghiogheny River over a hundred times in my lifetime. Ann and I were approaching this last rapid. It was not unusual. The water level was in the two feet to two-and-a-half feet range, no more difficult than what we had done so many times before, and there was normal, rafting-group traffic along the river. We waited for a raft to go through before we ran it, because we didn't want to get stuck.

The last rapid is called "River's End." It's called River's End because it has kind of a blind approach. You go in, and then, once you're committed, you have to make a sharp left through the big rapids, and then you have to make a sharp right once you get through the big stuff. We waited for the raft company to go through, and when they'd all gone through, we said, "Okay, we can go." Ann went first, and she did fine. She pulled up in an eddy before the last hard right turn that you have to make. I followed her, giving her a good fifty feet lead, then I went through the main part of the rapid. For whatever reason, this time, I flipped, and I couldn't roll my kayak. I couldn't seem to get up to surface level. Underwater, I thought, *What am I going to do?* I pulled myself out of the kayak, something I'd also done a lot. After this, I just held on to the kayak, keeping my head above water, so that when I got to a calm spot, I could pull the kayak over to shore, empty the water out, and climb in.

Everything was going according to plan. I wasn't scared or anything when I flipped in the heavy stuff before the hard-right turn. Then, I got to the hard-right turn. Remember, I now was out of my boat, floating in the water. I looked downstream, and all the rafts that went before us had stopped, and they were all piled up with each other—not necessarily in an eddy but all across the river. They weren't moving much, and here I was, coming down upon them. I wasn't in my kayak, but it was close by me. I really had nowhere that I could go to escape the logjam of rafters, and because they weren't moving, but the water underneath them was, I basically got swept under this logjam of rafts. So I was underwater, holding my breath, holding my breath, and holding my breath as long as I could, but I could not find the surface of the water; all I found was the bottom of more rubber rafts. I held my hands up trying to get to the side of a raft so I could get up and breathe air, and luckily, someone grabbed my arm and pulled me up to breathe. It was a close call, to say the least. It was no one's fault—stuff happens sometimes, and it wasn't my time to go. I've cheated death a few times in my life.

CHAPTER 49

I BECAME FRIENDS WITH MARK Gibson. He was chairman of OB-GYN at the West Virginia University School of Medicine. He was a full professor and a distinguished researcher, but he also loved the outdoors. Our relationship was both a professional one and a friendship. He and I did some adventures together, primarily winter hiking up in the Adirondacks, and we skied together on multiple occasions in Canaan Valley, West Virginia. Mark was very interested in learning to canoe.

One of the things that you learn about canoeing is that canoes are big objects. If they tip over, they fill up with water and often get caught on rocks or other obstacles that the water goes around. When you've got a big, big canoe, one that's sixteen feet long, it often doesn't behave the way you want it to.

Mark, his wife, Mary, and his son, Tim, went canoeing with Betsy and me. We were on Shavers Fork, which flows into the Cheat River eventually. Shavers Fork is an easy river, I must admit. Mark and his family were in a canoe, and for whatever reason, they broached. In other words, they floated sideways to a rock in the river. Their canoe did a classic broach, with the hull up against this rock, and with water pounding on it, trying to bend it around the rock. Now, the good news was that the water current wasn't that strong. Nonetheless, when you look at this situation, you're going to ask yourself, "How can I get this canoe off this rock that it's trying to fold around?"

Mark's canoe was an ABS, or plastic, canoe, so it had a certain amount of bend and give to it. I wasn't worried about it getting damaged. The trick was to get it off the rock. Fortunately, I had learned a skill, but I'd never had to try it out before. I was told that the skill was called the "Slim Ray rope trick." Basically, you attach a rope onto one of the thwarts, and you wrap it around the canoe so that you can pull on the rope to rotate the canoe. In other words, if you attach it onto the upper edge of one of the center thwarts and wrap the rope around and underneath, you can pull on the rope, and the canoe will rotate. Rather than the inside of the canoe getting the water, if you are able to rotate that canoe around, the outside of the hull, or the bottom of the boat, will get the force of the water.

When that happens, nine times out of ten, the boat will work its way around the rock, because the water is not hitting the inside of the boat; it's hitting the outside so that it's not filling with water. With help, I was able to rotate the boat around. Once that happened, the boat slid right around the obstacle. Luckily, the Slim Ray rope trick worked. It was the only time I had to use it. They dumped the water out of the canoe and got back in. I think part of their gunwale broke, but we continued on, with no other incidents.

WE MADE ANOTHER CANOE TRIP with Mark and Mary Gibson, their two children, and Mark's older daughter from a previous marriage. Heather was a fourth-year medical student at Harvard University. She was visiting her dad during a break in the school year. We all decided to run the Smoke Hole section of the South Branch of the Potomac River in West Virginia. The Smoke Hole section is in eastern West Virginia, within the mountains. It's absolutely gorgeous, but it's very isolated. We had about an eight-mile section of river to travel.

Mark and his son were in Mark's canoe; Mary and their daughter, Alex, were in one of our canoes. Heather was in our kayak. All went well for the first few miles. We must have decided to pull over to the shore for lunch or a snack. Most of us were already on the shore, getting out of our boats, when Heather came around the corner and flipped over in the kayak in some rapids.

She didn't know how to roll the kayak back up, because it was her first time in a white-water kayak. No one had seen her get out of the kayak, either. All we saw was the bottom of the boat, bobbing up and down through the little rapid. A few people in our group immediately rushed over to her. They reached for the kayak, pulled it to an upright position, and grabbed her to get her head up in the air so she could breathe. "I thought I was going to die!" gasped Heather. So now she could breathe again, which helped, but she was in major pain.

I looked at her shoulder and knew she had dislocated it, because, as the story goes, I had told her before we got on the river to never let go of her paddle. I told her to hold onto it because she wouldn't want to be up a creek without a paddle. Basically, you depend on your paddle to get you where you need to be on the river.

When she went through the rapid and flipped, her kayak paddle got stuck between some rocks on the riverbed. She didn't let go of it, and the force of the water was pushing her downstream, as she held onto a paddle stuck in the rocks. It put her arm in a precarious position, and the shoulder dislocated. She was in pain, so she couldn't push herself out of the boat.

I didn't panic, because her dad was with us, and he was a doctor. I thought, *He'll know what to do.* We got her to shore and sat her down. "Mark," I said, "her shoulder's dislocated. You need to reset it."

"I can't do it," Mark replied. "She's my daughter." He was very upset, knowing how much pain she was in.

"Okay," I said, "I guess I have to do it." I did the classic thing. I said, "This may hurt a little bit." She was already in pain with this dislocated shoulder. I had her bite on a stick, just to give her something to distract her.

We had to relocate that shoulder. We were in the middle of nowhere. We still had many miles to go to get to our take-out point. Luckily, I've had different first aid courses, and I kind of knew the dynamics of dislocation. That doesn't mean I've had that sort of dislocation or that I had reset one, but I'd heard about what I needed to do.

I had her lie down, and had her hold onto my arm with the arm of her dislocated shoulder. I started to say, "I'm going to—" as I took my river shoes off, and I put my heel into her armpit, holding her wrist, having her hold onto my hand. Then, I gently rotated her arm so that the shoulder popped back in. She didn't scream, because she was biting on the stick.

Once we got the shoulder relocated, we needed to isolate the arm. When you're a boater, you always have duct tape with you. We also had a T-shirt that we could tear up and make it into a sling, and then we duct-taped it to her body so that we could keep the arm against her chest.

Obviously, she couldn't kayak anymore. We basically had her in the canoe with her dad, who could handle the canoe from the back. She swapped places with Tim.

"No problem, Dad," he said. "I can do this kayak thing." Tim was not a little kid. I think he was just starting high school. He did fine.

We still had several miles to go. I remember just cautiously canoe-ing. Betsy and I would go first to check out the best route and basically do everything we could to make sure they were going on the best path. We had to go all the way to an outfitter's place, because that's where our cars were. We made it safely to the take-out.

This is one of those adventures that reminds me that all accidents are freak experiences. Little did Mark's daughter know that, when she flipped the kayak, her paddle would go down vertically in the water and get stuck between rocks. Normally, that doesn't happen. But strange things happen when you're boating.

CHAPTER 51

EVERY SPRING, FOR A NUMBER of years, I always tried to do an overnight canoeing/camping experience on the Smoke Hole section of the South Branch of the Potomac. One spring, (I can't remember exactly which one, but it was probably in the 1990s or early 2000s), I invited Larry Harris, Cindy O'Brien, and Greg Good to go with me. We had two of my canoes, and we went to the Smoke Hole. You always had to hit the river at the right level. You needed it to rain a few days before the trip to bring it up to a navigable level.

In the afternoon, we went down to the river and ran across another group of people that we happened to know, including Chip Chase, the legend of White Grass Ski Touring Center in Canaan Valley. Chip's an amazing person and does many, many things. Every year, he takes a group of people on the Smoke Hole section. As it happened, that night, we ran across them again, although we didn't camp with them. We camped downstream, but we visited with Chip and his group first. We ate supper, and everything was going fine.

However, that night, it began to rain, and it rained all night. When we woke up in the morning, we looked out at the river, and it was totally different than the day before. It was high and running fast. We were in an inaccessible area, and the only route out was on the river. We had about five or more miles to go to get to our car, which we had parked in a special parking place by taking a dirt road that follows the river. I had parked there before on these overnight trips, and there had been no problems in the past.

When we woke up and looked at the water, I said, "Oh my gosh. This river is rising higher and getting close to flood stage." Then I thought, *What do I do?* We were out in the middle of the wilderness, and our main transportation—our only transportation—was canoeing, so we got in our boats to run it out. Originally, on the first day, we put Larry and Cindy in one canoe, and Greg Good and I were in my other canoe. Even with the water at the normal level, this arrangement wasn't working, because Larry and Cindy were novices on moving water.

"Greg," I said, "I think you and I need to split up. I'll take Larry, and you take Cindy, and we'll have them canoe with us in that way."

Something you learn while boating is that the water volume and waves are significant. Rivers are living things. Their dynamics change when there's more water; they become faster, and the rapids significantly increase in difficulty. The whole dynamic of a small rapid changes. With a normal flow, the rapid is predictable, but when the volume increases, the peaks and valleys get a lot higher and lower. With a normal river flow, some rocks will show, and you can pull into eddies behind them. But, as the volume increases, those same rocks are now underwater—even if, under normal conditions, those rocks are three feet out of the water—so, with the volume increasing, it forms a whole new rapid, and it certainly doesn't make boating easier. Those were the conditions we were dealing with.

We got on the river, and we headed downstream. I had Larry with me in the front of the canoe. "Larry," I said, "there is no problem here. We're going to do fine, but I want you to do exactly what I ask you to do, when I ask you to do it." Larry obviously agreed, and I'm sure Greg and Cindy were having a similar conversation.

Back in North Carolina, I had run a river at flood stage, but I had no idea it had gotten to flood stage. I didn't have the skills then to know how the river's dynamics worked, and thought that with the increased volume, it would wash out the rapids. Not so. That flood-stage river was way out of my league, and I had been very lucky. I'd never climbed out of my league, but I'd boated on potentially dangerous rivers. Now, on the Smoke Hole section, I had better skills. Experience is a great teacher, if you can live through it.

So we got to the point where the North Branch of the Potomac meets the South Branch, and obviously, when you have a new river flowing into the river you're already on, the volume of the water increases. It, too, was running high. I remember, however, that when we got to the confluence, there were some people from Chip Chase's group there. Everybody was talking, excited that the water level had come up significantly and also that the sun had come out.

"Larry," I said, "Let's pull over and say hello and get out of our canoe, because the sun's out." I was getting hot, because I had all my rain gear on. I took off my watch and put it on the top of the canoe.

Then someone said, "It looks like the water is rising some more. We better get back in the boats."

For whatever reason, I either left my watch on the canoe, or I put it back on my wrist, but two hours later, after a rapid, I looked at my wrist, and the watch was no longer there. I had lost my watch on the river.

Larry and I did fine, and Greg and Cindy did fine, yet we were cautious. We made it to our car and then looked downstream to see if the water level was still rising.

"Oh, man, we've got to get these canoes onto our car," I said, because the stream was rising up over the road that we needed to drive out on. We could see it coming up, and it was starting to lap up against the road. The day before, the road had been twenty feet from the river. Now, the river was basically there, at the road's edge.

This was kind of midday, and you have to realize, with the water level being up, you're moving fast, so it doesn't take you four hours to run the river. It only takes you two hours to get off the river. So we got lucky. We got the canoes on top of my car, and we all got in. I had a four-wheel-drive Jeep, so I had some road clearance, and we drove through a little bit of water on this old, dirt road. Once we got to higher ground, we were able to get out and pick up the car we had left at the put-in. We stopped to eat, and when we got home, we heard that the river was in flood stage. We were very, very lucky to get off it in time.

CHAPTER 52

ONE OF THE THINGS THAT Betsy and I wanted to do was develop our skills as a tandem-canoe team, so we hooked up with a guy out of Pennsylvania, Bruce Penrod. We became friends, and he often offered canoeing lessons or adventures.

One weekend, Bruce called me and said, "Jamie, the Cheat River is running. How would you like to go down the Cheat Canyon with me and a few others? You could develop some of your solo-canoeing skills."

"Sure," I said, "I would be glad to go."

We put in on the Cheat River Canyon at its regular point near Albright, and we started heading down the river, but we noticed that the river seemed a lot pushier, meaning that there was higher water than we had expected. It had rained for a couple of days prior to us putting on, so we figured that, as we headed downstream, the water from tributaries had been pouring into this section of the Cheat River. No problem. This made it more exciting.

The first rapid we came to was bigger than I had ever seen it, so I basically skirted it, because it was really an instructional lesson to develop our canoeing skills right from the first rapid. Basically, I put my canoe exactly where I wanted it to go. The next rapid was at the High Falls of the Cheat, and it's a long, quarter-mile rapid. It has holes and big waves and rocks. I took a good line through that, and I felt pretty good. Yet I had this feeling that the water seemed to be rising slowly, rather than peaking out and declining. The water was browner, and more pushy; the waves were bigger, and we were making a lot more progress than I recalled from previous trips on the Cheat River Canyon.

We were coming upon the crux of the run, which was called Coliseum. Coliseum had a hole that you had to go through called Recyclotron, and then it had a horizontal, angled wave, which was actually more than a wave. It was a part that could flip a boat if you didn't hit it right. Downstream of that were some other big rapids, all occurring in about a quarter-mile section of the river.

"Hey," I said, "this looks like fun." The best run of the Cheat is from two to three feet, according to the gauge at the put-in, but I knew it was now probably in the three feet range.

"This is bigger than I've been on before," I said.

Everybody else on our trip shared my sentiments: "Yeah, this is great. Let's have fun." And we were having fun.

There were about three or four solo open boats, and I was one of those. One of the first guys that went through the rapid took the sneak route to the left and avoided the big Recyclotron. There was also a diagonal-wave hole that you had to go through to take on the crux of Coliseum. Coliseum was an area full of several big rapids, and there were several Class IV+ rapids. We'd done it at lower water before and had fun.

The next guy who went through was actually the instructor. So he went, following Recyclotron, going through the diagonal-wave hole, and then, he flipped immediately. We said, "Whoa, what's going on here?"

It was my turn. The first trick in an open boat is to get through Recyclotron without taking in too much water. In an open canoe, you've put in airbags to displace water so that it can't fill the canoe. So, when I took in a little bit of water at Recyclotron, my mistake was that I didn't push the canoe by paddling hard to hit the diagonal-wave hole. I got into it, and I said, "Whoops, I'm going to have to surf." Yet my canoe paddle was on the upstream side. I tried to brace and immediately got flipped over. You can't brace upstream when you're in a diagonal-wave hole.

I flipped pretty dramatically, got out of my canoe, swam to the upstream side, and then got hold of my canoe again. About one hundred feet down that particular piece of the rapid, I found a rock kind of in the middle of the river to stand on, and I held my canoe until I got it upright. I had my bailer to scoop out as much water as I could, and I was able to get back in the canoe and then hold it in place until I was ready to hit the next part of the rapid. I thought I had my act together, but I must admit, I was a little shaken from the first disaster on the Recyclotron.

I got to the next hole, which was a big up-and-down wave, so you go down the wave, and then you go up the wave. To successfully navigate that wave, you needed to have a lot of boat speed. Well, that was my problem with the first disaster. I was not feeling confident. I went down in the hole, and I didn't have enough boat speed to get up out of the hole, so I slipped backward, and guess what? I flipped again, and this was only within an hour or less of previously getting my boat cleaned up.

To make a long story short, it was a day where I lost a lot of my confidence boating. The good news is that, if you look at it in a positive way, I was not the only person who experienced difficulties. The instructor and every other so-called student—and we were good boaters—all crashed and burned at Coliseum in one way or the other. You learn from experience, usually upon reflection on that experience after you're off the river.

When we got off the river, we rechecked the gauge, and it was over four feet, which means that's the highest I've ever run the Cheat. I think they used to run commercial raft trips in that range; however, they had cancelled raft trips because of safety issues. That day, we were on the upper limits of boating on the Cheat. I don't know if it made me feel better. It basically made me feel that I had a genuine experience being on a river, and it wasn't that I was just having a bad boating day. The river was kicking our asses.

Out on my adventures, I was cautious, and my caution index depended on my experience. Some people said that I was doing crazy things, but I only did them when I had confidence in my experience and had developed skills. That's how I approached climbing, and except for the early days, that's how I approached boating. I never considered myself to be a daredevil. It's what I'd call natural confidence. Ability, experience, and wisdom have come together and allowed me to do things some consider risky. Honestly, the greatest risks often came while driving to all the places I liked to play.

In the Bluegrass Wildwater Association, when I first joined, I learned through their outrageous beginner trips. There was another beginner with me, Mike Weeks, who was nicknamed "Mr. Danger" because he was on the water purely for the thrill. He would do crazy rapids for that reason, but I wasn't boating for the thrill. I wasn't after the most difficult rapids. For me, it was about the art of how I got down river, finding a natural, artistic way. I worked to apply my skills so that I could experience the river as artistry in motion.

As my skills increased in kayaking, instead of trying more difficult rivers, I did the same rivers, but in a canoe. A canoe is a much different craft to maneuver in white-water than a kayak. The canoeing allowed me to increase my skill on the same rivers by boating with a less nimble craft.

Canoeing had other benefits. Betsy and I were able to tandem-canoe the rivers we had done in a kayak. And as we increased these skills, it would lead to even bigger adventures for the two of us together. In a tandem canoe, Betsy and I were not separate. We were together on the water.

There is a beauty, a symmetry, of flowing water, and there is something about the ability to be a part of it. I am drawn to rivers and being able to use them to get where I want to go, from eddy to eddy, with the river flowing downstream around me. That symmetry of nature is seductive.

When I think back on the lower Youghiogheny, which I've done more than a hundred times, I remember that my kayak felt so natural. Done right, it's elegant. I'd traveled the Youghiogheny in canoes, C-1s, and kayaks, and even with a group of people in a raft, as their guide. Canoeing solo or in a kayak, it was sometimes like the river was my friend, and other times it was like this friend was out of control, like he was on drugs or steroids.

On the Youghiogheny, from the entrance rapid, I would hop from eddy to eddy down the river. Boating is like a dance, and it's the nimble stroke here, the crossover stroke there, the planting of the paddle that creates a movement that's not about where I was going but how I got there.

A Photo Album

James McBride Shumway holding Jamie, J.M. Shumway, Jr., in 1948

Berte Alden Scovel, Jamie's mother, with her son Jamie in 1949

Jamie in his Maryland Street yard in Fairfield, California, circa 1952

Jamie, his mother Berte, and younger brother Ralph, circa 1958

Jamie kayaking in his grandparents' pool in
Marin County, California, circa 1958

Jamie with his Austin A40 before a road rally, circa 1966

Jamie in Yosemite National Park in the California Sierras, circa 1967

Jamie cuddling Guinevere circa 1969

Jamie *on* belay while climbing at Seneca Rocks, West Virginia, circa 1978

Betsy Pyle married Jamie, her canoeing instructor,
in March 1984 in Lexington, Kentucky

Sierra Club outing in Canaan Valley, West Virginia, circa 1986. L-R: Meg
Weesner, Mary Wimmer, Jamie, Betsy, Cindy O'Brien, Jim Kotcon

Jamie in an eddy when kayaking on the Cheat
River in West Virginia, circa 1987

Greg Good (L) and Jamie (R) waxing skis in
1987 in the Adirondacks in New York

Jamie (L) and Betsy (R) canoed the Colorado River through
Grand Canyon in 1988 in their tandem open boat

With Wesley in a backpack, Jamie introduced his
son to cross-country skiing in 1991

Jamie (L) hands an early grant check for the West Virginia Rivers Coalition to Roger Harrison (C) in 1991 as Mac Thornton (R) looks on

Father and son near Dunnottar Castle in Scotland in 1992

Wesley with Jamie after a 1995 WVU Health Sciences Center graduation

Resting during a family bicycle trip through the
Blackwater Canyon in West Virginia, 1997

Jamie at home from work for lunch with the family's puppy Shasta in 1999

Jamie's sabbatical in Dundee, Scotland, in 2000
advanced his medical education skills

Jamie and Betsy with Shasta before their 2001
Rotary Club presentation about Scotland

Jamie and Wesley in Scotland at Dunnottar Castle
in 2002 to recreate their 1992 photo

Betsy and Jamie in Glamis Castle in Scotland in
2002 for a medical education meeting

Jamie walked with snowshoes during his last winter camping trip in West Virginia on Canaan Mountain in 2008

Jamie enjoyed fly-fishing for trout on Appalachian streams and western rivers like the Yellowstone and the Upper Sacramento, circa 2008

Father-son toast to a good day on the slopes at Big Sky, Montana, in March 2009 – Jamie's last ski outing due to the progression of ALS

Jamie (R) guided Tahnee Bucher (L) down the Youghiogheny
River in Pennsylvania in August 2009

Jamie (L) and his brother Ralph (R), visiting from Hawaii
in 2011, in Pennsylvania's Ohiopyle State Park

Jamie celebrated Christmas 2012 with Wesley, his mother Berte, and Betsy

3-D movie outing in 2013 with friends Maria and Paul Provencher (left), another Morgantown family affected by ALS

Wesley with his parents after his 2013 graduation
in the West Virginia University Coliseum

Friends gathered in Blackwater Falls State Park in January 2014, L-R:
Betsy, Molly Carr, Mary Wimmer, Jamie, and Mac Thornton

Renée Nicholson (L) and Jamie presented their work
to a WVU wellness class in July 2014

Genelle Botje (R), who provided physical therapy
for Jamie, visited him in August 2014

Exploring the Wild in
Wonderful West Virginia

CHAPTER 53

I HAD CLIMBED SENECA ROCKS, in the east-central part of West Virginia, with Wesley Byerly, well before I moved to the state. This was back when I was still living in Chapel Hill—in 1978 or 1979—and I climbed the Gendarme, a fabulous pinnacle that no longer exists there. It was a classic climb. Of course, when I went to Seneca Rocks, I had no idea I'd end up living in West Virginia.

Going to Seneca Rocks was the epitome of climbing in the East: it was a technical, big rock. This would be true also for the New and Gauley Rivers, which are in West Virginia, and they are the epitomes of white-water in the East. So living in West Virginia gave me good proximity to the things I loved.

CHAPTER 54

NOT LONG AFTER I'D MOVED to West Virginia, in the mid-1980s, I took one of my first winter camping trips with Greg Good. I convinced myself I could do this because Greg, when he was in college and shortly thereafter, had had many experiences doing extreme, winter, snow-based camping trips. He had also made a significant trip above the Arctic Circle in Northern Canada on one of the major snow islands, Bylot Island.

Greg had come from Canada. Although he's an American, he lived in Canada for eight years and did a lot of trips in the winter in Ontario and Manitoba. He had also gone on a couple of trips in the arctic and subarctic in the 1970s, so going up and camping in the snow was not a big deal for Greg. He had the skills, and I felt comfortable going with him. Now, I'd never done anything like this, but I'd done many, many backpacking trips during spring, summer, and fall, so, of course, I was up for this adventure.

"Jamie," Greg said, "let's go up into the mountains of West Virginia in the winter and spend a couple of nights."

I thought it was a great idea. It was in January or February, because there was a lot of snow on the ground. We were both young college professors, and I thought, *What a great opportunity to go to an area that is only a couple of hours away from where we are working, yet we could be totally isolated in the woods.*

We put the trip together. Greg knew that one really good possibility for snow camping in West Virginia was up on Mount Porte Crayon and

Flat Rock Plains. This place is now a wilderness area, but back when we did the trip in the 1980s, it was just an unprotected bunch of trees that was overlooked by the Forest Service and the timber companies. The crew was comprised of Greg, Adam Polinski, Paul Turner, and me. The four of us skied up part of it, up through pastures and on an old railroad grade. Then, we came to a place where the trail left the railroad grade and climbed steeply. So we strapped everything onto our backpacks. It was, in round numbers, almost 4,800 feet at the top of Mount Porte Crayon. I recall that we camped just below the high area. So, at this steep point, we climbed certainly over one thousand feet. It might even have been a 1,200 or 1,300 foot climb.

We spent the night, and then, the next day, we took day hikes from our camp. That was one of the best trips that I ever did in terms of getting to places that were inaccessible any other way. For people who live in a city, this really was a wild place. One of the places we went to on this trip was Haystack Knob. I remember that this was primarily a trip where we used our cross-country skis to get around. So it wasn't really a hiking trip; rather, it was a cross-country-ski type of trip. I think that was one of our incentives for doing this, and we felt that if we wanted to have snow that was reliable to ski on, we needed to pick our weekend. We hoped it wasn't snowing and that we had picked the weekend after a big snow. On this trip, we got lucky, and the conditions were pretty good. At the bottom, there wasn't enough snow, so we had to tie our skis onto our packs and hike, but when we got to the very top, there was a lot of snow. When we came back down, there was more snow, because it had snowed while we were up there. When we were up on top, we were always on skis. We skied everywhere. Altogether, we probably put in twenty or thirty miles of cross-country skiing at a good, Appalachian altitude on that trip.

We spent two nights on top of the mountain. The second night, it snowed maybe six to eight inches. Luckily, we all had our cross-country skis. We could ski down the trail that we had to walk up when coming up the mountain. Little did we know that it's actually more difficult to cross-country ski downhill than it is to go up hill, especially with a heavy backpack with tents, sleeping bags, food, and stoves. But we were young and gung ho. Paul Turner was probably the most impervious to cold temperatures and other hardships of the whole group of us. I think the only person who had any real physiological difficulties was Adam Polinski. It turns out that Adam has something called Raynaud's syndrome, and the circulation in his fingers, toes, and extremities generally is not very good. This trip was the first time that Adam started to figure out that he actually had to be concerned about his circulation in cold temperatures. To Adam's credit, he continues to do all kinds of cross-country ski things to this day. He just needs to be careful about how he manages the blood flow in his body.

It was my first winter experience camping overnight, and I really liked it. Before we left, I was a little worried. I'm thin, so I didn't have a lot of insulation and was concerned that I would be cold. But that did not turn out to be the case. I felt good and stayed active and ate properly. I remember Greg always telling us to eat more carbs.

We were able to come down on the third day, in the morning, and we made it down safely. Each of us fell about five or six times, though. The snow had kept falling, and it was turning to sleet and ice. We didn't have very far to go, as the crow flies, to get back to Morgantown, but the road surface was simply terrible. This was something that we got used to over the years, because Greg and I kept going every year to do one trip or another.

Of course, when we came back to tell our stories, we developed a bit of a reputation—not necessarily a reputation of saneness. Of course, we probably embellished our stories a bit. We developed a reputation among our friends in the Sierra Club for going on these "macho" trips. I understand how other people feel that the term applies, even though the people who do the trips don't. Out there, you don't get to take a shower. You don't have any chance to wash up at all, because all the water's frozen. Any water that you melt on your stove is precious, and that is consumed. You drink that water. There's no chance that you would waste it on washing off your face or your hands. Well, maybe you'd do that much, but you wouldn't do anything more than that. It's pretty rugged.

However, we were so lucky to have this resource in West Virginia that we could enjoy. What we were trying to do with Sierra Club is to help ourselves and help others appreciate the natural surroundings around us, and with trips like this, we could get to very beautiful, natural surroundings and just have a great experience. This was my first winter backpacking trip, and I was hooked. I must admit, the next week, I was exhausted. I had lost a few pounds, and I'm thin to begin with, so when I lose weight, it really affects my physical ability to do things. But I knew, a year later, that I would like to do this again.

CHAPTER 55

AFTER MY SUCCESSFUL TRIP THAT was organized by Greg Good, I had the opportunity to go winter camping with someone that I had known for a number of years. His interest in winter camping was unexpected. He was also my dentist, Don Smith. I had been seeing him as a patient for routine dental care. When I told him of my winter camping trip, he said, "Jamie, I also go winter camping."

"Really?" I said. "Well, maybe you and I can go winter camping sometime."

The following winter, we went up looking for a place to camp out. We wanted snow, because winter camping in the snow made it so much more interesting, as we could use our cross-country skis. We also didn't have to worry about the grass that covered the countryside, because, hopefully, it was all snow-covered.

On my trip with Don, it was just the two of us heading out to camp. We drove up toward the Monongahela National Forest along Highway 33 that runs from Elkins to Seneca Rocks. We headed toward Seneca Rocks, looking for the best place to do our winter camping. The first thing we did was turn north toward Canaan Valley to get to Laneville Road, a road that people often use to get up into Dolly Sods Wilderness Area.

"Boy, I hope we can get up this road in the winter," I said. "That's the place where there'll be the most snow and a good winter camping experience."

196

As luck would have it, we only got up about a couple of miles on the road. It was snowed over, and we found ourselves in a bit of a situation, where we discovered that we couldn't go any further. We were up a few miles above Laneville on this road that goes up into the high country. We somehow managed to turn around, but I said, "Don, you're going to have to get out of the car and keep it from sliding into the ditch on the side of the road."

"What do you mean?" he asked.

"As I drive the car very slowly, you're going to be walking in the ditch, pushing on the car," I said. It was very slippery. We had to do it, though, to keep the car from going in the ditch, or we would have been stuck for I don't know how long.

Don guided the car, but it wasn't very safe for him to be on the downhill side of the car if it were to roll over. It could have rolled onto him. So we quickly abandoned that idea. Somehow, we got off the Laneville Road and back to Route 32 that runs south to Highway 33. So it was an adventure just trying to get to a place to camp. I think we ended up in one of the wilderness areas on the way to Seneca Rocks, and we had a great winter hiking time. We spent the night, and everything went fine.

Since we both worked, we started trips on Fridays. We tried to spend the nights somewhere along the way on Friday nights and then get to where we really wanted to go early on Saturdays. It's really just Saturday nights that were the official times for camping out. I think I did a couple of trips over a couple of winters with Don Smith, and they were great. Don is a calm soul who also has a lot of confidence in taking care of himself in the outdoors. I always appreciated doing these kinds of adventures with Don, up in the high country of West Virginia.

CHAPTER 56

THERE ARE A COUPLE OF more winter camping trips that I want to recount, including one in 1987 and one that happened in the early 2000s. Both were with Greg Good. Greg was what I'd call the outdoor guru of the West Virginia chapter of the Sierra Club. One of the places that Greg had introduced me to was outside West Virginia; we went to the Adirondacks with Paul Turner.

In 1987, Greg, Paul, and I decided to put our winter camping adventuring to a test. As you know, we had developed this reputation of doing winter camping in the 1980s. We were made fun of by our friends who described these trips as "macho" trips. I think we had done macho one, macho two, and macho three. In February of 1987, we decided to get serious about winter camping and not just camp in the high country in West Virginia, which is about four thousand feet up. We were going to drive north, into the real winter lands.

We planned a winter-camping trip in the Adirondacks, in upstate New York, for about a week at the end of February. Up in the high country of the Adirondacks, it's a lot snowier, and, obviously, it's a lot colder. We thought that our West Virginia camping trips would prepare us to go out for a four- to five-day winter-camping trip in the Adirondacks. As the three of us left warm West Virginia, we were really looking forward to consistent snow and cold.

When we got up there, the first place we stayed was like a hostel that also housed other people who were going out cross-country skiing and climbing in the High Peaks region of the Adirondacks. The Adirondacks are mountains in the northern section of New York. The character of these hills and ridges was very Western, because they were a lot steeper and more dramatic, and you saw much more rock structure than in West Virginia.

So this area was a perfect place for us to get a more Western-like, high-mountaineering experience. The place we stayed at the first night was basically a little lodge. They fed us breakfast. Many of the people who were using the Adirondacks region in the High Peaks part of it would stay here, doing day hikes. Others, like us, would use it as our first base and then go out and camp for four or five days.

I have some reflections about winter camping in the Adirondacks. It was at the end of February, which was the peak season, so we were guaranteed snow and freezing conditions. When I thought of freezing before this trip, I figured on anything under thirty-two degrees. I did not expect our temperature to be subzero. Many, many mornings, it would get down to ten or twenty below zero. It was definitely a cold experience. Much of the time, when we were climbing in the High Peaks, we didn't have adequate wax to make our skis really stick to the snow, because it was so cold. After leaving the base on the first night, we used a tent, but after that, we decided to stay in the Adirondack shelters. These were three-sided with an open side; they were wooden, lean-to shelters. They weren't large, and we didn't have fires in them. All of our camping was done with propane stoves to melt water to drink. Then, we would keep that melted water in the bottles close to our bodies, to keep them from freezing at night.

What we experienced was a true, winter, mountaineering-style experience. Our ultimate goal was to climb Mount Marcy, which was one of the highest peaks in the High Peaks region of the Adirondacks. We were thirty to forty miles out from any civilization. We felt that we were prepared. After all, we were "mountaineers" from West Virginia. I remember that we were hoping to do most of the trip with our cross-country skis. We had thirty- to forty-pound backpacks on our backs, and we had skied like that before in West Virginia. In the Adirondacks, the snow conditions were so cold that, no matter what we did to our skis, we couldn't get them to stick, so skiing wasn't very efficient. We only had a couple of days where we could cover a lot of territory with our skis, and they didn't help us go up hills. On the last day, coming off Mount Marcy, we had about a fourteen- to fifteen-mile hike back to our home base, which was the shelter, where we could stay overnight.

I remember coming off Mount Marcy. I had lost fifteen pounds. I beat up my body pretty badly on that trip. That's not unusual for me, since I've been pretty much skinny all of my life. I needed to do this with two good friends whom I trusted. Greg and Paul had previous winter-mountaineering experience. I didn't struggle, but I knew what my limits were. Greg and Paul went out on day one, and I stayed at base camp and took it easy. I was pretty much spent, and I knew that, next, we were going to have to climb up Mount Marcy and then ski down to get back to civilization. This was a once-in-a-life experience for me.

Another winter camping trip with Greg Good in the mid- or later-2000s was over a weekend in February, and it was below zero up in Canaan Valley. I believe that there was snow on the ground. He decided we'd hike to a shelter at the junction of the Plantation Trail with the Allegheny Trail. We drove up to the beginning of Canaan Valley and hiked out Canaan Mountain to a lean-to shelter that was available. Greg knew it was there.

We started hiking, but we wanted to make it a trip where we were using our cross-country skis. There wasn't enough snow for cross-country skis, but there was enough snow for our snowshoes. They provided more stability and support so that we weren't sinking down in the snow.

The first obstacle we came upon was one small creek that we had to cross. It really wasn't a creek. It wouldn't have existed in the summer, but in the winter, it held enough water to be a creek. Greg tried stepping over the creek but missed and caught a rock, and his snowshoe broke. The strap that held it on his foot snapped off where the joint onto the snowshoe was, breaking it. Greg was stuck without a snowshoe the rest of the trip. However, because my snowshoes still worked, I was able to make it across the creek without getting wet. Luckily, I had no water in my boots. I broke trail, and Greg carefully took his broken snowshoe off and followed me.

Greg knew where he was going, and I trusted him to get us to the Adirondack-style lean-to to spend the night, because we had not brought a tent. That was going to be our shelter. Eventually, after a couple of miles, we arrived at this shelter. It was a beautiful night but very cold. Greg built a little fire that we could burn in front of the shelter, and we could look out from the ridge and see the stars.

Before we went to sleep, Greg said, "Make sure that you keep a warm bottle of water with you when you go to bed. One, you'll have something to drink if you get cold or if you get thirsty. Two, if it's warm, you can snuggle up with it, and it keeps you warm, and you'll keep the water in liquid form throughout the night by having it next to your body." That sounded good, so I got out my canteen, which was basically one of those Nalgene bottles.

We put hot water on and then filled the Nalgene bottle. I closed the lid. "Be sure to put it in your sleeping bag to warm it up," Greg said.

"That makes sense to me," I said. About half an hour later, though, I went back to my sleeping bag. "Greg, there's a problem."

There was a big puddle of water coming out the side of my down sleeping bag. Of course, the down wasn't functional, because it had gotten wet. Apparently, what had happened was that there was an ice crystal in the top of the lid that I screwed onto the bottle. It didn't seal properly, so it leaked. The hot water ran out and saturated my sleeping bag, one I had borrowed from Don Smith because it was very warm. It was a high-density down sleeping bag, which had a lot of loft, much more than my zero-degree sleeping bags had. This one was rated to a temperature of negative forty. It was a wonderful bag, but the bag was wet and totally ineffective.

So, here we were, probably around midnight and in the middle of subzero weather up on the top of a mountain in Canaan Valley. I still needed to get some sleep. We dressed me up in as many clothes as we could get on me, and Greg had me climb into the sleeping bag, even though part of it was not very functional because it was wet.

Unfortunately, the wet part covered my upper torso, where I'd normally get the coldest. I had a very difficult night sleeping. We woke up very early in the morning, because I couldn't sleep, and we both came to the conclusion—because Greg's snowshoe had broken and my sleeping bag was basically dysfunctional until I dried it—that we should say "To heck with cooking any food!" that morning. We were going to walk out and go to a restaurant in Canaan Valley and get some food, after only one night out. We had planned the trip to be a couple of nights. We at least had a great story to tell others. It was also my last winter camping trip.

CHAPTER 57

MOST OF MY ADVENTURES ARE stories that I tell people, meaning that I tell them orally. But, in a few cases, I have written down my adventures. Actually, Betsy wrote about one of our adventures, too. The following story is one I wrote for *Mountain State Sierran* in the May/June 1988 issue. It was originally titled "An Adventure: Dark Waters of Laurel Fork."

"This is unquestionably the best run of the Cheat basin," says *Wildwater West Virginia*. Early in the week we were anticipating our opportunity to paddle the Laurel Fork. The weather service forecasted rain for Wednesday and Thursday. I encouraged Mark to get a raft for Friday so he could film the remote canyon, and invited some friends to go along with us. Wednesday came, a little rain, Thursday a little more. The Parsons gauge was 4.2 feet and rising at 7:00 Friday morning. We all wanted to believe the middle and southern part of wild and wonderful West Virginia got more rain than we received up north.

We arrived at the Laurel Fork at 11:00 AM Friday. The weather was 75 degrees and sunny. The party consisted of Kenyon and Sally Stebbins, Brad Losh, Mark Samels, Betsy Pyle and me. Betsy and I paddled a tandem open canoe, while the four others paddled an eight foot Avon raft. Kenyon and Sally had been rafting before. Brad was an experienced river guide.

Mark began kayaking last season. Betsy and I were experienced kayakers and open boaters. We looked at the water in the Laurel Fork; it looked a little low. But our enthusiasm led us to overlook signs that it might actually be falling rather than rising.

Wildwater West Virginia and *Appalachian Waters V* stated that a reading of five feet on the Parsons gauge was necessary to run any of the upper Cheat tributaries. Brad said he could get the raft down the river. We agreed; we were eager to run the thirteen-mile Cheat tributary which had the reputation of being one of the most scenic and remote rivers in West Virginia. The shuttle was surprisingly straightforward, given the remoteness of the area. The Laurel Fork Canyon north of US 33 has been designated as a 6.2 remote habitat area in the Monongahela National Forest Plan. This management prescription is as close to a wilderness designation as any, mainly due to remoteness and ruggedness of the terrain. We were eager to see the area since access was mainly by the river and we had heard so much about its beauty. We returned from the shuttle and put on at 12:00 noon. About three miles into the run, we realized we weren't making the progress we had hoped for, yet we said to ourselves that we would be off the river before it got dark. At 4:00 PM we reached the falls approximately seven to nine miles into the trip. We now knew that we had to hurry if we were going to be finished before dark. Low water conditions had slowed our progress considerably. On many occasions, we had to get out and drag our boats over the exposed rocks.

The three miles before the falls consisted of two-to-four feet river-wide ledges, which we ran after scouting where the most water went over the drop. The gradient was approximately sixty feet per mile for that stretch. After carrying around the falls, we proceeded down the next two miles. In this section, the canyon walls became steeper, the river narrowed down, and the drops became more frequent and steeper, dropping at a gradient of approximately seventy to eighty feet per mile. The scenery was outstanding, as we viewed it with fading light. Rock cliffs lined the river, with nearly vertical canyon walls rising 600 feet. Rock outcroppings were apparent near the top of the canyon. The green hues of hemlock, rhododendron, and laurel dominated the streamsides. In certain aspects, the scenery reminded me of the Red River Gorge in Kentucky, and the white-water and stream size were like the "The Mile" section on Slippery Rock Creek in Pennsylvania or the Tellico River in Tennessee.

After a short and exciting two-mile section following the falls, the river widened but continued to drop at a gradient of approximately sixty feet per mile. By this time it was getting dark; we were still on the river and the amount of dragging increased, due to the widening of the stream bed.

Darkness was upon us and we were still paddling and dragging. With the help of moonlight, we progressed slowly. Someone remarked that it was 10:00 PM, surely the confluence with the Dry Fork was just around the next bend, wasn't it? We thought we saw a white house in the distance, but it was another exposed rock wall. Betsy and I were hit by a branch that hung over the river. We didn't see it in the dark and consequently capsized.

We continued on in the dark and anticipated other strainers, and lined around them. In the dark we would paddle fifty feet and drag the same distance. Where was the confluence with the Dry Fork? Progress at this time was measured in yards. At 11:00 PM we stopped to talk things over. We were fatigued after having been on the river with little extra food and having gone through our supply of water. Every one of us had the sincere desire to keep going, because we felt we were close to the confluence with Dry Fork and to our cars. But were we? After eleven hours on the river, the group decision was to get out and bivouac for the night. A level spot of ground was found, and we leaned the raft and canoe against a fallen log to provide shelter. The airbags came out of the canoe to provide a small measure of comfort and insulation between the ground and our bodies. We huddled together as we tried to sleep, but most of us just waited for night to pass, lying awake, letting our exhausted bodies rest.

We got up with the first light. The temperature had dropped to the low 40's because the cloud cover had dissipated. The wetsuits and synthetic fleece did a marginal job of keeping us warm at night. Those with dry suits did better. After first light we waited until 7:30 AM and put on. We shared three granola bars, drank river water and shared the future possibility of "beaver fever" (Giardia). We were on the river for the second day of what was originally scheduled for a day trip. The water level had dropped steadily since putting on the previous noon. There were too many exposed rocks. The stream bed had widened and was filled with rock debris left over from the 1985 flood.

We paddled and dragged for another hour or so, covering approximately a mile. We realized we were not making much progress. A group decision was made to carry out on an old logging grade. The sun had come out, we warmed up, and began our carry. About 200 yards down the grade, we heard voices and one of us saw an ATV in a pasture. We immediately struck a deal with the driver to be shuttled to our cars. We were about three miles from them.

There are many lessons to be learned from the experience. I have always said "don't believe everything you read" especially with respect to river guide books. This turned out to be false and true in this case. We now wish we had heeded the advice on the impractically of the run at less than the recommended water level, even though they were using a correlated gauge rather than one on the tributary itself. *Wildwater West Virginia* said the run was thirteen miles; *Appalachian Waters V* indicated sixteen miles. When no one in the group has experience with the river you'll be running, bank on the longer estimate. Next time I go paddling on a remote river, I will carry iodine for water purification, matches to start a fire, a flashlight, and a candle lantern. We had a first aid kit, but it didn't contain those items. Long and remote rivers require us to take a broader view of "first aid" than the usual aspirin, band aids, or ace wrap that initially come to mind.

We used questionable judgment in running an unknown shallow river with a sixty feet-per-mile gradient in the dark. We could have had serious trouble with strainers and foot injuries from the dragging; we were lucky. It was our good fortune to be wearing wetsuits, dry suits, and fleece garments. While wet, these kept some of us warm at night. One also needs to be mentally prepared to deal with the unexpected while paddling in remote areas. The human spirit in this case was a wonderful thing. All of us were supportive of each other and kept our confidence and composure under difficult and uncomfortable circumstances.

I highly recommend this river, but not under the circumstances that we experienced. Wait for more water. Look at the water level at the Highway 33 Bridge and use good judgment. Do this river in a group. It is far too remote for one or two paddlers. At adequate water levels it would be a class III–IV run with several river wide potential keeper hydraulics. Never boat alone, especially on this river. The flood of 1985 has changed the river; it widened it in spots and filled others in. This is especially true the closer you get to the confluence with the Dry Fork; many strainers were present; be on the lookout.

What Is Leadership?

CHAPTER 58

MEMORY, I HAVE FOUND OUT, is a funny thing. I don't remember everything or even attempt to tell every story. Many of my stories are about adventures, most of which I took with others. I guess I have been lucky to have a wide group of friends and associates that provided opportunities for me. I find it easy to make friends, even in coincidental meetings. I get along with a diverse group of people, and I've kept up associations with them, even if I didn't agree with their positions or didn't prefer their general styles. I have learned that if you treat people with respect, even if you don't agree with them, you can still learn from them. I believe that there is good in everyone and there is something to learn from anyone. That's one of the credos that I've followed in life, work, and play.

There have been times that this outlook has been challenged. One time was through my work on the faculty senate at WVU. I am comfortable in groups, and I work hard to be a part of various groups. It's been my modus operandi throughout my life. And this was true when I was elected to the faculty senate. I spent a number of years as a senator from the School of Medicine. I had been nominated chair-elect, but there was a particular group of senators that had a deep, innate hatred of anybody, regardless of the person, in an administrative position. When I was nominated chair-elect, I was also an associate dean in the School of Medicine. This group of senators rose to the debate when I was nominated and did anything they could to impugn my integrity, simply because I was also an administrator. As it turned out, it happened to be a small group who could not come up with another candidate to run against me.

Still, I was criticized through the nomination process, and I felt bad about being criticized for my role as an administrator. The ringleader of these criticisms and debate had some issues and would later leave the university. I'm not sure whether it was his decision to leave or whether he was fired because he wasn't doing his job as a teacher. He left, even though he had tenure. This ringleader saw himself as a junkyard attorney, even though he was a professor in the Department of Sociology. He'd taken law courses, which contributed to his persona. He also had an ax to grind with any administrator, and I just happened to be the target of the day.

During the process, I sat and answered questions from this junkyard lawyer and others. I just had to be myself. People asked me questions to be sure that I wasn't just an administrative person and that I understood what faculty do. In answering them, I explained that I also taught and that I held an academic appointment, just like any other faculty member. I also wasn't involved in the hiring or firing of faculty. I found a way to get through the interview, and I stayed calm and composed. But it was like getting the third degree, even though I hadn't done anything to get myself in trouble. Some people defended me. The president of the university, David Hardesty, even called me at home and apologized on behalf of the university for the actions of a few.

In the end, the same things that helped me in other groups helped me with the faculty senate. Over the years, my approach to life and challenges have stood the test of time and served me well.

Outside my professional context, I have found certain qualities in the diverse individuals who participated in outdoor adventures with me. Especially on extended trips, these groups included people who kept patient under unknown conditions. They were calm in difficult situations and had an unbridled respect for others, even when there were differences of opinion or disagreements. I always approached disagreements with the idea that I should take the opportunity to walk in another's shoes, to think about where they're coming from and why. At least, I try to do that.

The diversity of my adventures has always been attractive to me. But I don't like to do things alone, and I want to share them when I'm doing them, not after they're done. Whether I am dealing with publications or outdoor adventures, my pattern is to work with others. Interpersonal interaction is just a motivator; it's just my nature and the way I'm wired.

Because of my interactive skills, if I find a group and stay with the group long enough, I tend to assume a leadership role. I also believe in the concept of synergy. In any group, the output or product of the group is greater than the sum of individual contributions. That's what synergy is, and so I promoted and participated in group activities. It's another one of my patterns. Said in a more flippant way, I'm a groupie, and I always have been.

CHAPTER 59

ONE OF THE THINGS THAT I was asked to do was to be a representative of the environmental community when a decision was being made in the central part of West Virginia about the Gauley River. I was appointed by the Secretary of the Interior of the United States for this role, because I had been nominated by the West Virginia Sierra Club. The appointment allowed me to represent the state's environmental community on the Gauley River National Recreation Area Advisory Committee. The committee would help determine the future of the US National Park Service's management of the Gauley River.

For a number of years, the Gauley River was used primarily as a rafting river by many rafting companies in West Virginia. Each company had their own approach for their patrons to access the river. If you were to go down the river, first, you would see one company's access; you'd go down a mile, and then you'd see another company's access, and so on. Basically, the beautiful Gauley River was being carved up by all these rafting companies, each with their private, individual access.

The park service, which now had the management responsibilities of the Gauley River, wanted a recommendation on what to do, so they formed the advisory committee. In this group, I was the lone representative for the environmental community. Each rafting company had its representative, and the local merchants had their representatives, and there were also some people who were in state government who had responsibility for other interests in the Gauley River, primarily fishing.

It was an interesting committee to be a part of, and I had major responsibilities to help the members understand the philosophy and wisdom of not cutting up and piecemealing the river, which is what was happening. So I attended a number of meetings down in Summersville, West Virginia.

One of the first issues that came to our group was this: should there be an access road in the first mile of the river? Remember, people put on right at the base of the dam, where they had a brilliant view of the big tubes coming out of the base of the dam, which filled the river with water for rafting. The best rafting level was a release from the dam of about three thousand to four thousand cubic feet per second. This formed the best ride down the Gauley River.

I tried to get an understanding of the environment of this area from where the proposed access road would be to the first major rapid, about a mile downstream from the dam. The rafting companies tried to use the safety argument. If we could only access the river at this point, which happened to be near the first difficult rapid, then we could help save lives if there were an accident at this first big rapid.

The fishermen argued that the road could provide access for stocking the river with trout. Trout trucks could run down this road and, through tubes from the tanks on the back of the trucks, put trout into accessible areas for the fishermen. Many of the fishermen on the Gauley wanted to fish for cold-water trout. Each of the constituents on the committee had an argument. The difficulty with the road was that this was an area of the river that had basically been untouched by modern man. It had beautiful, old-growth trees and other environmentally important aspects.

One of the things that I proposed was that we have a walking tour of the area before we made any decisions about where a road should go. There was a natural bench above the river, about one hundred feet up, that was part of the ridge that outlined this part of the river. It was also walkable. So I arranged for a trip. Anyone on the committee who wanted to could walk to this bench with me one Saturday afternoon. I arranged this so that the committee could look at the area where commercial rafting and fishing groups wanted to put a road. Those who volunteered to meet me that Saturday walked with me to this bench. We found large trees that would have to be brought down if we decided to put a road up there.

After this walk, I made a written report to the park service of what we found. The bottom line of my report stated that we wanted to follow the philosophy of the US National Park Service to maintain this wild area for future generations. To build the access road would be very inappropriate, given the philosophy of little impact by the park service to preserve natural places. That was the gist of the report that I wrote. I had pictures and videos of the beautiful surroundings, including some rock formations with little caves that animals had stayed in. It was very pretty and pristine as a natural area. I gave the report to the group.

I was outvoted.

A few people, most of whom were locals, supported me. It was clear that I was definitely in the minority with respect to my particular position of what should be done with this area. Still, the arguments of the fishermen and the rafting companies didn't sway me. I ended in the minority. The majority report, in the board's final recommendations to the Park Service, said that there should be a road, and they could do it in the best way possible. Of course, it would provide more access to fishermen and would provide a safety access road for those rafting customers who were either hurt at the first rapid or wanted out before the first rapid. My report argued that this was an absolutely a pristine and gorgeous area and that any road would harm the natural environment.

So we got to the point where we were finalizing our recommendations as an advisory committee. We were meeting with the park service higher-ups, who would make the final recommendation. The spokesperson for the majority, who happened to be one of the directors of the Fish and Wildlife Service of West Virginia, gave the majority report. However, I was provided the opportunity to give the minority report, as well. There were a few local people who understood what I was trying to do, and they were supportive of my position. The committee, as a whole, was not. I can't say that the rafting company owners who were on the board liked me for it, but I think they respected me and the manner in which I disagreed with them. For the rafting companies, access and safety meant more customers. I understood where they were coming from, according to their financial point, but I didn't agree that this particular area should have a road.

I'd been down the Upper Gauley several times on private rafts. I also had been down it on a commercial raft. I had either canoed or kayaked the Lower Gauley on multiple occasions. I felt that it was very important to present my report, too, even if it was the minority point of view.

Six months later, we got the park service's recommendation. It turned out that the park service agreed with my minority report. There was no need for an access road in this pristine, beautiful area. They did not accept the position of the rafting and fishing interests. In the end, I don't think it was a financial decision. I think it was a decision that came down to the preservation of wild land for future generations.

CHAPTER 60

MY US NATIONAL PARK SERVICE experience is not the only way I tried to help protect the environment. In 1990, Mac Thornton and some American Whitewater Affiliation board members met at my house to discuss something with me, because they knew I was involved in the Sierra Club in West Virginia. They had an idea—basically, a proposal to form a rivers protection group in West Virginia. We decided that it would be called the West Virginia Rivers Coalition, or the WVRC.

Mac and I did some more communicating throughout that spring. He also knew that I was a white-water boater, and protecting rivers for recreation was a primary purpose of his planned organization. White-water boaters have tendencies to get to know each other. He also had heard that I was one of the early leaders of the Sierra Club in West Virginia. In his mind, I seemed like a natural fit. As soon as we met, we hit it off, and we remain good friends to this day.

We all had a common interest in protecting the beautiful rivers and streams of West Virginia. We thought that forming a new conservation organization, whose sole purpose was to protect rivers, was the way to go, because there weren't any groups focused specifically on rivers. Other groups, like the Sierra Club or the West Virginia Highlands Conservancy, were primarily land-based, focusing on trails and other areas.

A few other members were connected to various West Virginia organizations that had environmental input, and we got together and formed a board of directors. I was one of the original board members. Mac, who lived in Washington, DC, was another board member. Mac brought in a woman, Pat Muñoz, who was wonderful. Pat was a staffer for American Rivers, which was based in Washington, DC. American Rivers is a conservation organization that supports all rivers in the United States and tries to provide support services to groups who are interested in protecting their local rivers. So, there was a natural connection between Pat, Mac, and me, and we all became friends. We enjoyed rivers. We boated. We all had a need to conserve our natural resources flowing in our blood.

After a number of months, we were successful with writing some grants. I wrote a grant and got some money to help support our hiring of an executive director. Mac and Pat wrote grants, and American Rivers gave us money, so we had enough to actually pay someone a reasonable salary, around $30,000, to be an executive director for the first year. From that point on, we would continue to seek funding sources to support the West Virginia Rivers Coalition. We were successful in getting money, and we established an office in Buckhannon, West Virginia, because that was where our first executive director lived. His name was Roger Harrison.

Roger was a young college graduate, full of vim and vigor, and he was very good at working with people. He was also good at making public speeches about the value of protecting rivers. He traveled throughout the state, going to different rivers, as well as going to different organizations, talking about the value of maintaining the current status of rivers and protecting them. Roger did a great job in the early years of the Rivers Coalition. Our board had expanded, because we needed more people who could raise funds or at least have some influence on fundraising, as our budget had grown from $30,000 in the first year to $150,000. We had a larger staff and greater expenses.

There was a lot of pressure on the board members to help us raise money. One of the things that we learned quickly is that most young people who were involved in river running, whether it be running the

Gauley River or running the Cheat River, were very interested in protecting the rivers in West Virginia. The Rivers Coalition is still strong today. Of course, the executive director has changed a number of times, and the board has changed a number of times. Basically, during the mid-1990s, Mac, who was chairman of the board of directors, asked me if I would be interested becoming chairman, because it was time for him to step down and do some other things. Mac was always a very good thinker and leader. In his professional career as an attorney, he rose to be the Chief Counsel to the Inspector General of the US Department of Health and Human Services in Washington, DC.

So, with Mac's encouragement, I became chairman of the board, and one of my first responsibilities was to find a new executive director. It took a significant amount of my extra time, of course. And it was all volunteer. As you know, I was working full-time, but this was an opportunity that I felt deeply committed to, and it was very rewarding. I met great people, and I got to visit many of the rivers and streams that we were able to work on.

Since we had lost our executive director, I needed to find a replacement. After many tries, I found an individual who I thought would be a great executive director, but he only stayed about six months. Then, another director only lasted about a year. Being executive director of a 501(c)(3) organization is difficult, because you have to raise money to support your purpose and goals. You really don't have a life of your own. It's stressful, but well worth it when you see the benefits of what the organization has done.

In 2014, I can say that the WV Rivers Coalition is alive and well and is strong today. The coalition continues to focus on the rivers. However, our primary original goal was to gain federal designation for some rivers as wild or scenic in the State of West Virginia. That never happened, because the legislature changed the rules to get rivers designated as wild and/or scenic. West Virginia's Department of Natural Resources, especially the fish and wildlife personnel, fought that federal designation on many of our beautiful rivers in the State. Sadly, there is only a 10.5-mile protected section of the Bluestone River in southern West Virginia designated as scenic today. The period during which those designations were very popular was in the early 1980s. Since that time, wild and scenic designations for other rivers throughout this country have been few and far between.

Even though the WV Rivers Coalition couldn't achieve its original goal, it matured into an organization that tackles many important river-related issues. In 2012, a new executive director, Angie Rosser, decided to move the coalition's office from Elkins to Charleston so that they had a stronger presence in the state capital. She also contacted Mac and me and asked each of us to write our recollections of the history of the WVRC for their fall newsletter, as the organization anticipated its twenty-fifth anniversary. Angie called me at home sometime during the fall of 2014 to let me know that the coalition would celebrate this important milestone at Canaan Valley State Park on April 25, 2015. It felt good to know that the organization I helped to establish was still providing a strong voice for rivers and clean-water issues in our state.

Canoeing the Colorado River
through the Grand Canyon

CHAPTER 61

IN THE WINTER OF 1988, Betsy and I were at a film festival put on by the Bluegrass Wildwater Association, back in Lexington, where we went every year and where we still had many friends. We attended the party that followed the film festival. At the party, we overheard some people talking, and we went over to listen. A group was putting together a boating trip—but not an ordinary one. This would be a trip boating the Grand Canyon, and the organizers were looking for people to join. I quickly conferred with Betsy and then asked if they would like a tandem, open canoe to join the trip. The organizers laughed, but we were serious. In boating culture, the spirit of independence is valued, and as long as we were willing to take responsibility for ourselves, we were welcome to join.

Before we could say yes, I had to check with my boss at the university, Bob D'Alessandri, to see if I could get thirteen days off. It was a little tricky, timing-wise, as the trip began over the Labor Day weekend and school would just be starting for the fall semester. However, Bob knew me well and understood the importance of this trip, and because part of it would be over the holiday, I was able to go. Betsy was able to arrange a leave from the university as well. Some others going on the trip would be driving out West and could take our canoe and some other gear. So things came together.

We got out to Arizona with a free day before the put-in, and did a day hike into the canyon to Plateau Point for a better view of the river. We stayed in a mom-and-pop hotel that night with the whole group. Our gear had arrived, and we were set to go. Betsy captured the trip beautifully in her published article, "Tandem in the Canyon: A Double Dose of BIG WATER," in *American Whitewater: Journal of the American Whitewater Affiliation* in the March/April 1989 issue. It is included here:

Sure, a tandem open canoe is a great way for a couple to share whitewater action...but isn't boating the Grand Canyon taking togetherness a little far?

The longer you boat, the more you hear about rivers. Rivers of mythic proportion. The lure of big water is a powerful thing. Inevitably, the Colorado becomes an obsession. You learn the names of the rapids by heart: Crystal, Lava, Hance, Hermit, and Grapevine...finally you're hooked. You have to see them for yourself. You have to find out if you have what it takes.

For a long time we'd known we wanted to run the Colorado. The question was when and how. Jamie felt more confident in his kayak than I did in mine, so I always assumed that I'd wind up riding the support raft. But that assumption changed dramatically after we'd moved to Morgantown, West Virginia, and spent a couple of solid seasons tandem open boating. We developed confidence in our ability to put the canoe where we wanted it on the Cheat Canyon, the New River Gorge, and the Lower Gauley.

We believed in our boat, a Mohawk Scamp custom outfitted by Bruce Penrod, and we practiced "Zen and the Art of Canoe Maintenance," carefully fine-tuning it to our idiosyncrasies. We felt we were as ready as we'd ever be to tackle Big Western Water. We were told that all eastern boaters needed to do was dig in and confront the power of western rivers. And so we said, "Let's go for it."

The reaction from our paddling acquaintances was mixed, to say the least, when we announced our intent to paddle a tandem open boat through the Grand Canyon. "You guys are crazy," was an all too familiar retort. Some of our "friends" took delight in listing the names of the drops they thought we would swim. Words of encouragement were few and far between.

In September of 1988 our dream came true. Our group assembled at Marble Canyon Lodge, a few miles from Lee's Ferry. The trip was organized by Bill Atkins of Knoxville's Chota Canoe Club with Colorado River and Trails Expeditions providing raft support. Two other members of Pittsburgh's Three Rivers Paddling Club joined us, Meg Weesner, a ranger at the New River, and Paul Kammer. Meg had only been kayaking for a little more than a year. Paul had lots of eastern boating experience but had to be convinced that he was ready to challenge the Really Big Water of the West.

The remainder of the party consisted of five kayakers from the Winston-Salem (NC) club, an open boater from Lexington (KY), and three solo open boaters, two kayakers, and a C2 team, all from Tennessee.

At the put-in we swapped stories about our sleepless night. The anticipation was overpowering; we felt like children on the night before Christmas.

The Colorado was crystal clear at the put-in but it didn't stay that way for long; at mile one the Paria River added a load of silt, compliments of thunderstorms during the preceding week. After the Little Colorado joined the river at mile 61, the river attained the color of chocolate pudding.

Because of the drought the Bureau of Reclamation was conserving water, releasing only enough through the turbines at Glen Canyon Dam to meet the demand for power...and not a drop more. That meant low water conditions for us. But lower on the Colorado does not necessarily mean easier. At diminished flows more rocks are exposed and juicy holes open up. Bill told us that, during the preceding year, flows ranged from 20,000 to

30,000 cfs, while we experienced flows from 4,000 to 15,000 cfs.

Why had I believed them when they told me that the Colorado would just be open chutes, no rocks, few holes and bigger waves than I had ever seen? At the first major rapid, Badger, I learned differently. It looked big alright, but there were many rocks and holes. Rapids on the Colorado are rated one through ten. Badger was a seven. Could this be extrapolated to a 4.2 on the AWA boating scale?

Yes, we swam the first rapid, a disappointing start. Yes, it was a cold swim, and yes, it was a long one. But we had company, though Paul and Meg didn't make the list.

And then we swam the second big rapid, Soap Creek. I managed to hang onto my paddle and stay with the boat, enjoying a more buoyant ride than my unfortunate husband, who was swept away from the boat and bounced over a number of rocks before taking sanctuary in an eddy midway through the rapid.

Afterward we had one of those heart-to-heart talks that are so necessary for maintaining a serious tandem-boating relationship, not to mention a marriage. Some encouragement from veterans of previous trips on the Colorado helped. We had been trying to stay out of the really big action to avoid swamping our boat, as a consequence we had been getting caught in the pour-overs near shore. We were advised to commit ourselves to the well-defined "V" of each rapid, then turn it toward the right or left to meet the reactionary waves coming in from the sides.

What a difference! Our redemption came later that day with a flawless run of House Rock Rapid, rated an eight. The cheers we heard as we eddied out at the bottom of that rapid with a boat full of water made me feel great. Better still was the compliment we received from another tandem open boat team sitting in the eddy.

Frankly, we were surprised to see another tandem team on the river; far fewer canoeists paddle the Colorado than kayakers, and even fewer canoeists try it tandem. These new acquaintances, natives of Salt Lake City, paddled a Mad River Explorer with a customized spray cover.

When we told them we were from West Virginia they didn't look a bit surprised.

"We knew you must be from the East," they observed, "since you're paddling a *real* open canoe."

We encountered them one more time during our trip, near the junction of the Little Colorado.

"Got a spare gunwale?" they called from shore. They had broached on a rock near the bottom of Kwagunt Rapid, just a few miles upstream. We knew the rock that had caused their trouble; we'd had a closer look at it than we would have preferred.

On day four, I spotted the Desert View Watchtower on the South Rim. How well I remembered standing up there, peering down at the river, wondering what it would be like to run it. Not far ahead lay the Granite Gorge section of the Canyon, where the pace of the action and the scale of the drops really escalates.

We stopped to scout Hance Rapid, a long class nine, from the right shore. When the C2 in our party was devoured in a large hole at the top, we quickly decided not to attempt that route. Instead we followed Bailey Johnson's Sunburst canoe into an eddy behind some large boulders near the top center, then worked hard to the left. Success!

We maintained our confidence with great runs through Sockdolager and Grapevine, both rated eight. We were managing to stay upright but our boat looked like a bathtub full of water at the bottom of each rapid. This came as no surprise because our boat was designed for solo use. We rode low in the water and banked upon our combined power to maneuver the boat when it was full.

The steep walls of the Granite Gorge blocked the late afternoon sun and it seemed to be getting dark. Our group had dispersed after Hance, with most of the kayakers paddling ahead. We were tired and hungry, and as we rounded each bend we hoped we would find our camp. Jamie and I were starting to remember our April Fools' Day experience on the Laurel Fork of the Cheat River, a voyage that was interrupted by an unexpected cold night's bivouac in the middle of nowhere. Finally we spotted our party on the shore just above the Kaibab Trail suspension bridge. Several of us had warned the raft crew not to pass Phantom Ranch before camping; we were determined to have our postcards packed out by mule-train.

The following morning we rehearsed the order of the Big Ones. Horn Creek, Granite, Hermit, Crystal. It would be a day to remember.

Mark Tygeson, the commander of our support raft, estimated the flow at Horn Creek to be 8,000 cfs. It was nasty. Larry Steven's *Colorado Guidebook* rated it a ten at that level. There were huge holes and pulsating waves that intermittently revealed the top of a rock near the bottom of the drop that didn't look inviting. We elected to portage, as did the team in the C2.

The others all ran it, with varied success. Mark Copeland kept his squirt boat, a Ferrier, vertical through most of the drop. But poor Meg experienced what I believe to be her first bona fide swim at Horn Creek. Her only other swim occurred just a few miles downstream at Granite, a class nine.

We dumped at Granite as well, halfway through the best roller coaster wave train I've ever experienced. We analyzed our swims and decided that every time we flipped it was on Jamie's side. His resolve to perfect his brace paid off in the class nine wave train at Hermit Rapid. As we dropped into the big hole he leaned way out, head in the water, and sculled until he could snap us up and on our way again.

Even at low water the top two holes at Crystal were impressive. Much bigger and much nastier than anything I wanted to sample. Some of us carried around the holes, others snuck along the shore. Hugh Worthy, paddling a Mohawk Scamp, was the only brave soul to run the meat of it, heading left at the top of the two holes. His run was flawless.

The river mellows out a bit after Crystal. Most people enjoy the change of pace and take the opportunity to hike up some of the spectacular side canyons, like those at Tapeats, Deer, and Havasu Creeks. We also explored the Elves' Chasm, another enchanting location.

At Deubendorff, another class eight, Meg drifted too far to the left and straight toward a gigantic hole at the bottom. She was so surprised when she crashed through it upright that she stopped stroking and flipped in the backwash. But Meg executed one of those bomb-proof combat rolls that she had been perfecting and joined us in the eddy.

Paul Kammer, who hadn't been sure he was ready for Big Water but clearly was, had a moment of glory at the Upset Rapid. This seldom mentioned class eight gem featured a nearly river-wide hole that is, at low water, every bit as impressive as the one at Crystal. Everyone carried or snuck along the right shore except Paul, who stared at it for a long time from shore, then touched the edge of the hole. His run was perfect and he arrived in the eddy at the bottom grinning from ear to ear.

Jamie and I each shot a roll of film at Lava, perhaps the Colorado's most notorious rapid. Most of our group ran right, heading into a V created by two enormous, crashing diagonal waves. Many, but by no means all, finished upright in their boats. Paul Kammer had a clean run, while Carolyn Kerr, the only woman in our group who challenged Lava, was separated from her Dancer near the bottom.

Andrew Carr bow-and-stern squirted his kayak through the whole rapid. Spectacular, but intentional? Ben Van Meter eddy-hopped his Mad River ME canoe through the turbulent water located on river left.

Our hero at Crystal, Hugh Worthy, discovered that Lava looked different at water level and missed his line, sailing directly into the dreaded hole at the top. He enjoyed (?) a momentary surf, then his open boat endered out of the hole. We held our breath until his yellow helmet surfaced in the bubbling, brown water, a long way downstream.

After Lava everyone relaxed a bit, though camp life remained lively. We hiked to the Indian pictographs at Whitmore Canyon, played volleyball and tried to chip away at our inexhaustible beer supply. The meals provided by our outfitters exceeded our expectations.

Colorado River outfitters often compete with one another on service criteria, rather than price. We had fresh fruit for breakfast each morning and entrees like grilled salmon for dinner. The lunch spread was a veritable delicatessen, with tomatoes, red onions, avocados, and lettuce—all the trimmings. The river did a good job of chilling our beer and sodas and the raft crew cheerfully tossed us a drink on demand.

Tension in camp was minimized since our commercial support team did all the work. We were free to devote all our energy to enjoying the river, canyon explorations, and the company of those in our group. Boaters were responsible for getting their gear to the raft each morning and not much more. The raft crew handled all the cooking, clean-up, and the party's sanitary needs. Concerned about maintaining a quality environment, the National Park Service requires that all solid waste be packed out of the Canyon.

A commercial trip is more expensive than a private one, but there are advantages. We avoided the long waiting lists for private trips and were able to schedule during a pleasant time of the year, early September, after the rainy season, with daytime highs in the 90s and balmy night-time lows in the 70s.

On the thirteenth and last day of our trip we paddled the last few miles to Diamond Creek, 225 miles from the put-in. Knowing that we'd replay this scene often in our minds, we tried to enjoy the rapids and soak in as much of the scenery as possible. Many of the boaters in our party had run the Colorado before, and now Jamie and I knew why.

It is impossible to explore all the side canyons in a single trip. We had been unable to visit the fluted rock passages of Matkatamiba Canyon. Others wanted to see what the big drops looked like at different water levels. Paul Kammer, now a Big Water specialist as well as a consummate photographer, wanted to take more action shots.

Now that our first taste of western whitewater is behind us, we're like the others; we hope to return and perfect our tandem open-boating skills on the Really Big Water of the Colorado.

We never really doubted our ability to make it down the river—but did we fully realize the proportions of the challenge?

The answer is probably "no." But we'd be ready to go again tomorrow!

Fulfilling a Dream

CHAPTER 62

DURING OUR GRAND CANYON TRIP, Betsy and I had another challenge. Up to the time of the trip, we had been trying for a baby. I was giving Betsy injections to try to boost her hormonal system so that we could get pregnant, even as we were on the Grand Canyon trip.

We tried and tried and tried to have a child, but nothing would work. We sought medical advice. After all, I worked in the Health Sciences Center, so we went to the fertility clinic. Betsy found out that she had very severe endometriosis, which is a kind of tissue around the reproductive organs that can affect fertility. We were very frustrated that it was difficult for us to produce a pregnancy. The recommended approach was to artificially inseminate Betsy with my sperm, which could be inserted directly into her uterus at the right cyclic time. We tried that for two different cycles.

Unfortunately, in the spring of 1989, Betsy developed a pelvic infection. It was a very serious infection, and Betsy was admitted to the hospital. She was in the hospital for about twenty days and was extremely weak from this aggressive infection. The good news is that we were eventually able to arrest the infection, but the bad news was that the doctors ultimately needed to remove all of her reproductive organs to arrest this very persistent infection. We were sad and then disappointed, but that's the way life happens sometimes.

By the summer of 1989, we knew for sure that we were physically unable to have a child. It is at that point that we became more serious about trying to look for a way to adopt a child. We'd heard about adoption options before, because we had been trying for several years to have a child. We knew now that she would never be able to give birth to a child, and we were okay with this option. Our friend Candice offered to be a surrogate mom or to be birth mother to a child for Betsy and me. That could be done through artificial insemination so there would be no "hanky-panky," as Candice said. A potential adoption was already in the works, but we were keeping all our options open at that point.

We made it clearly known to as many physicians, social service agencies, and adoption agencies as possible that we were very interested in adopting a child. In December of 1989, we got a telephone call from a local physician, saying that one of his patients, a younger college student, had become pregnant unexpectedly and was considering giving her child up for adoption. He recommended our family to her as an opportunity for a private adoption. It was wonderful news, but we still didn't know if it was going to actually happen until closer to her anticipated due date, which was early or mid-February of 1990.

At the time, our feelings were hopeful, but we also prepared ourselves for disappointment. It was a difficult time to really think through how I felt, because it was very emotional. In early February of 1990, the physician contacted us again to inform us that his patient was, at that time, still comfortable with having her child placed for a private, anonymous adoption. This meant that the physician still recommended our family, but the anonymity of the birth mother and anonymity of the child's future parents would be ensured. So it sounded like we might get the baby. The physician also asked the birth mother to meet with our attorney about her decision. She told the attorney that she definitely was interested in the private-adoption option, and we agreed to pay all medical expenses related to her delivery, as well as counseling if she was interested in that service. He also clearly explained West Virginia's laws regarding adoption to her.

In the middle of February, our friends from Washington, DC, were visiting us with their young son. They were friends of mine from my

Chapel Hill grad school days. Dedun and Rob were there to share in the good news when our attorney called us after the birth to say, "It's a boy!" He cautioned us that the birth mother had seventy-two hours before she could legally relinquish custody of her son, but said she seemed firm in her resolve to proceed with the adoption.

Dedun and Rob were relatively new parents themselves, so they said, "I guess we're going shopping tomorrow!" Betsy and I felt optimistic about the adoption, but hadn't bought a single thing—just to be cautious. So, the next day, we went to the mall and bought all the things we needed to have an infant in our house and transport him in our car. We basically only had a few days to get what we needed—in other words, the bare essentials—so that our home would be ready to go. It was helpful to have the advice of our friends as we shopped, because they had acquired all the same things so recently. I think their son was about eighteen months old during that visit. After lunch, they headed home and wished us luck.

On the day of our child's arrival at our home, our friend Candice had actually invited us over to talk again about the potential of being a surrogate. But that afternoon or evening, we called and said that we couldn't come over for dinner, because our child had arrived. All of our friends were very supportive of us adopting a child. Many of our friends from the Sierra Club had children, and they were growing up, and now it was our turn to become parents.

Earlier in the day, our attorney had called us and said that the birth mother had agreed that she would place her child with us for adoption and had signed all the legal documents. He said he and his wife would bring the child over to our home. I remember that it was a bright, wintry day. We got a call from our attorney, and he said, "He's coming home this afternoon."

So it worked out that, all of a sudden, that afternoon, we had a baby boy with us.

Naming our new baby boy was easy. Betsy and I, about a year or two earlier, had run the Grand Canyon in our open boat. While on the trip, right there in our canoe, we decided that if we were able to have a child, a boy, that we would name him Wesley after John Wesley Powell, the explorer who was first to run the Colorado River through the Grand Canyon. It was also the name of my good friend Wesley Byerly from my rock-climbing days in North Carolina, a good coincidence. And Betsy's great grandfather's name was William Wesley Pyle.

Of course, having a baby changed things. We cut back on the outings, so now neither Betsy nor I had the freedom to go. And even if one of us did want to go do something, we realized that the other person would be taking care of our new child alone. Over time, we figured out how to share responsibilities and provide each of us a psychological break when we needed it. We did it in a positive way. Love changed our lifestyle.

CHAPTER 63

WESLEY WAS FUN TO HAVE around from the beginning, because little children—babies growing up into children—are fun at all different stages. Wesley was a talker, and even as a baby, he would try to communicate with us about what he wanted and what he didn't want. He was the master of the "no" word, and he would turn around the lessons we were trying to teach him and say what we would say, only adding "no."

During Wesley's early years, I enjoyed taking him on cross-country ski trips. I would put him in the backpack every year when we would go to the cabin at Blackwater Falls, West Virginia. Greg Good and Lynn Sobolov, Betsy and I, and a few others would cross-country ski the trails in the area. We had little backpacks that we'd place our kids in, so we'd be skiing through the woods with Wesley and Anna, Greg and Lynn's child, who was just one month younger than Wesley. This is one of the things I remember most during the early years. We all had a great time.

We took Wesley out to Suisun Valley to go visit my mother in California every summer, and I remember him loving to play in the toy room in my mother's house. My mother had remarried, and this room was full of his kids' toys. There was a big closet, and Wesley would pull the toys out and have all sorts of fun with them. There was a long hallway in the house on Willotta Drive, and Wesley would run up and down that hallway, just having a great time. He'd run from the toy closet to one of the bedrooms, which was his little domain.

Wesley always wanted to play outside, and he liked playing sports. We introduced him to kids' soccer when he was just a little guy. At that point, kids' soccer looked like "bunch ball," where there would be these little groups of kids following the ball and trying to kick it. Of course, they would end up kicking each other. But Wesley had a good time playing, even when he was really young.

When he entered grammar school, he also played basketball, and he was a pretty good shooter, but he was not as tall as all the other kids. He even went to one of the WVU camps and won the award for being the best free-throw shooter in his age group.

When Wesley was young, I had pretty much an eight-to-six job, but I always made it a point to do the work at the office and not bring it home. That way, I could be with my family in the evening. Sure, I worked hard, but there was one year where that was an exception. Wesley was a little kid, probably younger than five years old; it was in the mid-1990s. I was working in the School of Pharmacy all that year. The Vice President for Health Sciences of West Virginia University asked me if I would be interim dean for the year until they could recruit a pharmacist to be dean. I was working very hard, coming home later in the evenings, and I remember that Wesley and his mom always wondered where I was. So there was that year, when I didn't spend much time at home during the week. And often, on the weekends, I had academic events that I needed to go to, as well. However, I enjoyed it. In fact, I thought I did such a good job that, even though I wasn't a pharmacist, I thought I could be a permanent dean of that college. Even though that was not the plan, I had stepped in to fix a problem that the school had. They had various, warring faculty, who were doing everything they could to make it difficult for other groups in the school, even though it didn't make any sense. By the end of the year, I was able to resolve that situation and help us recruit a good pharmacy dean.

My permanent position was as the Associate Dean of Medical Education. After my year in pharmacy, I went back to my previous position but older, wiser, and certainly with more experience. I think that helped me continue to assist faculty in medicine do the right thing. I always felt that faculty always wanted to do the right thing, but they didn't necessarily know what that was, given the challenges that they were facing. I've always felt that my job was to help or facilitate people to reach their maximum potential, to solve problems, and to help others solve problems. I guess that is what I've always done in my academic role. I was always the facilitator.

When Wesley was a little tyke, Betsy was working full-time. She was a faculty member at West Virginia University, teaching geography classes. Then, when Wesley got a little older, she changed positions and was working in institutional research. She worked in an office that supplied all the statistics about the university and gathered decision-support information for administrators to help them run the university. Those were the types of things that Betsy did.

Because Betsy and I both worked, we had different daycare situations for Wesley. Some of them were good, some mediocre. First, a college student took care of Wesley in our home. Then, we found a woman in the neighborhood, a couple of streets over, who had two or three kids at her house, so she could watch Wesley for the day. After about six months, she decided that the boys had all become too mobile, and she couldn't keep up with all of them. We found other arrangements, but they weren't completely satisfactory. We were concluding that home care or babysitting, or whatever you want to call these arrangements, weren't the best options for us. Eventually, we did find a woman who took care of several kids in her home. She had run a daycare company and was actually doing a pretty good job. Wesley was with her for a while until he got old enough to go to preschool. During this time, learning from somebody was a good thing, because it was more like preschool. The kids were getting academic input, as well as child care and socialization. We felt good about that. Then, Wesley got to go to Chyleen's Twos and Threes, and later to Morgantown Early Learning Facility (ELF). At ELF, he was able to have a full day of kindergarten before the county school system switched to make full-day kindergarten mandatory. From that point on, he was in his normal schooling years. We were fortunate that there was a small, neighborhood public school where he attended first through third grade, and it was only a few blocks from our house.

CHAPTER 64

IT WAS IN HIS GRADE school years that Wesley started to develop skills as a soccer player. When he was even younger, maybe six years old, the city of Morgantown had community soccer for little kids. We read about it in the paper. It took place on a soccer field, and there were all these little kids that would run and try to kick the ball, all at the same time. They used little groups, maybe five or six. It was hilarious.

That was his first introduction to the sport. Then, we noticed that Wesley figured something out: don't go with the group where all the kids were trying to kick the ball. Wait on the outside, until the ball got kicked out of the group, and then take the ball where you wanted to take it. He figured that out pretty quickly as a little kid, and, consequently, he would end up scoring during these bunch-ball soccer games. Wesley liked it, and he certainly got a lot of praise from everyone.

Soccer was something he liked doing, and he was good at it. But when he was younger, I also introduced him to snow skiing. He was eight or so, and I really enjoyed doing that. I tried to get him to ski like me. We started with skis, but he saw other kids on long, wide boards.

"Dad, I want to do what those kids are doing," he said. So he took up snowboarding and developed some good skills at it.

For many winters, we managed to go out west to have family vacations at ski resorts. We were able to do that through Wesley's middle school and high school. Betsy and I skied, and Wesley snowboarded.

When Wesley was a young boy, we both took piano lessons. We had common ground playing the piano. He could learn things a lot quicker than I could, but I had more discipline to practice than he did. I wish he would've continued to play music, but I stopped playing piano when I was a kid, too.

In some ways, Wesley and I are very similar, and in other ways, we are quite different. He's smarter than I am and more athletic than I am. However, we're very similar in our political views. He's more liberal than many of his peers. I think it's from the influence of his mother, Betsy, and from me. We always tried to look at different points of view. It can be called an exposure to "diversity," in the broad sense, or the idea that one person's opinion can't be right all the time. You have to learn to walk in another's shoes to understand why the person believes as he or she does. We tried to instill in him the ability to make friends, no matter who they were, or where they were from, or what their backgrounds were. In certain respects, I think we've been fairly successful. The ability to play soccer gave him the ability to meet and relate to other kids his age outside of school, too.

Wesley didn't need to rebel to get attention, because he got attention for his athletic abilities. I guess you could call him a jock, but he wasn't a football player or a basketball player. He was a soccer player.

Since Wesley was our only child, and since we were fortunate to have the opportunity to adopt him, I suspect he was spoiled, to some extent. He didn't have to compete with a brother or sister for our attention. We pretty much gave him what he wanted, within reason, and we loved him, hoping that he would turn out all right in the end. To our knowledge, he has. I think his becoming involved in a very engaged and positive way with developing his soccer skills really kept him out of the trouble that smart kids get into because they're bored. We were older parents. I was in my early forties, and Betsy was in her late thirties, when we adopted him, so adopting another child might have been over-the-top for us. Our only regret—and it's really not a regret in my mind—is not having a brother or a sister for Wesley. We did have Shasta, though, a golden retriever, who lived for almost fourteen years. Wesley often teased and referred to her as his sister.

Every fall, Wesley played on the local soccer teams, and those soccer teams grew into traveling teams. For many decisions you make in life as parents, you have no idea whether your choice is the right thing to do, but we were lucky with soccer. And we learned all we could about the game. I was one of the parent assistants when he was playing club soccer in Morgantown. We also took him to camps or training sessions sponsored by a semiprofessional team in the region. He had a serious soccer beginning. He was asked to join a club team in Dundee, Scotland, when we went there during my sabbatical, and he played with kids who traveled throughout the towns in the local area. Even though we were only there for six months, he got a great opportunity to play with them. He was the second-leading scorer, so we thought, *Something is going on with this kid.* He knows how to play soccer, and he loved it; little did we know that he would have quite a soccer future in his pre-high-school and high-school years.

We came back from Scotland, and Wesley was one of the stars on the local club team in the Morgantown area. But every time he would play, he would be frustrated with the other kids. In his mind, many weren't playing at the level that he would prefer to play.

For some reason, Wesley got the idea (and I don't know how he got it), that he wanted to play on a club team in Pittsburgh that was really good, a team with a great reputation. I didn't know how he got the Beadling soccer team's information, but he did. Betsy reminded me that I had taken Wesley to a semipro game in Pittsburgh, and this team had won the state championship for youth soccer, so they were introduced at halftime. That's how Wesley learned about the Beadling Soccer Club.

"Dad, can we go up and watch one of their games?" he asked. So I took him, and we went up and watched one Saturday.

After watching, he said, "Wow, these kids know how to play." It was at a much higher level of skill, and of course, they won.

During the car ride home, Wesley said, "Dad, I want to join that team."

"Do you have any idea of what it would mean for us to take you to Pittsburgh if you tried out and made the team?" I asked.

"Yes," Wesley said. "I'll do anything you want me to do. I'll get A's in school. I'll do my homework."

So Betsy and I drove him to Pittsburgh, and he met this team for tryouts. One had to be invited to join this team, and they didn't take all comers. The team had a long-standing reputation of attracting the best kids in the region, and they had won multiple state championships as a club team. Wesley went through the tryouts. He liked the kids who were already on the team, and he felt that he'd fit in. A few days after the tryout, the coach called us.

"If Wesley is interested," he said, "we would like him to join the team."

Practice for the team was in the South Hills area of Pittsburgh, and they were one to two times a week. Here we were, in Morgantown, realizing that getting Wesley to practice required a drive of an hour and fifteen minutes. Of course, as his parents, we gave in and wanted our son to have the opportunity he wanted. Wesley started going to practices, and I think that he got along fine with the kids, even though he was an outsider, being from West Virginia.

Wesley went through a little reality check or culture shock. First of all, the driving every couple of days to the Pittsburgh area got to him. "Can we stay home? Can I miss this practice today? Can't I stay home and play with my friends?" he'd ask.

"No. You wanted to join this team, and you knew what it would take," I said. It was a growing experience for him.

Then came the early games, when Wesley was one of the newbie kids on the team. When he got in to play, he was really, really nervous. He didn't always know where he was supposed to be. He didn't look like he belonged, and he also got tired of the other kids from the Pittsburgh area teasing him because he was a "hillbilly" from West Virginia.

Wesley and a few other kids were subbed in and out during the games. Wesley wasn't one of the starters, because the kids who were bigger (though not necessarily older) were well-established, and they were very good players. Eventually, he calmed his nerves. Someone crossed the ball in front of the goal when Wesley was playing an outside mid or forward position. He ran up and kicked it in the goal, and his attitude changed. The attitudes of the other kids on the team changed as well. They said, "Maybe this player from West Virginia isn't so bad after all."

After that, the kids began to accept him, and he felt more like a part of the team, so things were very good for him the first year. He had scored, and he had a regular playing rotation. There were obviously more than eleven kids, so the coaches substituted kids in at different times. The coach liked Wesley's work ethic, and things went well. The Beadling team defeated their rival and won the Western Pennsylvania championship. Wesley scored a goal in the playoffs.

Here's the deal, though. A player doesn't know if he gets to continue on the team the next year. Each player has to wait until the coach calls and asks him or her to be a part of the team for the next season. After the season, a week went by. We didn't get a call, and Wesley was getting nervous. Then, we finally got the call, and the coach asked if Wesley would continue on the team for the following year. And he did.

Wesley was smaller than the other boys on the team. His growth spurt hadn't kicked in yet, whereas some of the other kids' growth spurts were kicking in full-scale. The second year went well, and he again contributed to the team getting into the finals of the club-team state championship.

Each year, for the five years that Wesley was on the team, besides going to Pittsburgh two times a week to practice for an hour and a half, we would be traveling in the spring to who-knows-where all over the eastern continental United States. There was no question that we drove a lot. Betsy and I both tried to go to all the games, and my work was well-established, so I really had no problem doing that. If there was a time that I was out of town, or if something had to be done during the weekend, I would stay, and Betsy would take Wesley, but those times were few and far between. During the week, Wesley got out of school at three, and Betsy would have Wesley in the car at three thirty, heading to Pittsburgh for a two-hour practice. Wesley did homework in the car, because that was our deal.

By the third year into his time with the team, Wesley was getting a little tired and discouraged because he wasn't one of the starters. He got to play in the games, but he wasn't in a position to score a lot, even though he probably had his share of goals in some tournaments in the spring. He was also playing for Morgantown High School, but high school soccer was in the fall, and most of the Beadling games were in the spring and early summer. I believe that the Beadling team got beaten for the state championship by their archrivals sometime during the last couple of years that Wesley was playing for them. The coaches, two brothers, became more difficult. One brother was a high school teacher, and the younger brother had just graduated from college and was working part-time jobs, delivering pizza and what have you. The younger brother took over more of the coaching responsibilities. Wesley's relationship was with the older coach, who had asked Wesley to join the team a couple of years earlier. The younger brother was more old-school and depended on the players who had always played for the team.

CHAPTER 65

DURING WESLEY'S TIME WITH THE Beadling soccer team, he grew up a lot and learned a lot of skills. We also got to go to Spain at the invitation of an international organization that matched up high-level kids' teams with others from around the world. Barcelona was the host city of the tournament. We all got to go. Not everyone had the means to pay the $1,500 to $1,800 it would cost each kid on the team to go, however. So, as a club, we raised about $25,000 through donations and a special gambling event held one night in Pittsburgh, approved by the Commonwealth of Pennsylvania, where the money went to the kids' fund for the trip. Every kid on the team was paid for, regardless of the parents' ability to pay, and the coaches' trips were also paid for. Those parents, like Betsy and me, who had the means to pay their own ways, also went.

The team all stayed together, and the parents stayed together, but in separate hotels. The kids were fifteen years old and had a curfew. They also had to stay in shape and play the games. While the kids practiced, the parents would tour the different parts of Barcelona and the surrounding region. Betsy, because she was learning Spanish, became a tour guide for all of us American gringos who really didn't speak the language. Betsy would talk to the bus driver or the tour person to get us to where we wanted to go. So, we got to see sights that we would otherwise have missed if the bus driver had merely dropped us off at the normal tourist sights. We became friends with the parents, and although we were not part of the leadership, Betsy's Spanish skills provided a little benefit to all of us non-Spanish speakers.

One thing in particular that I remember was a famous cathedral in the downtown area that is an architectural wonder because it has two halves. One half looks like a cathedral from the 1400s, but the other part looks like a dark-magic, Harry Potter-like structure with a mythical, movie-like presence. It had rounded edges, and the stone looked like it was seeping out, like a sandcastle. The cathedral, Sagrada Família, designed by Antoni Gaudi, was still under construction.

Not all the games were in the city of Barcelona. There were several villages on the Mediterranean Sea that hosted games, so we traveled the coastline. The trip was timed over the public school spring break, and kids who weren't on break got special permission to miss school by writing a report on their travels. The trip was considered a cultural opportunity, and it was.

In Barcelona, Wesley's team didn't do very well, because they were a young team. The organization of the teams wasn't in our favor. Wesley's team of fifteen-year-olds had to play in the sixteen-year-old bracket. Kids could always play up a year, but the kids could not be older and play down, so our competition from the Spanish club teams was very difficult. However, Wesley was one of the kids to score in a game, one of two scores that the boys made in the tournament during the first game. The second game that was played in the Barcelona tournament was against the youth-club team of FC Barcelona.

FC Barcelona was one of the world's best professional soccer teams, so this was a club team sponsored by the professional team. They won the game, three to nil. However, we got some great pictures of Wesley playing with kids who are probably on the professional team today. There's a great quote by a historic coach that applies to the way soccer is viewed in places like Barcelona. It goes something like this: to win or lose a soccer match is not about life or death; it's more important than that.

In the fifth year, Wesley debated hard whether he wanted to stay with the Pittsburgh club team. By this time, the younger brother had taken over the head coaching job and had his favorites, kids who had always played. They were bigger kids. Wesley, even though he had started his growth spurt, was still relatively small, compared to the other kids. During that season, Wesley wanted to quit, but we said no, because he made a commitment. It was a difficult season for him. The Beadling club team lost to their rivals in the finals of the state championship that year. It was during the same year that Wesley finished high school. He had a very successful season. He played in the fall for the high school team, and he enjoyed that and did well. At graduation, Wesley got the outstanding player award for the high school team. During his senior year with his buddies on the high school team, they went to the state tournament and ended up third in our state.

In addition to playing on the club team and high school team, Wesley also was a starting center-mid player on the State of West Virginia's Olympic Development Program (ODP) team for several years. This is where states would put together their best players and play against other states, usually in the summer. He would occasionally see some of his club team players, who were representing Western Pennsylvania at the tournament. The ODP teams that we played were generally from the Northeast.

Of course, Betsy and I would not miss a game that Wesley was part of. We did a lot of traveling and would often take some of the kids up into northeastern Pennsylvania and New England, where the ODP games were played. It was quite an adventure. I think that if you look at it in retrospect, you could say that Wesley's time as a teenager was filled with soccer, which kept him away from the normal mistakes that young teenagers often make. It kept him busy. We all traveled on the weekends. He wasn't hanging out, bored, getting into trouble. He was focused.

CHAPTER 66

WESLEY HAD A SOCCER PORTFOLIO that made him known to regional university coaches. One of the coaches who actually knew Wesley pretty well was Bob Gray, the coach at Marshall University, in the southern part of West Virginia. Bob Gray knew Wesley because he had seen him perform on the state's ODP team, and he had known that he was on a high-level club team in the spring in Pittsburgh. Bob saw Wesley as a potential recruit to Marshall's Division I soccer team. Of course, as parents, we liked Bob Gray, but being from WVU, we were not overly impressed with Marshall University as an academic institution.

Yet Wesley was invited on a recruiting trip to Marshall, and we all went down. We got the complete show. We met with people in the admissions office and were given a tour of campus. Then, we were shown all the facilities that the Marshall soccer program had to offer by Bob and his assistant coach. Wesley got to hang out with members of the team at night. This was in the fall of his senior year in high school, when his high school team got to the state championship series. They played in the semifinals. The Marshall coach watched Wesley play and was disappointed in how he was playing in the position (as a forward) that our high school coach had him playing, because Bob saw Wesley as a natural center-midfield player.

By the time Wesley was considering Marshall and the options he had at other schools, it became apparent that Bob Gray considered Wesley a developmental recruit, not someone who would start as a freshman.

He seemed to want to red-shirt Wesley as a freshman because of his lack of size and upper body strength. This discouraged Wesley from going to Marshall. In the meantime, Wesley made visits to other universities that were interested in him, including another Division I university in South Carolina. They offered Wesley a spot on their team, but it was a small private school, and he decided he was not that interested in going that far away.

There were numerous Division II and III teams that were interested in Wesley, and one of those teams was in the middle part of Ohio, not too far from Ohio State. It was called Ohio Wesleyan University, and even though they had a Division III team, this school always had a national soccer reputation. The coach had seen Wesley play with the Beadling team in a tournament in Ohio and had an interest in Wesley. So we went on a recruiting trip to Ohio Wesleyan and met Coach Jay Martin.

"Wesley has a future here," the coach said. "I see him as one of our premier recruits."

It was clear that Wesley was on his radar screen. When it came down to Wesley making a college choice, he really didn't know what to do. I think he would have gone to Marshall if he thought he would play as a freshman. WVU had never shown any interest in him as a soccer player. Marlon LeBlanc was in his first or second year and was recruiting big, athletic kids. There never was much interest in Wesley, even though Marlon had seen him play ODP soccer, nor had Wesley shown any real interest in WVU soccer by attending their camps during high school. That's fine. Wesley was maybe disappointed, but it wasn't to be, so Wesley chose to go to Ohio Wesleyan, and he played with Ohio Wesleyan in the fall of his freshman year. However, he really didn't like it. I don't know if it was a maturity issue, whether the school was too small, or what, but at the end of the fall semester, he wanted to come back to Morgantown and attend WVU.

I believe that it involved a few factors. One was the smallness of the university; it wasn't a big-time state university like WVU. The second thing was that he had a girlfriend here in Morgantown. It was difficult for him to be away from her when he was going to college. She was a year younger than he was, a senior in high school. He also knew that he would get West Virginia's merit-based scholarship if he returned after just one semester. He said he'd rather spend our college savings for him on study-abroad experiences rather than private school tuition. Let's just say that all those factors helped him make the decision to come back to Morgantown.

So, as it turned out, Wesley came back to WVU and had a scholarship because of his high school academic record and test-score performance. It was called the PROMISE scholarship and paid all of his tuition and fees for eight semesters. He also qualified for another scholarship, which covered his books and some other expenses related to college. It was actually a no-brainer for him to come back to WVU. Of course, after a few months back, he and his girlfriend broke up. And he tried out for the WVU men's soccer team.

There was a tryout, and later that week, Wes got a call from the assistant coach, encouraging him to come back for another session. Whether he was burned out on soccer or whether it was because of being up and down in his relationship with his girlfriend, he decided not to go to the call-back session. He would later regret this decision, but that's where maturity comes from in the long run. Wesley decided that he would go back to the open tryouts the following semester, but he sprained his ankle during the session, and that meant he was no longer a viable walk-on for the team that year.

However, Wesley continued to stay involved in soccer. He coached at a soccer academy in Fairmont, West Virginia, and he played for a high-level community soccer team. I wouldn't be surprised someday if he doesn't take on his own team, if he continues coaching. He's also been asked to serve as a travel soccer coach, but we'll have to wait to see where Wesley's soccer future takes him.

It's Never Too Late to Learn New Skills

~~~

CHAPTER 67

IN A POSITIVE WAY, I'D been exposed to classical music before and during college. A couple of my best friends in college ran the local public radio station, as both were classical music buffs. As a little kid, I listened to classical music with my grandfather and his wife when we would go to visit. I'd started piano lessons as a kid, but, stupidly, I stopped playing. I decided to start playing the piano again after many years, since I'd taken lessons as a boy. The good news is I that asked my mother to ship the piano that I had had as a little kid across the country to Betsy and me. She did, and it held up. One of the front legs broke, but we could still use the piano. So I had a piano at home.

Wesley actually began piano lessons in Morgantown before me, and then I decided to start with Wesley's piano teacher, too. By the time Wesley was in middle school, he didn't want to stick with it. I continued for a few more months, but the teacher decided that she wanted to focus on flute lessons rather than piano. Around this time, I discovered that the WVU music program, in the College of Creative Arts, offered piano lessons. The students who were getting their advanced degrees as young pianists and artists offered private lessons. I decided that it was a great opportunity. I signed up for private lessons and was very fortunate to get a young student who was working on her doctoral degree in performance. She was a very good pianist. Her name was Sylvia Atmadja, and she was from Thailand.

After I had practiced a little bit, Sylvia decided that I was at the intermediate skill level. I was very interested in learning to play classical music, the works of Tchaikovsky, Rimsky-Korsakov, and composers from the romantic, classical era. I dug in, and I took lessons from Sylvia for about five years. I also got to be on her doctoral committee since I was a professor at WVU. Since I happened to be one of her students, I could analyze her dissertation, offering what I call a layman's perspective. So I became the outside committee member for her dissertation.

I came back to piano because I enjoyed the ability to learn a skill that required an intellectual mastery. This is a repetitive pattern for me—finding activities that require learning and practicing a skill. Piano was the preferred instrument for me, because it required good hand coordination. I also had good reach between my thumb and small finger: an octave plus one or two keys.

As I was taking piano lessons, my teacher told me she would like for me to play in a recital. I thought, *Why not?* At this time, I was a professor and was used to being in front of audiences. So I agreed.

At the recital, when it was my turn at the piano, I had classic stage fright, with all the motor releases and adrenaline.

I thought, *Hell, I can do this.* I performed a difficult piece, Debussy's *Clair de Lune.* When it was my turn, I got up and started walking to the piano. I was the oldest "kid" in the recital, and there were about forty people or so in the audience. My heart pounded in my chest. *Wait,* I thought, *this can't happen.* So I turned to the audience and said, "Let me tell you a story before I play my piece."

Then, because I was comfortable talking to audiences, I started telling the audience why I took lessons and why playing the piano was important to me. I was completely comfortable giving my little speech to the group. After I finished talking, I walked to the piano with no heart thumps, and I could play my piece. It sounded like when I'd practiced, not different or special. Because I'd taken the opportunity to calm down and change the environment into something I was familiar with, I lost my stage fright.

After I was done and the recital was over, many of the parents in the audience came up to me to say, "Your story touched me," and "I wish I'd done what you've done." Many were like me when I was a kid; they wanted to play, but they didn't want to practice. I was told many of these personal piano confessions by others. So my little speech was good for all.

When Sylvia finished her degree and moved away from Morgantown, a friend encouraged me to continue piano lessons. That friend was Rosanna Sikora. I'd known her for a long time, because she had been a resident in the joint medicine-pediatrics residency program that I originally was hired to work on in WVU's School of Medicine. She had been taking lessons with Carol Beall in the community music program for a number of years. The class was called "Piano for Fun," a perfect title. It really was fun, and Carol Beall was an excellent teacher. Each person sat at their own electronic keyboard in a classroom at the university's Creative Arts Center, and we all played music together. Another friend, Jan Reger-Nash, joined the class too, and the three of us would ride together from my home. Rosanna learned how to load my wheelchair into the van and, once a week, off we would go. We called ourselves "the three musketeers."

My hands were already getting weak from ALS, but the teacher and the others in the class, especially Jan and Rosanna, encouraged me to stick with it. At one point, I could only use my left hand to play the chords, and eventually, I had to resign myself to simply following the music and playing it in my head when I lost the ability to use both hands. Ultimately, it became uncomfortable to ride in the van unless it was necessary for doctor appointments or other such things. I was very sad to leave the class, but Jan and Rosanna continued to visit me most weeks before they went to class, and Carol Beall offered to come and play music for me in my home.

Having friends around the house was very important to me. In addition to visits with my piano friends, Martha Schwab would come and read out loud to me each week, because I couldn't hold books or turn the pages. We enjoyed some interesting books: a biography of Steve Jobs, a memoir by Cheryl Strayed of her backpacking trip on the Pacific Crest Trail, and a history of the USS *Intrepid*, the aircraft carrier that my father was based on in the South Pacific during World War II. Mary Wimmer also read a biography of Roy Williams out loud to me. We were both fans of his University of North Carolina Tar Heels basketball team after earning our PhDs in Chapel Hill, North Carolina.

One other friend who visited me regularly after I could no longer work at the university was Art Jacknowitz. He retired from the WVU School of Pharmacy right around the time of my retirement from the WVU School of Medicine. We were colleagues and friends. Art would arrive once a week with his lunch, deliver a copy of the campus newspaper to me, and fill me in on all the latest news from the Health Sciences Center. Visiting with friends helped to take my mind off my disease.

Shangri-La It's Not

CHAPTER 68

IN THE WINTER OF 1993, West Virginia University was approached by a group of private entrepreneurs. They asked if we would be interested in sponsoring and helping with a new medical school in Nepal by giving it our good, American curriculum. They were seeking support from West Virginia University's School of Medicine to give them some legitimacy in forming this school.

We asked, "Where?"

Of course, we all knew where Nepal was, but we had no idea what this group was asking us to do. After a number of months, we concluded that we really needed to go over to Nepal and visit the site and assess what the private entrepreneurs were proposing for an independent, private medical school. I was the educator in the group, because I was an associate dean for medical education. I understood curriculum, so it was my job to analyze what they were proposing. We were very interested in taking this rather exotic trip.

So five of us got on an airplane, and flew from Pittsburgh to Kathmandu, Nepal, the capital. We got to Kathmandu after about thirty-five hours of travel. Nepal was still a kingdom, so it had a king. As part of the visit, we got invited to meet the king of Nepal, since we were American doctors and educators thinking about helping a new, private medical school in this country. The school was being set up by Indian citizens, as the border with India was to the south of Nepal. Because Nepal was a close geographic neighbor, it had attracted some unscrupulous entrepreneurs. We came to find out later that their aim was to set up the new, private medical school to make money, but they couldn't deliver the product. There were many students in India wanting a Western-style, medical school education, and India had banned the creation of these private schools. Therefore, nearby Nepal offered a close location with less regulation. They also said they had US sponsorships, but we hadn't yet agreed. Students and their parents paid hundreds of thousands of dollars to attend these schools if they weren't accepted into US or European medical schools, and it ended up being a questionable proposition.

When we got to Kathmandu, of course, we were all jet-lagged, but we were also fascinated to be in a country that was so different from the United States. It was an incredible place. It engaged our senses. Things smelled differently there. Kathmandu, as a city where we spent most of our time, was severely overpopulated, and it had heavy smog. We knew that it wasn't a developed country but a third-world country. We had one heck of a time taking in the sights and sounds of our tour and getting around Kathmandu.

Of course, it was a very religious area, too, being a place where there is a combination of many religions. Obviously, the Indian influence of Hindu was part of Kathmandu. As well, there was a large Christian influence, which was surprising to us. In the 1950s and 1960s, there were many missionaries who came to Nepal to try to introduce the Christian way of thinking. It was a confused country as far as the culture was concerned, because everybody always had a romantic notion about Nepal. It was kind of like nirvana-land. They made movies about special hidden places in the mountains in Nepal that intrigued so many.

Our group did a lot of sightseeing, and I got wonderful slides to document all that we saw. Unfortunately, I couldn't record the sounds of Kathmandu. There are some areas where I heard religious sounds, and then there were also the sounds of monkeys, along with car engines and horns, and the ring-ring of bicycle bells, all mixed up together. The streets were very congested, like streets you might see in a B-grade spy movie. One of my observations was that the people who lived in the city were worse off physically and health-wise, even though they may have been making a little bit more money than the very poor people who lived on the outskirts, in the country. It was so evident that overpopulation in a small area really doesn't show the best of humankind. I had the chance to tour Kathmandu before we eventually took a bus ride to where the medical school would be located.

One of the things I witnessed in Kathmandu, which I thought was unusual, happened when I was walking down the street, just taking in the sights and sounds. I observed cows wandering around. Of course, in the Hindu faith, they were special. They could go anywhere they wanted, and they basically roamed around within the heavily populated area. One afternoon I witnessed a woman walking up to a cow when it was urinating. It was a female cow, so the pee came out of the back of the cow, and in a moment that was actually beautiful, the woman walked up, cupped her hands, and pooled the urination. Then she took some of the urine to her mouth. It was like a blessing in her faith, a blessing of the cow through the cow's urine. Of course, to this day I don't understand that, nor should I, because I'm not part of that culture. But it's a good example of one normal observation that I had early on in my visual walking tours of Kathmandu, where the cows roamed the sidewalks, even in front of commercial buildings.

Another observation I made walking down the street was that there were many vendors. If they figured that you were from the United States, the vendors would come up to you and try to ask for money, because poverty was rampant. One time, I was just walking down the street and looked to my right. I saw something unusual. I thought, *That can't be real.* It was a teenage child with what I initially thought was a monkey on a string, performing. I didn't think it was unusual until I looked closer at what I thought was a monkey. It had a cord on it, and it had a necklace on it. I looked again, and I realized that what I thought was a monkey was actually a human being, a little deformed baby that was malnourished. The other child was using this brother, if you can call it that, as a way to get money for the family by showing off the deformity of the child. The brother was using the little child to put on a show as if he were a trained monkey, like you see sometimes. It was quite shocking to me, and I didn't understand it. I've thought about it many, many times. How people can do what they do never ceases to amaze me.

The medical school group I was a part of toured the best hospital in Kathmandu. By all standards, it was ancient. It looked as if we had fallen into the 1800s in a poor area in some Western, developed country. It was really quite rudimentary and was unbelievable as far as our trip's goal of coming to help support a medical school to produce doctors for hospitals. Were the doctors going to work like they were in the Dark Ages of Europe? It was an amazing, eye-opening experience.

One of the things that I got to do before we left Kathmandu for the medical school trip was take a plane ride into the Himalayas. This was quite a highlight for me. The company that offered the rides actually went up to the part of the Himalayas where Mount Everest, or Chomolungma, as the Nepalese call it, was located. Obviously, I wanted to go on that sight-seeing tour. It was a small airplane, carrying maybe six to eight of us. We each had a window to look out. I had my camera. I took incredible pictures. I'll never forget flying between twenty thousand and thirty thousand feet in this this small plane, looking at the mountains. I got glimpses of Everest that would come and go, because we were flying in and out of cloud cover. It was incredible to be so close to the peaks, seeing it, and then not seeing it. It was otherwordly, and as a climber, it was significant to me to see such a storied mountain, the highest on earth. There is a mythical draw because of Everest's symbolic quality. It's also in a mystical place, like Shangri-La, and you have to journey there, walking for days just to get there.

Over my lifetime, I've read all the accounts of ascents of Everest, from those of Mallory in 1924 and Hillary in 1953, to John Krakauer's book, *Into Thin Air,* about a disastrous trip in the mid-1990s, when commercial trips to Everest were popular. The books became real to me as we flew by. The Krakauer book describes a commercial climb led by

Jim Hall, where paying customers died in a storm. There's just a short window in May and early June to climb, before the Indian monsoons arrive in mid-June.

The son of a friend, a former WVU medical student who became a doctor, made the decision to try to climb Everest recently. He may have paid big bucks for the trip. But because he noticed his feet were getting cold, and the line of people waiting their turn to summit was long, he declined to make a summit attempt. He knew the risks and made a good decision. It's all about knowing your boundaries. You'll remember that Wesley Byerly and I declined to make a summit attempt on Gannett Peak when we were in Wyoming because he wasn't feeling well. Personally, I've always climbed peaks on my own time frame, according to my own skill. I never climbed a mountain that was "sponsored," where a paid guide would take me up. I always did them myself. To this day, there are still companies that will take you up Everest. In April of 2014, there was a disaster on the lower part of the mountain, where many Sherpas died. The paying customers were rescued but not the Sherpas. The Sherpas have started to boycott.

Then came the time when we needed to leave Kathmandu and head out toward the region of Nepal where this new medical school was being built. Obviously, its investors were looking to us for experienced advice, curriculum development, and eventually some sort of accreditation. We didn't understand that at the time.

We got on the road from Kathmandu to Pokhara. Pokhara is the other large city west of Kathmandu, and the route follows the river. We're talking about a two-lane road, which was a major highway in Nepal. To the left of us were mountains, and on the right, about one hundred feet down, was the river. It was steep country. The road had been cut to follow the river, because that was the only way through the mountains.

The trip was going well until, traveling maybe about twenty-five or thirty miles an hour, we crested a little hill, and we saw a huge, roaring truck stopped in the middle of the road, blocking any way to get around it. The good fortune was that our bus driver, rather than trying to go to the side nearest the river to get around it—where we would've rolled down one hundred feet into the river—went to the mountain side of the road. We got wedged in and wrecked our bus. We all got out of the bus and figured out the only way to get us where we had to go was to commandeer another bus. An empty bus approached us, and we managed to flag it down. Since the bus was going in the opposite direction, the driver needed a little incentive to turn around and take us back in the direction of Pokhara. We managed to pay him some money, and he took us to where we were going, another four or five hours south.

We eventually got to the Chitwan Forest, a low-lying jungle, which was in the western part of Nepal, by the southern border with India. It was a lonely area, a forest famous for its Bengal tigers. We arrived at the International Institute for Medical Sciences, sponsored by the International Society for Medical Education. It was like some creature had hatched out little buildings with trees and arrows in this low-lying region of Nepal. And they were calling this area (what I thought was a camp) a medical school.

Our purpose was to evaluate this medical school to get a sense of whether we wanted to form a partnership with them. There were ceremonies to go through, because, after all, it was a big deal to have physicians and scientists from America. We participated in a lot of hoopla, a lot of ceremonies, a lot of dancing, the whole nine yards.

It was ironic that the person chosen as the leader of our group was not a physician but a scientist from Marshall University. In my mind, he had an idea what was going on, but he was along for the ride because it was great adventure. The whole thing was—let's just say, *sketchy*—from the beginning. Of course, we didn't know any of that. They showed us the facilities, and we were underwhelmed with what we saw. We talked to a few of the medical students enrolled and learned that they were from well-to-do Indian families, who had money and wanted their sons and daughters to attend medical school. These were Indians, not necessarily from the subcontinent of India but from Europe and from the United States. They didn't have the academic credentials to get into medical school in their own countries.

As it appeared to me, the leader of our group from Marshall, who really didn't know anything about medical education but was a faculty member and entrepreneur, made it a great vacation for himself and his group. They left two of us there at the medical school as they went jaunting off into the forest with a tour guide. What were they going to do? This "medical school" in southwestern Nepal was not up to Western standards. Nevertheless, they just went into the forest on safari and rode elephants, looking for tigers. It was the most bizarre thing.

Two of us who had some credentials, Ray, who was an international infectious disease physician, and myself, an associate dean of medical education and a member of medical-school accreditation teams, were left at this camp. Ray and I quickly figured out that we weren't going to have any good recommendations. It became clear to everyone that we weren't very impressed. Ray and I needed to figure out how we were going to get back to Kathmandu, because, in a day or two, we were leaving for the United States. Our flights were scheduled out of Kathmandu. We asked how to get back there, and it was suggested that we take a bus, like the one we came over on.

No way, we thought, *are we going to be on a bus on these roads for twelve hours to get back to Kathmandu.* So we asked if there were any alternatives. We were told that we could fly back.

I said, "Great! Where do we go?"

I was told that there was small airport, not too far from where we were. We were told that reservations would be made for us and that we could go to the airport the next morning and get on a plane and fly back to Kathmandu.

"That's great!" we said.

We arrived at the small, private little airport, and the planes were two-engine props that held about four or five, maybe seven people at the most. I had no problem flying in those planes, because I flew a lot when I was young with my dad in small planes. We checked in at the desk, saying, "We're here to get on the plane."

And we were told this: "We don't have you down for a flight to Kathmandu."

"What do you mean?" I said. "Someone was supposed to call ahead." The institute for the new medical school was supposed to be paying for it.

Again, we got the wrong answer. "We have none of that information."

"Well," I said, "we've really got to get back to Kathmandu."

In every adventure trip, there comes a time where you're glad someone gave you good advice. I never thought I'd need it, but, luckily, someone had shared a piece of wisdom with me.

"Ray, I have us covered," I said. "We'll be able to get on the plane." I'd been told by a wise person who had done a lot of international travel in third-world regions that I should always have on my body some US dollars in cash. It was recommended that I carry a few hundred dollars at all times, not known to anybody, in case I should ever need it. That time was now, and luckily, I'd followed that good advice.

"What if we gave you some US dollars to purchase a plane ride for the two of us to go back to Kathmandu?" I asked.

Of course, I was told, "No problem."

So I pulled out $200, which I thought was a fair price to pay, a hundred apiece, to get back to Kathmandu on the small plane. Lo and behold, they had space for us, so we got back. One of the sights that we got to see was Annapurna Massif, another famous Himalayan mountain, and one that was also a very difficult climb. So, on this trip, I saw two of the three great climbing mountains. The third, I would see on another trip. Annapurna was first climbed in the 1930s and is not as high as Everest but is often considered more technical and more difficult. Maurice Herzog, who first climbed the mountain, wrote a classic climbing book about Annapurna. The mountain was not too far north of Pokhara.

We arrived safely a day before our flight was to leave for the United States. This time, we got on the big plane, a huge jet, owned and flown by one of the premier companies in Southeast Asia: Singapore Airlines.

We made a stop to pick up passengers in Dhaka, Bangladesh. We stopped, loaded passengers, and took off again.

About an hour later, a flight attendant came up to me and asked, "Are you a doctor?"

I said, "No, but these two guys next to me are."

"We have a medical problem in the back of the plane," the flight attendant said. "One of our passengers is very sick and needs some medical attention."

Luckily, the two gentlemen sitting next to me were both internationally oriented infectious-disease doctors. The three of us went to the back of the plane to help this passenger who needed medical attention, because, in layman's terms, he was crashing fairly quickly. He was a passenger who'd been picked up in Dhaka and didn't speak any English. He was with his translator. We found out that this man left Dhaka, heading east, to get better medical treatment. The guy was very sick.

After talking to the translator, we found out that he had just had a severe, infectious disease and was also a diabetic. He had numerous things wrong with him. What we had to do was start an IV. The two physicians did the work, and I was the nurse. I held things, I found things on board, and I talked to the flight attendants to get the medical chart. We eventually got an IV line into him, where we could give him some fluids, because it was clear that the patient was very dehydrated. However, the needle for the line we got in him didn't have a big enough gauge to get enough fluids in quickly. Ray and the other physician spent an hour or so trying to get a good connection into the gentleman's weak body. I was holding up a bottle with the fluid in it, telling them if it was dripping or not, because they couldn't tell. The three of us basically took care of this guy.

The two physicians told me, "Jamie, you need to talk to the pilot." We needed to communicate that we had a medical emergency and needed to land and get this guy to a hospital as soon as we could. So I went and talked to the pilot.

We made an emergency, unplanned landing in Bangkok. We had kept the passenger alive and then passed him off to the medical team in Bangkok.

All of this was third-worldish, so what you see, and what people say, is not necessarily the truth. Basically, the EMT from Thailand came up and took him.

About fifteen minutes later, we asked, "How's the patient doing?"

We were told, "Oh, he's fine. He'll be okay." Of course, we didn't believe it. The good news was that we had been able to keep the patient alive under our care, and then, once we transferred him to another medical team, the patient was no longer our responsibility. We never knew what happened to the patient, yet we left with hopeful hearts that the patient did all right. We'll never know.

Then, we took off again for our destination. We had been up for hours and had not eaten anything on board. However, we were asked if we would like to fly first class, as there were a few first-class seats remaining. We had been in coach. Of course, we took the upgrade, because we had just been through a very emotional ordeal on the flight.

Once home, our recommendation to the Vice President for Health Sciences at West Virginia University was that we no longer have anything to do with this particular organization and the relationships they were trying to establish between us and the private medical school.

Adventures in Alaska and the Tetons

CHAPTER 69

IN THE SUMMER OF 1995, I was at a conference at Harvard University, an invitational conference where I was actually taking a course for associate deans of medical schools to catch up on some of the latest things that were happening. Four months before that, a friend of mine, Don Smith, approached me about a trip. Don, as you might remember, was both my dentist and one of the people I went winter camping with in West Virginia. "Jamie," he said, "one of my nieces is an aide to a congressman, and she is putting together a trip up in Northern Alaska to see the breeding range of the porcupine caribou and their migration in that area."

"That's hundreds of thousands of caribou," I said.

"Yes," Don replied, "and every year, in July, they come into the Kongakut River valley in Alaska to breed."

"Don," I said, "if there is ever an opportunity for an extra person to go, even at the last minute, let me know."

Well, when I was at this invitational conference at Harvard, doing my thing, taking a professional course, I got a call from Don.

"Jamie," he said, "my niece can't go, so there is an extra space in the trip. Would you like to go?"

So I had to tell Harvard that I needed to bug out a day early. A few days later, I needed to have my act together to be on a plane to begin this trip. I went home. I got my gear together, and within a day or two, I was ready to go up to Alaska.

We arrived in Alaska and then got on a smaller plane that flew up past the Arctic Circle to a little town that could handle very small, single-engine planes. That's how we were going to get to the Kongakut River. Then, we got on the single-engine plane. It was called a short-takeoff-and-landing plane. It had huge, rubber tires that would be able to land on a makeshift runway in a flat section along the river, and it had such power. It was able to take off from very short distances. I always flew copilot, because I had had previous small-plane flying experience with my dad. And so the adventure began.

We needed a raft guide, because we were taking rafts down this wilderness river. "Hey, I'm a white-water boater," I said, "and I can handle an oar-rigged raft. I know rivers and what to do in the rapids and everything." So I had the responsibility of handling one of the rafts.

Our trip had a purpose, which was to show environmental donors the beauty of the caribou migration and the importance of protecting the Alaska National Wildlife Refuge, or ANWR, region. There was a lot of controversy with oil companies wanting to drill in ANWR. One of the donors and his wife, who were older people, were heirs to Hanes, the underwear company, and they felt strongly about conserving this river valley and not letting it be developed for oil exploitations. The trip was sponsored by the director or former director of the Department of Fish and Wildlife in Alaska, with the aim of protecting the area from drilling. So donors and congresspeople were invited. Many of the aides went because they did the detail work, keeping the congresspeople informed of issues that needed attention.

We headed to the farthest northeast corner of Alaska. The trip was in July, when there is twenty-four-hour sun. You look up at the sun through goggles and protective glasses, and at nighttime, all you see is the sun moving in a semicircle. There was never any darkness. We celebrated the Fourth of July up there.

We had three or four rafts, so we could travel looking for the caribou migration through the valley. As it turned out, we missed the hundreds of thousands of caribou coming into that river valley, but we certainly saw thousands of caribou in the valley. There were many Dall sheep, which is a horned sheep. It was also a fishing paradise. I brought my fly-fishing rod, and of course, I broke it on the first day. I then had to figure out how to repair the tip of the rod, using tape and a little branch. It wasn't pretty, but it worked, and I was still able to throw out lines to fly-fish. There were these beautiful, beautiful fish in the river. It was strictly sport for me, and I used barbless hooks and caught and released the fish.

The Kongakut River is in Northern Alaska, above the Arctic Circle, and it's a relatively new river, compared to the old rivers in the Appalachians that I was used to. One of the things that this river had was dead-end channels. You had to be very careful what particular river channel you went down, or you might end up in a dead end. At times, we'd be stuck, and then we'd have to paddle ourselves back upstream. We did a lot of standing in the raft, scouting the main flow visually from the raft. We got stuck a couple of times, but we were able to get ourselves out of those situations. There was lots of wildlife around: grizzlies, black bear, Dall sheep, birds, and all sorts of critters, as well as fish. Also, there were several sections of ice that were in the shadows of rocks that we could actually use to keep our food cold. Even though we had rafts with professional iceboxes on them, we could resupply our ice containers.

There were no significant rapids on the river. We encountered a few rapids, but we were in good, oar-rigged rafts, and I knew what to do, even though I almost dumped the Hanes underwear heirs out of my raft the first day out. I got caught in a side eddy, and I pulled the end of the raft, where they were sitting, into a rock wall. The lower part of the raft kind of dipped under the water, and they almost went for a swim, but they didn't. My reputation for being a good raft guide pretty much went all to heck.

It was very pleasant, weather-wise, with temperatures in the seventies. There were twenty-four hours of sun, so we slept in tents to protect ourselves from the sun while we were sleeping. However, we had a bigger problem: there were constant mosquitoes. The mosquitoes there are big and numerous. To say that there was an infinite number of mosquitoes is really no exaggeration. Every moment of every hour was full of mosquitoes.

The best thing that could protect us from the mosquitoes was the wind, so we were pleased to have windy days. Walking up into the wind, there would be an eddy behind you, a wind eddy, a calm area, and that's where the mosquitoes would collect. There were hundreds of mosquitoes behind us all the time as we walked into the wind. We kind of made a joke that anything we ate had a special added spice—mosquito spice, because they got into our food, too.

I used an ointment from Avon called Skin So Soft to help fend off the mosquitos. There was something about the odor of it that kept some of the mosquitoes away.

At the end of the trip, which was about eight days, in flew the STOL, the short-takeoff-and-landing plane, and we all got the opportunity to wait our turns to fly back to town. One of the pilots whom I got to know was actually an emergency medicine physician who pretty much did his work as a physician during the winter. He was a bush pilot during the summer and took people like us into remote areas of Alaska to enjoy the beautiful country. I got to know him pretty well during our flight in to the Kongakut River, and during the flight out with him, I got to fly the plane a little bit through the Brooks Range. We wove in and out of mountains and valleys to get back to the Arctic Circle town. Then, we got on a larger plane back to Anchorage. On our way home from Alaska, we flew over Denali and got to see it lit by the moon.

CHAPTER 70

MY NEXT TRIP TO ALASKA was in August of 1996, when my mother invited me on a trip through the Inside Passage. That part of southeastern Alaska is like a spit of land that goes southeast toward the lower forty-eight states of the country. We took a small boat through the Inside Passage. When I say a "small boat," I mean that it held about eighty of us, compared to the big liners where there are two thousand people. In our boat, we were able to go places in the Inside Passage where the large boats couldn't go. That provided us the ability to see far more wildlife. We saw a ton of wildlife. The most significant things that I saw were bald eagles. Sometimes, we now see bald eagles even here in Morgantown, but there were a ton of bald eagles flying around in the Inside Passage.

Alaska, being in the western part of the country, is very mountainous, and traveling through the Inside Passage, we saw many peaks. A standard routine was to stop at a community, go out and explore during the day, come back to the boat to have dinner, and then go to sleep. While we were sleeping, the captain of the boat moved it to our next port or destination point. It worked really, really well.

Each day, we chose the activities that we wanted to do, whether it be getting in a jet boat and exploring a particular inland river, or hiking in an area, or getting on a narrow-gauge rail train and going up a mountain. We had lots to do. One day, I even got to fish for salmon, and that was a lot of fun. The company put them on ice and sent them to West

Virginia on a designated date. Unfortunately, when they arrived, they had spoiled, so we couldn't eat them. They screwed up with the dry ice. It was worth the try, though.

One morning at about five, when we were making our way to the next stop for the day, the captain sent his mate to wake us all up. We wondered what was going on. Twenty whales surrounded the boat, and, unbelievably, put on a show for us. They would come up and blow their air out; then, they would go down, and we saw their tail fins go out in the air. That lasted for about half an hour. It was a wonderful thing to see.

Our trip lasted for eight days. We made our way up through the passage, north to Glacier Bay. Our top terminal of the trip was Glacier Bay, and we went specifically to see all the glaciers that came down from the ridges to the Inside Passage itself. One of the cool things, when you got close to one of the glaciers, was seeing what is referred to as "calving." This is when the snow and ice break off from the glacier, hitting the water. These are huge calves, very large, and if we waited a few minutes, we felt this incredible swell, and the boat would bob up and down—I'm talking twenty to thirty feet swells. This was an example of the type of thing that was available in the small boat tour. If you were on a big ocean liner that had two thousand people on it, you couldn't get into these bays, and you couldn't experience the swells from the calving of the glaciers.

Again, during the days, we got to explore different regions. On one of the days, we took a narrow-gauge rail route up the mountain, and it actually paralleled a historical route that the Alaskan prospectors took up over the ridge to get to the Yukon gold deposits. As you know, in California, there was a gold rush in 1849, but the Alaskan gold rush was later that century. Nonetheless, it attracted thousands of people to Alaska through the Yukon to stake their fortunes in search of gold. We took this narrow-gauge railroad up, paralleling the walking route, and we saw historical pictures of people—thousands of people—in lines, going up the trail.

One of the things about going on a small-boat tour was the incredible wildlife I got to see. We saw many birds that were part of that region, including puffins. It was really cool seeing puffins all around our small boat, just watching what they were doing. We also saw a bear from our boat, in one of the little inlets. At one point, we saw some wolves, which were extremely uncommon for people to see. When you're in the small inlet, however, the animals pretty much don't worry about you.

Of course, since this was a sponsored tour, there were different activities for all of us. One of the activities was to stop at an Indian reservation. Now, understand, these were Alaskan natives, primarily in the United States. Of course, we were tourists, so on certain days, they had festivals or shows to welcome us. We got to learn a little local lore and get a sense of what old-time Indian life was about. Alaska is still a wilderness area. Many of the areas, rightfully so, are still undeveloped and in natural states.

We were in Alaska in August, and it was still light because of it being so far north. If you have light all day and all night, you're there in the summer. My mom and I had a wonderful adventure exploring this part of Alaska. I made friends with other passengers, including a woman who was traveling alone. She became my traveling friend, and we did things together. I remember one of the things that we did, which was maybe a little unusual. Because we had such a wonderful crew on this trip that went above and beyond and out of their way to take care of all of us, my traveling friend and I organized a party, in cahoots with some of the crew. We wanted to do something special for the captain, his crew, and the tour guides, because they had done so much for us during the trip. I remember organizing this party on the last night of the cruise. Of course, in my style, I got to give a little speech to thank our crew for such a wonderful trip. Maybe that happens on all of the trips, or, perhaps the chemistry was right on this trip. My mom and I had such a good time, and it provided a good opportunity to do something very special with her.

CHAPTER 71

IN THE SPRING OF 1998, I heard about a conference being offered at the Jackson Lake Lodge in Grand Teton National Park. I thought, *What a beautiful area! I wonder if I could submit a paper with my colleagues and see if we could get it accepted so that we could go to this conference.* Of course, there was an ulterior motive in my thinking. It would provide us an opportunity to see a wonderful area. The paper got accepted. Michael Elnicki, Barry Linger, and I were off to Jackson Hole and the Grand Teton National Park in October of that year.

Barry Linger and I arrived, and Mike had not gotten there yet. So I talked Barry into taking a little hike—about a ten-mile, round-trip hike with a three-thousand-vertical-foot climb up to a mountain lake. We hiked on a trail that led to the base of Grand Teton Mountain, a climbing area that I had read about. It was a day hike up and down to see Amphitheater Lake.

Michael Elnicki had arrived, and we got to our conference, ready to present our paper. We were good to go and gave our paper successfully. People liked it. We felt so good about the work we shared. The next day, we thought about another adventure. "Here we are on the Snake River," I said, "running along the base of the Tetons. We should do a trout fishing adventure."

So Mike and Barry and I hired a guide who had a fishing boat, and we fished for a day on the Snake River. The next day, we decided that while the conference was winding down, we would attend meetings in the morning. In the afternoon, we decided to go out fishing again, but this time on our own. We got our gear together and went out and fished on a little creek coming into the Snake River.

When we were walking out to the creek, I thought, *There's something unusual going on.* We saw many hunters. We didn't know it at the time, but it was opening day of elk season. "Whoa," I said. "We don't necessarily need to be out here fishing in the woods with a bunch of hunters, hunting for elk."

So we got back in our car and drove back. On the way, we saw a big bull elk running to the hills, making noise because he was being pursued by a hunter. We saw people pulling huge elks out of the woods. It's just part of Western life. Mike was salivating because he and Barry wanted to be out there hunting. I was sad because these beautiful animals were being shot.

This adventure is an example of another pattern for me. Let's just say that these types of locations, where I could find other things to do, are but one opportunity to present papers. What you don't know is that I was also presenting papers at big conferences in Washington, DC, Chicago, and New York. The Jackson Lake Lodge conference was what I call a "boutique meeting," where there were also opportunities to go to areas that fit my interests. These were fun places to go. Meetings were usually three days at the most. I'd go in a day or two early, at my own expense, or stay a day or two after. During the conference proper, the university would pay for my registration fees and lodging, provided I had a paper to give.

As it turned out, Betsy, and Wesley, and I would go back to the Tetons several other times during our family vacations to ski in the winter and hike in the summer.

To Scotland and Beyond

CHAPTER 72

It was 1991 when Betsy was asked to go give a paper in England, but she traveled to Scotland for a few days before her conference began. She had such a wonderful time there. "Jamie, if you ever get the chance to give a paper in Scotland, go for it," she said.

Then, in 1992, I heard of a conference in Scotland. Wesley was two years old, and I decided that the three of us would go to Scotland, and I would give a paper there. So I applied, my paper was accepted, and the good news was that we were off to Scotland. What I didn't know was that a few years later, in 2000, I would actually do a sabbatical in Scotland. This trip to Scotland helped us decide that it would be a great place to do a sabbatical. I developed a relationship with Scotland, and my family took various trips to there. We went to the conference in Dundee, where I gave my paper. I really didn't make any significant contacts. It wasn't until a few years later, in 1998 or 1999, that I really made significant contacts. Yet the people I met at that conference in the early 1990s turned out to be especially helpful when it came time for me to arrange my sabbatical. The one individual with whom I studied and worked, who was actually knighted a few years later, was Ronald Harden. He and I developed a significant relationship when I did a sabbatical with him. Because of what he was interested in and what I learned about, we authored several papers together.

This first trip included a three- or four-day conference. Then, in our rented car, we toured from one bed-and-breakfast lodging to another, seeing the countryside. When we arrived in Scotland, we confirmed the reservations that we made previously by mail or e-mail. If we didn't have a place to stay, we would stop at a tourist office and find the nearest bed-and-breakfast. It worked out well. We got a traditional Scottish meal every morning, which was bacon or sausage, eggs, some sort of bread, fried tomato, and oatmeal.

There is one thing you do not want to eat in Scotland; it's called haggis. It is a stuffed sheep stomach with whatever meat and organs from animals they can chop up and put in it. It has a creamy, odd-tasting flavor that I didn't care for.

Scotland is like returning to a world of the past, meaning that what we saw there was a lot of history. There are so many places to visit; it's overwhelming. Luckily, it's small enough to visit many of those places. Between 1992 and 2008, I had the chance to visit Scotland several times with my family. Scotland is a very diverse and interesting country, because there are many palaces and castles. The terrain of Scotland is varied: it is both flat and mountainous. In fact, Scotland reminded me a lot of West Virginia, with respect to its landscape. Of course, it rained a lot. The mountains in Scotland are not that high, maybe peaking out at three thousand or four thousand feet at the most, but some rise straight up from sea level. They were old and worn. Because of the way we planned our trip, we were able to see much of the countryside.

In this first trip for me, we primarily stayed on the west coast portion of Scotland. We mostly saw and hiked in the highlands and the more mountainous regions. One particular place that we really enjoyed was the Cuillin Hills region on the western part of the Isle of Skye. It was a beautiful, mountainous area, which we hiked with Wesley. Skye is almost like a peninsula that goes out from the western coast of Scotland and kind of sticks out to the north. It really is an island, though, and we took a ferry to reach it on the first visit. By the time we returned for the sabbatical, a bridge had been constructed, eliminating the ferry at the island's main access point.

When we got to the United Kingdom, Scotland being part of it, we drove on the opposite side of the road from the United States. When we landed at the airport, we had a rental car waiting for us, and our first challenge (rather, *my* challenge) was to get in the car and drive on the left. Then, we came up to our first double roundabout. I had to make sure, after spending all night on the airplane, being a little sleep deprived, to turn left in the roundabout and not right. With Betsy's help, we managed to safely get out of Glasgow, which is where we landed. Wesley was in the child's car seat we brought with us, because he was so young.

Scotland has a beautiful countryside, but I also discovered that many of the highways and roads when you're touring Scotland are very narrow. Often, I went down what were really one-lane roads and had to try to stay left if I saw other cars coming toward us. It took a bit of time for me to convert.

Of course, I was looking for outdoor activities—not that I would be able to go canoeing or kayaking, but I discovered other cars that had kayaks on top of them. Since this ended up being a pre-trip to the sabbatical, I knew that these outdoor activities were possible, so that knowledge came in handy later.

CHAPTER 73

SINCE I WAS AN ASSOCIATE dean in the School of Medicine and I was interested in curriculum development, I wanted to get more of an international perspective of what was happening, curriculum-wise, in different parts of the world. Since I'd met Dr. Harden a few years earlier, I contacted him to see if it was a good idea to come to Scotland to do a sabbatical with him. He was overwhelmingly enthusiastic about me doing this sort of thing. I needed to convince my dean that it was okay for me to go away for a semester from WVU. You can take a sabbatical, or a professional leave, and receive a full salary for the semester.

My idea was to research how we could develop a more mature curriculum in medicine that helped young people become doctors. It would help them make the right choices when they decided to go into medicine rather than doing it for the typical reason of "Oh, it's a high-paying job." If you look at the traditional medical curriculum, the first two years are all the basic sciences you would ever want to know. However, it's quickly forgotten. Then, in the latter two years, the students are in apprenticeships, working with physicians and learning what they're doing. I thought, *There's got to be a better way of educating the doctors in the United States.*

Then, I began thinking, *Well, maybe in the United Kingdom and in Scotland, where the medical schools have international reputations in medical education, I could learn about how different systems work and how to approach the medical education curriculum in new ways. Who better to work with than the father of medical education in Europe, Ronald Harden?* So I went to the source, and he and I developed a terrific relationship, one that has lasted throughout my career, one that has provided me with many opportunities, and one that has significantly contributed to the medical education literature.

I was still receiving my salary while in Scotland, being on academic leave, professional-development leave, or sabbatical, as I call it. It's basically the same, but the university system differentiates it, depending upon how you approach them. To me, it didn't make any difference. It felt like a sabbatical; I did academic research, I learned, and I taught. Ronald Harden, who was the director of the Centre for Medical Education at the University of Dundee, had international students coming in the fall semester. These students were being taught and would receive, after completing their work over the course of the year, a master's degree in medical education. I worked with these students while in Scotland.

It was interesting to try to plan a sabbatical. The first challenge was bringing my family and figuring out where we were going to live. I was told, "Don't worry. We'll find you a place."

When we arrived, we learned that we were staying in an apartment that was created from rooms in an old mansion. "Wow!" I said, "What a place this is." The rent was £600 per month, which was not too unreasonable, and we handled that fine. We were in Dundee, which had a history of millionaires who imported and processed jute. Dundee fortunes were made producing all sorts of burlap products, everything from ropes to food bags. These millionaires built mansions on the River Tay estuary. So, we overlooked the River Tay in the top apartment of one of these mansions. It was an unbelievably beautiful setting; we were really lucky to be living in this converted mansion apartment. We were in an area that was on the outskirts, only a mile or two walk, or about twenty minutes to the downtown of Dundee, or city center, and it was an even closer walk to work for me. We couldn't have lived any place better. It was just fantastic. It was also arranged for us to rent a car.

Because it was for such a long time, the rental wasn't very expensive at all. Having a car gave us the opportunity to travel on weekends and see much of the countryside on our adventures during the sabbatical. We really lucked out. We gave our house back in the United States, at no cost, to two graduate students that we knew. "Don't worry about paying us rent," I said. "Just support yourselves, and live in our home."

While in Scotland, I would teach, and I would read. I would also have meetings with people. Then, I was asked if I would be interested in a project. Ron Harden was a very creative person. He was always pushing the edge in education, trying to figure out ways to help others. In that sabbatical year, he put together a small group of people, and I was one of them. "I have been thinking of creating a system, an international medical education system," Ron said, "that could really help develop physicians for work in underdeveloped countries. Because, as countries, they can't afford to have their own medical schools. But as nations, they could work with other nations and support an international medical school that would be different in how it functions yet rely upon the basis that the Western and European medical schools use."

He came up with this idea, which I was part of, called "IVIMEDS," an international, virtual medical school. He received funding from the United Kingdom's health service to come up with this concept. We had funding, and then we recruited all twenty international medical schools that would be involved, including some that I recommended from the United States. Other countries that were included operated medical schools in places like Spain and Germany, primarily Western European countries. Yet there were also a few Asian countries that supported this idea of IVIMEDS.

Of course, I talked to our dean and vice president, Robert D'Alessandri, and he helped support the project, too. The medical schools contributed some money to support the infrastructure. Bob D'Alessandri contributed me as an external staff member to help them develop the project. That was the foundation of my subsequent visits back to Dundee, Scotland, in the following years after my sabbatical. It was during the sabbatical that Ron Harden and a small group of people, including me, created this international, virtual medical school. The foundations, or what we in the United States call the basic science years, were going to be electronic. The clinical years were going to be partnerships, featuring the placement of international students into more traditional, rotation-based hospitals that were affiliated with established medical schools throughout the world. I believe IVIMEDS still exists, but it never grew to its potential. Maybe it was a thought before its time, but like all great thoughts, there'll be other similar thoughts in the future that will develop.

When I wasn't working, reading, writing papers, and contributing to the development of IVIMEDS, Betsy, Wesley, and I were traveling on the weekends. The great thing about Scotland is that it is small enough to drive a few hours and be in a totally different area. Dundee, where we were living, is on the east coast, on the River Tay estuary, but in three or four hours at the most, we could cross Scotland and be on the west coast, which is totally different, because of the Atlantic Ocean and the climate.

I have to say that, if it didn't rain every day in Scotland, then something was wrong. Dundee actually had one of the more moderate climates in Scotland. It didn't rain every day—perhaps every other day—but if you went to the west coast, you were getting pounded with rain frequently. No matter what you did, you needed to be prepared to be wet. We had great raincoats, and we had great umbrellas; we got a lot of use out of them. There were many, many trips that Betsy and I took on the weekends from Dundee with Wesley.

However, Dundee had a horrible reputation in Scotland. It was the fourth-largest city, yet it was one of the poorest areas in Scotland. Everybody from bigger towns and cities would always be critical of Dundee. This poor reputation stemmed from its history. At the turn of the century, it was a city that was a port town, and many sailing vessels were built there. That's not a bad thing, but the labor was cheap and undereducated.

The second thing about Dundee that attributed to its poor history is that it was a city in which industry was slow to develop, not because it wasn't a laborer population, but because the people who came produced cheap products. These were primarily made out of what's referred to as jute, and these plants produced a fiber that you could use to make ropes and inexpensive cloth. Because of the cheap labor to produce this cloth, there were many, many old apartment buildings that one could see in town that were now dilapidated and deteriorating. They had housed factory workers. So, Dundee never got the reputation of being where people wanted to be. They'd much rather have been in Edinburgh, the capital, or at Glasgow, the big city that had more "culture." Betsy and I, however, realized that Dundee was the real Scotland, once we got to know it. It was the Scotland of hardworking people, the Scotland of history. Much of the Scottish monarchy came from close to Dundee. It was a small port city and had wonderful access to the North Sea. We always felt that Dundee and the surrounding areas got a bad rap historically because people liked the bigger cities, which they thought had more culture.

It's interesting; you are often attracted to live in places that are similar to where you're from. Betsy and Wesley and I felt right at home in Scotland, because it was a mountainous country, like West Virginia. Dundee had a poor, working-class population, like West Virginia, and it had the beauty of the outdoors, like West Virginia. We were very comfortable there. I took my best professional job and position in West Virginia. I've loved West Virginia. It's home, the birthplace of our child, and a wonderful place to live. In certain respects, Dundee was the same sort of place. It got no respect, like West Virginia gets no respect.

However, when we first got there, we were very lonely. We didn't know anybody, and it took us a while to meet friends. However, the first or second weekend we got there, we saw that there was a soccer camp in the afternoon, sponsored by the Scottish women's national team. Since Wesley had been playing soccer in Morgantown, we decided to take him to this camp. While he was at this camp, we took care of some of our business. Some things took much longer than expected. For instance, we went to the bank to open checking and savings accounts. It was a major operation. They had to interview us and go through all sorts of security, asking us about everything. We thought it would be simple, just like opening a checking account in the United States. To make a long story short, we looked at our watches and said, "Oh no; the camp is ending, and we are twenty minutes away, if we can find it again." We had only been in town a short time. We got in the car and realized that the camp had ended half an hour earlier.

We drove to the camp and realized that almost everybody had gone. We said, "Oh my gosh, what have we done?" Remember, Wesley was only ten years old at the time.

We had left Wesley all by himself. When we looked carefully, there was one other car there. When Wesley saw our car, he ran out and grabbed us. "Mom and Dad, you won't believe it, but I found a new friend," he said.

He had found a friend, Michael Dand, and his parents and sister were there, too. During our time on sabbatical, they became our best friends. Wesley's new friend also talked to the coach of the kid's soccer team that he was playing for. He said that he met this kid from America. Wesley joined the team and played soccer with Michael and developed his soccer skills. Graham and Merry, Michael's parents, lived across town, only a ten-minute car ride away. Then, a year later, they moved closer when we came back, so I could work for a month during the following summer. Michael and Wesley were happy to be able to walk between their homes. It was a great relationship, and we still see them every couple of years.

School started a couple of weeks later, and life got even better. Wesley made friends, and he had a great time. As parents, we also had new friends. When he went to school, he met a boy. His accent was Scottish, but his family was from Iraq. They had left Iraq many years earlier to come and work in Dundee. Wesley became a friend of their son, Mustafa, who went by the nickname "Mussy." Wesley and Mussy had a common love for the game of soccer. They would kick the ball 24/7 if you let them. I remember that Betsy and I were invited to their home, too. Mussy's dad could speak English, but his mom could not. She still spoke Arabic, and for some reason, she never learned to speak English, even though she had lived in Scotland for many years. Mussy had an older brother who was in his late teens. There were other Arabic-speaking people in the community, too.

Mussy was a great kid, and he later turned out to be a very good soccer player. I remember reading something about him a couple of years ago, where he had gotten a summer job to come to the United States to teach soccer at various camps across the country. It's something similar to what Wesley does today, but Mussy was with a national soccer camp company that moved from one big city to another, whereas Wesley teaches soccer locally in West Virginia. It's very interesting how both of them kept a similar love for soccer. Because of that game, they started a friendship when they were ten and twelve years old, and they still keep in touch.

CHAPTER 74

ONE OF THE OPPORTUNITIES THAT Betsy, Wesley, and I had when we were on my sabbatical was to do some traveling. At that time, Betsy was learning Spanish, and she had a great interest in anything that was Spanish-related. So, that fall, during Wesley's school break, we decided to go to Spain. It wasn't very far, just a short air trip from Edinburgh, Scotland to Bilbao, Spain.

We got on a plane, landed in Bilbao, and rented a car. We left the airport in Bilbao and drove west to stay at a small hotel in a small village called Benia de Onís. It was great driving there, because, on the Continent, people drove on the right, just like in the United States. One of the reasons that we went to this northern part of Spain was that we had friends from WVU who were on sabbatical in Oviedo, Spain. They had invited us to visit them and to do some hiking in the Picos de Europa National Park. The Picos were mountains with rough terrain, unlike anything back home in West Virginia, but more like the mountains in the American West. It was a nice climate—not quite Mediterranean, but it was in the seventies and comfortable.

We hiked a trail along a river gorge, and the trail was right on the edge. Wesley was ten, and we hiked this trail for six to eight miles, to an even smaller village, where we had lunch. Our lunch consisted of room-temperature soda, bread—kind of like French bread but different—and a good-tasting, blood-red sausage called chorizo, which is cured with peppers, so it's spicy and rich. It tasted great but probably wasn't that healthy for me.

After lunch, we had to hike back the six or eight miles to our car, so the round-trip hike was more than twelve miles, the longest that Wesley had been on. He kept asking, "Are we there yet?" The last miles were like a death march.

We had a good visit, and Betsy's Spanish was improving all the time. We could get by. We asked the normal questions, such as "Where is the bathroom?" and food-related questions. We actually had no problem communicating the basics, and obviously, Betsy was a great help. She thoroughly enjoyed it. Besides hiking with our friends in Spain, we visited a famous, old cathedral in Burgos and the modern Guggenheim Museum in Bilbao, which was designed by Frank Gehry.

CHAPTER 75

ANOTHER SABBATICAL SIDE TRIP I wanted to take was a trip to the Netherlands. There was a colleague there in Maastricht who had written a lot about medical education. It was my excuse to go visit him and do some touring while back on the Continent. I met with my colleague, and we talked about his latest manuscript, and we talked about my sabbatical. He invited me to consider doing something with him in the future if I ever had the opportunity to take a sabbatical or an extended trip to Europe again. We agreed to keep in touch, and since it was just a day-long meeting, we were able to see a little of Belgium, as we had flown into Brussels.

This was the second time I was in the Netherlands. I was in Amsterdam in 1983 as one of my stopovers in the Aramco consulting that I did in Saudi Arabia, before Betsy and I got engaged. On the way back, we had stopped over in Amsterdam for a day and a night. We had the opportunity to see the various sections of Amsterdam. At the time, being young men, one of my colleagues and I decided to go into the red-light district, not to do anything but to see the sights. The red-light district had a history of women looking out the windows and showing their wares, so to speak. We saw a very liberal and open culture, where trading sexual favors and legally smoking marijuana were not big deals.

My colleagues and I took a ride through the city's canals. I think the most important part of Amsterdam is the canals, where a good part of the transportation happens throughout the city. It's built in a delta area, so there's lots of water from rivers and the ocean. It was quite beautiful, and there were plenty of ways to get around on the land also. It wasn't totally water-dependent, like the Italian city of Venice.

Right before Wesley went to college in 2008, we traveled to visit an exchange student named Sean in Belgium; he had once lived with us, and the four of us went to Amsterdam. We wanted to meet Sean's family, but before we did, we had Sean meet us in Brussels, where we landed. Then, the four of us boarded a train to Amsterdam. That happened to be during the time of the 2008 European Cup. There were all sorts of "Euro" parties and celebrations going on. At that point in the quarterfinals, the Netherlands national soccer team was still in play. As it turned out, Spain won the European Cup that year. When we were in Amsterdam, Wesley and Sean, being college-aged, got to see all sorts of things, including a walk, I hope, through the red-light district so that they could see the wares being offered.

But I digress. The main side trip we took in association with my meeting in Maastricht in the Netherlands was to Paris. I have been to Paris twice. The first time was when I graduated from high school. I attended a summer-abroad program. For six weeks, I took local courses in a school in northern Wales, in the city of Bangor. It was a summer program, and I had not started college yet, so I was probably eighteen years old. There were two weeks of travel. One of those weeks was in Wales and in parts of England, and then, we spent five days in Paris. I was with a bunch of American students, and we were all studying abroad. Most of them were younger than I was.

In Bangor, I met a local girl, and she took me to her parents' house. They let me drive one of their cars. Luckily, I had no accidents. I drove a car that was like an antique, a 1920s or 1930s car. It looked like a Model T, but it was an English version. Maybe it was an Austin, which was a car maker back in the United Kingdom a long time ago.

Then, when we were in Paris with this group of young people, I remember holding one girl's hand on one side and another girl's hand on another side. I remember walking with one of the girls who was from Southern California. We walked by the ponds and waterfalls at the base of the Eiffel Tower, which were water gardens, sprays, and different things. We splashed around, and it was good for me, because the girl I was with was cute.

On the last night in Paris, we were invited to a party in our hotel. I remember that our chaperone was an older, spinster-type woman, who really had no idea what we young people were doing. So we got invited to this party in our hotel, and it was in one of the rooms. The deal was that, to be able to come to the party, you had to bring a bottle of wine. We went out, and I think I bought a very inexpensive bottle of wine, like maybe four or five dollars in today's currency. We had lots of wine at this party, and even though there were some adults there, they didn't mind us drinking. They weren't our chaperones. However, they were nuns. The next day, we flew home. All of us at the party were pretty hungover, so we got on the plane and flew home, exhausted.

When I was older, when I was more mature and married, and had a son, I made my second trip to Paris during my sabbatical in Scotland. We had flown to Brussels, because I had a meeting I needed to go to in Maastricht. We drove there from Brussels. Then, we took the high-speed train, the TGV, from Brussels to Paris. It was less than a two-hour ride. We arrived in Paris and spent three days there. Betsy, Wesley, and I did everything we could think of. Wesley was only ten, and he was up for doing all that we wanted to do. We walked, and we walked, and we walked everywhere around Paris. We chose a little European style bed-and-breakfast hotel next to the Luxembourg Garden as our place to stay. We went to Paris on a beautiful week in November. It was not as touristy as in summer seasons. The weather we had was fantastic; it was in the high sixties and low seventies.

Although it's divided into sections, all of Paris is beautiful. Neither Betsy nor I spoke French, but I had taken some French in high school and maybe even in college. I would be the one trying crudely to ask for directions or food. What we found, contrary to what we had heard about the French people, is that they were extremely courteous and kind.

They were not rude at all. They could understand that I didn't speak French, so if they could speak English, they did as much as they could.

We went to the Louvre and the Orsay museums and saw primarily impressionist paintings. Then, we went to Notre Dame Cathedral and walked around it. Basically, we did all the tourist things that we could do in the city. If we got hungry, we stopped for crepes on the street where they sold them, or we ate in cafes or brasseries. My general impression of Paris was that it was a beautiful city that was very walkable. You really don't need much other transportation. There is public transportation, including a subway system that we used to get from one section to another. For example, when we went across town to get to the Arc de Triomphe, we took a subway. When we went to the Sacré-Coeur, we took a subway, too, but where we were staying pretty much provided us the opportunity to see much of Paris. In three days, we saw all the highlights.

CHAPTER 76

BESIDES TAKING TRIPS AROUND EUROPE, one of the things I wanted to do while on my Scotland sabbatical was to go fishing. Now, in Scotland, there was no open, public water. All the water was owned by someone, and you had to pay to go fishing. One of the friends that we developed through Wesley's relationships with kids playing soccer was a young man, maybe a few years younger than myself, who loved to fish. Over there, they fly-fished. We would get in kind of a rowboat and row out into these lakes, where big lake trout lived. The owners of the lake would stock it, and if you caught a trout—and there were good odds that you would—then you would pay them so many pounds based on the weight of the trout. My friend invited me to go fishing.

"Sure. I think that would be great," I said.

We went out early in the morning and rowed the boat out to a certain area and fished all day. We brought our lunch, and when we had to pee, we just peed over the edge of the boat. It was a guy-bonding experience.

CHAPTER 77

I GOT TO RETURN TO Scotland in the summer of 2002 for a month, because I was asked to be the recording secretary of a significant conference that was happening in Dundee. This was a kick-off conference for the concept of a computerized medical education program that could be developed for third-world countries that couldn't afford to have medical education like that provided in the United States or Scotland. Instead, they could have training and education to provide healthcare through IVIMEDS. The whole concept of IVIMEDS was created when I was first in Scotland on my sabbatical. In 2002, I was invited and hired to document the proceedings of the conference. That's one of the roles I played in this highly controversial, yet forward-looking, approach to meeting the medical needs of underdeveloped countries. It was also the perfect way for us to go back to Scotland. I saved up all my vacation time to spend a whole month there.

The IVIMEDS conference included a "royal" dinner that we attended. It was out in the country at one of the castles, Glamis Castle, where the queen's mother had lived as a child. It was a multicourse dinner, with drinks beforehand, all very Scottish and formal. A man in a kilt played his bagpipes as we entered. We got a tour of the castle and were shown historical rooms, where the queen's mother stayed. It was a great evening for Betsy and me. Wesley was staying at a friend's in Dundee while we were out at the castle for this special dinner.

Another of the castles that we visited on the weekend was called Dunnottar, and it was on a cliff overlooking the North Sea. I have a photo taken during my first trip to Scotland in the early 1990s, when Wesley was two years old. I was holding Wesley for a picture, with Dunnottar Castle in the background. I remembered that picture, so I talked Betsy into taking another picture now that Wesley was twelve years old. That made him a lot heavier, but I picked him up, and we tried to duplicate the same picture from when he was two years old.

We had a much shorter stay in Scotland during the 2002 trip, so we stayed in the country and on the weekends, we got the opportunity to tour some of Dundee's historical sites. As I explained before, Dundee was the hemp, or jute, capital, because it had an industry to make jute into ropes. These ropes were used on all of the sailing ships that were produced at that time. We stayed in a different apartment in the same, old jute-baron mansion. Maybe Ronald Harden had some sort of relationship with this particular house, so this was where he would put up his visitors.

My routine was to work five days a week and vacation on the weekends. Ronald and the University of Dundee had pretty much paid for my visit there, so I had a lot of work during the week, but on the weekends, there was time to travel and do what we wanted. While I was working, Betsy and Wesley kept busy. Since it was the summer, Wesley had time to visit his group of friends. Betsy would go do different things. And since she had friends, too, she went off to visit them as well.

CHAPTER 78

ONE OF WESLEY'S FRIENDS FROM school was a young lad who was the son of a politician in Dundee. He represented the Dundee district of Scotland in the British Parliament in London, England. Being a politician in Scotland was difficult, because there was the Labour Party, which he was a member of, and then there was the Conservative Party, or the Tories, I think they were called. In Scotland, there was also a Scottish National Party. This party was more radical, because they wanted independence from Great Britain. You see, Scotland has always considered itself a separate country. The British took it over after many, many different battles and wars. To this day, Scotland has never felt that it is part of England, and instead, the people always felt like they were uniquely Scotsmen. Through Wesley, we met this politician, and we became friendly with the family. In fact, the first time I had met this politician had been through his wife, when Wesley was in school, two years earlier. By the time of our return in 2002, he had been elected to Parliament, representing Dundee, so it was really, really neat. One weekend, we traveled with the family to London and got a personal tour of Parliament. We also cruised on the River Thames with them to Greenwich to see the Royal Observatory and stand on the famous Greenwich meridian line.

Sadly, the politician's wife, who was a wonderful woman, had been diagnosed with cancer. Within one year of our fourth family trip in the summer of 2008, she died. She had been treated for the cancer several times, but ultimately, it claimed her life. We had been in touch with the family, back and forth, through the years. It was a tragedy. In addition to their son, who was Wesley's age, the couple had two younger daughters.

Unexpected Heart Surgery
and More Travels

IN JANUARY OF 2003, I was cross-country skiing, and everything was normal. For many years prior to that, I knew that I had a heart murmur in the mitral valve of my heart, but it was no big deal. Physically, I was doing everything I would normally do without side effects. Like most adults, and certainly because I was working in the Health Sciences Center, I had a regular doctor appointment to see my general internist once a year or once every six months. Every year or two, I would have an echocardiogram of my heart. It was just normal care. In February or March, I was sitting at home but working, and my general internist called me.

"Jamie," he said, "according to your last heart echo, you need to come in and talk to me."

I went in and talked to him, and he explained that, even though I had no symptoms or shortness of breath or anything, and no physical signs of anything, he had concerns. "You have a significant regurgitation of good, oxygenated blood leaking backward in your heart from your mitral valve into the part that's pumping it," he said.

Leaking backward doesn't do any good, and so I wasn't getting enough good, oxygenated blood pumped through my body. More importantly, the pumping chamber was showing signs of enlargement, because it was working extra hard due to the blood leaking back into it.

"But I don't feel any difference," I said. "I've had no symptoms."

"Jamie," my doctor added, "this is significant enough that you will probably have to have heart surgery."

"Are you out of your mind?" I replied. "Who in their right mind would have a heart surgery without symptoms?" I was only fifty-six years old.

"I want you to see your cardiologist," he said, "and we'll do another scan of your heart."

They did, and it showed that, yes, I had too much blood leaking back from the mitral valve and that it wasn't a good thing. I could have significant troubles in a short period of time. It was perplexing because I was physically active. I was downhill skiing, and I was cross-country skiing. I had no side effects that would suggest something was wrong with my heart.

Like a good, health sciences person, one who is teaching medical students, I said, "Okay, if I have to have open-heart surgery, so be it." The first decision was this: what would be done to my heart to fix the regurgitation? Common practice was to put in a plastic or metal artificial valve. After the surgery, I would have to be on some sort of prescription to keep the valve clean and not have anything happen. After maybe ten years, I would have to replace the artificial valve, which meant heart surgery again.

"Is there an alternative?" I asked.

"Yes," I was told. "We can try to repair the valve." The surgeons would tighten it up and repair the opening so that when the flaps of the valve would close, they would close around a smaller opening that wouldn't stretch out and leak. So I went into surgery with the expectation that they were able to fix the valve with my own tissue, just cutting, or resecting, it a bit, so that my normal valve mechanism would not leak. The surgery took a long time, of course, but I had no idea, since I was under anesthesia. The cardiothoracic surgeon was at it for more than seven hours. It was a major reconstruction of that valve.

It was a big deal. Within a day and a half of the open-heart surgery, I was told, "We need to get you up and moving around." My heart was working fine. It was not missing a beat or speeding up, and the murmur was gone. I walked around on the floor of the hospital. Of course, I walked around with everybody nearby. No one would let me fall. I had an entourage of nurses and med students, all part of my care team. Then, an hour later, my heart started beating irregularly, meaning that it had some sort of problem going on. It was a dangerous rhythm, like part of my heart was trying to beat two cycles for every one. The atrium was beating too fast. There was a mismatch of the regular pattern, so my heart was not in normal sinus rhythm.

This irregularity would come and go. I was told later that the electrical system in my heart that keeps it beating regularly was probably stressed by such a long surgery—a surgery that was necessary. It wasn't like the physician did anything wrong. It was just the trauma of working on the heart for so long.

During surgery, my blood was artificially bypassed from my heart, a normal procedure in any heart surgery. My system was overly stressed, and the electrical system in my heart, the one that keeps it beating regularly, got out of sync. To this day, that's what I've been living with, an irregular heartbeat.

In order to rehabilitate from the heart surgery, I worked on the treadmill every other day for a good six to eight weeks as part of the normal routine of recovery for open-heart surgery. I remember that there was another gentleman, a maintenance worker at the Health Sciences Center, who'd had a heart attack and also had open-heart surgery. He was doing the same physical exercises that I was doing, just to bring back the endurance of the heart to maintain a certain level of function that the body requires when it's working. Any time you manipulate the heart or have surgery on the heart, whether it be for a valve repair, which was mine, or a heart attack, you actually lose some muscle within your heart. The muscles atrophy a bit, and you have to build them back up to the same level of performance that they'd had before. You have to build your heart back up so that it can endure normal levels of physical activity.

Following my heart surgery, I needed to be on Coumadin, which is a blood-thinning drug that keeps the blood from clotting unnecessarily. Because I have an irregular heartbeat, the blood could pool in my heart, and clots could be formed. My heart could send a clot to my brain, and I could have a stroke; all sorts of bad things could happen. Over a period of time on Coumadin, I kept my blood at a level so that clots would not form, even with my irregular heartbeat.

For a number of years, I was managing well, until I began to develop ALS, which basically meant that I was a fall risk. At this point, my doctors didn't want to risk me hitting my head, which could result in bleeding on the brain. They eventually took me off Coumadin, the preferred method of handling the situation. While they were trying to diagnose the ALS definitively, they withdrew a lot of spinal fluid to analyze. I ended up with the "headache from hell" that wouldn't go away for weeks, probably because no one advised me to lay flat after the procedure for several hours. I got up, got dressed, and went home, like everything was normal. Eventually, they did a CT scan to see why this headache persisted, and it revealed micro-bleeds in my brain. With so many micro-bleeds in my brain and ALS making me a fall risk, we decided that it was best to stop the Coumadin.

Unfortunately, a few years later, in 2011, I did have a stroke, and it did affect my brain. I've had to recover from it, on top of dealing with increasing ALS symptoms. It's made it difficult for me to access some of my memories. I lost vision in the upper-right quadrant of both eyes. I adapted to that, and now, it doesn't particularly bother me. When the stroke occurred, it occurred in the area where there is a connection between the two hemispheres of the brain. The human brain is an amazing thing. It can adapt to the circumstance that it is given.

One odd occurrence was that, immediately following the stroke, I could read, but I could not tell anybody what the words were that I was reading. I simply couldn't tell anyone what they meant. I was asked to write things, and I could write things correctly. Then, I was shown what I'd just written and asked to read it, but I couldn't say the words.

Through all this, I could still speak normally and respond to other questions. Now, over time, that's gone away; but I still don't read as well as I used to. There's a lot of weird medical things that have happened to me that I've had to adapt to. Each one is linked to ALS in some way. For example, I stopped taking blood thinners because ALS made me a fall risk, but it put me at risk for the stroke I ultimately had.

I needed to adapt to how I did things. The stroke has affected, to a certain degree, my quality of intellectual life and my memory. ALS also affects my physical life.

CHAPTER 80

ONE MONTH AFTER MY HEART surgery, I got a call from my colleagues in Scotland, saying that they were going to be at a conference in Bern, Switzerland, the de facto capital of that country. They wanted someone to talk about the work that I had done when I was on sabbatical and to come up with a way of introducing medical education to the masses in underdeveloped countries.

When they called about the conference, of course I wanted to go. "What about me coming to Switzerland and giving the talk?" I said, since I had done the original background work and had the data. I had also interviewed colleagues at other medical schools in Europe about the concept.

I was invited and able to go on the fully paid, round-trip journey to Switzerland to present the data. Of course, the Alps are in Switzerland, and I very much wanted the opportunity to visit some of the famous areas I had always heard about and read about there. One of the towns that was centrally located in the Alps and had a lot of history was Grindelwald.

I went over to Switzerland a week before the conference. *I just may be able to have an adventure for myself by going to Grindelwald,* I thought. At Grindelwald, I hoped I would be able to walk by the base of the Eiger, which is a huge mountain with a very exposed north wall. There were other places there that I wanted to see, as well. I arrived at the airport in Bern and immediately went to the train station. The great thing about Switzerland is that their train system goes anywhere you want. I caught the train going to Grindelwald. It was a great adventure: we passed by a big lake, and then we got into the Alps. The trains wove in and out between mountain ranges, and I had incredible views. Eventually, I made it to Grindelwald.

The town of Grindelwald was really a ski destination and vacation place in the winter. Just imagine this beautiful little Swiss town, with all the mountains around it, with many ski lifts, trams, and things going up into the hills. If you're a skier during the winter, this is the place you would want to go.

When I arrived, my first assignment was to find an inexpensive place where I could stay for the night. I went to the tourist office and they recommended a place, and it was €100 a night, which isn't that unreasonable; it was about $135, so it was not out of control. I arrived and got settled, and the first night, I went out to find a place for dinner. I took a walk down the street, and there were tons and tons of places to eat. I was looking at all these ski lift trams that were going up from the side of the street into the surrounding mountains, too. I stopped at this one restaurant, where all the tables were outside. It was a nice, beautiful evening, and I said, "I'm going to eat here." I sat down, and this extremely attractive waitress came up to me. Luckily, she spoke enough English, because I didn't speak any German.

"How can I help you?" the attractive waitress asked.

I looked at the menu, and I ordered what I wanted. Then, my waitress turned around. As she was leaving my table with my order, I noticed that across the small of her back was what some refer to in the United States as a "tramp stamp." It's a big tattoo that covers about six inches above the buttocks and wraps around about a foot or so at the small of the back. It's called a "tramp stamp" because it is thought to indicate a certain looseness. Whether that's true or not, it is something that has developed that reputation. Nevertheless, I had a fine dinner and then went back to my accommodations and went to bed.

The next day, I decided to explore the area. One of the neat things coming out of Grindelwald was a small-gauge railroad, which went up the mountain to a high peak at the base of the Eiger; then, it went around the mountain itself and ended up at a very high altitude. This was summer, but there was snow at about fourteen thousand feet, and you have to realize that Grindelwald itself was probably at three thousand to four thousand feet already. It was a big climb on this narrow-gauge railroad, and it took me to an area where I could see for miles around. It was a beautiful view. When I got up on top, there was a tourist area that people could explore. At that point, I was walking around with a walking stick, or trekking pole.

I walked about a half-mile to a post office. It was obviously a tourist post office, but I walked up there with a specific purpose. That purpose was to send a post, a letter, to the surgeon who had worked on my heart five months earlier, thanking him. I also wanted to let him know what I was doing to exercise my newly repaired heart, and it was a fun thing to do. When I got back to Morgantown later and I saw him, he got a real chuckle out of receiving this letter mailed from about fourteen thousand feet in Switzerland.

Then I walked around, exploring. I got back in the train and started heading down. On my way down, in the narrow-gauge train, I ran into another English-speaking individual. I can't remember if he was from the United States or the United Kingdom, but we hit it off, and we decided to get off the train halfway down the mountain and walk back to Grindelwald.

We got off basically halfway down, at a specific place where we could hike up to the base of the Eiger. The Eiger is an extremely difficult climb, and it's not a place where recreational climbers would go. Both of us had seen the Clint Eastwood movie that features the mountain, and we understood the significance of the Eiger. I had read the accounts of when the Eiger was first climbed in the 1930s. After Everest and Annapurna in Nepal, this was the third very significant mountain for climbers. With my new friend, I walked to the beginning of the climb and gauged its difficulty. Of course, I had done my climbing in the 1970s, and my companion had never climbed, but he had a sense of what it would take to get up to the Eiger from that Clint Eastwood movie. It was a pretty neat place, and we had the sense of the adventure that a climb on that mountain would entail. We did walk at the base of the Eiger up to where we anticipated early climbers would go to start their ascents up the rock.

One of the significant things about the Eiger is that on the route going up, there's a snowy place, snowy even in the summer because of the nature of the rock. It was called the Spider. It was always a difficult place to get around in any attempt at the Eiger. Certainly, climbers made their attempts in the summer, when most of the rock is dry. There is often rock-fall out of the Spider, because of its wetness from the fact that snow that stays there year-round. That always causes difficulties for climbers.

We went back to our route, walking down to a place where the next train would stop, and we waited for it to pick us up. It wasn't but two or three miles from Grindelwald. We could have walked it, but we decided that we would take the train.

The next day, I decided to do a hike on my own up in the high mountains surrounding Grindelwald. To do that hike, I took the ski tram up to the top of the ridge. I think I was a little out of my league as far as taking a solo hike. I didn't have any problems, but I thought if I were to slip, have an accident, or get tuckered out, it would be days before anybody found me. I followed a trail until it led to another little village, high in the mountains, and I eventually ended up at a tavern in this little town.

The Swiss often speak English, so I asked, "How do I get back to Grindelwald?"

"Just wait here," said a guy. "There'll be a bus coming in a couple of hours." It was a regular route, and I got back to Grindelwald. I did leave a message at the hotel about what I was going to do that day; in case I didn't show back up, they had an idea of where to look for me. Even though it probably wasn't the safest thing to do alone, it was something that was important for me, because it was outdoors, it was hiking, and it was exploring a new area. Most importantly, it was a blessing that I was able to do this after my heart surgery. It had only been four or five months earlier. How miraculous was it that I was able to do it?

Eventually, I did get back to Bern and gave my paper. That went well, and then after my paper, I was still in the mood to take another hike. Outside of Bern, I had the opportunity to take another hike up a smaller mountain that overlooked the city. To get there, I took a lift that went straight up from the valley floor. It was a funicular, like they have in Pittsburgh. I took it to the top and hiked around. It was interesting when I was on top. I didn't hear anybody speaking English, nor did I get the sense that people could speak English, so whatever directions I was asking for, people didn't understand. It was interesting getting back down. I did find my way to the route that I could walk down. In West Virginia, we would call this place a mountain, but in Switzerland, it's just a big hill. It was a couple of miles to walk down. The whole trip allowed me to connect again with climbing, since this area was a historic place for climbers.

CHAPTER 81

In 2003, West Virginia University was approached by a group of businessmen to see if we were interested in helping to start a private medical school in the Sultanate of Oman. Oman is on the Gulf Sea, which is on the eastern side of the Arabian Peninsula. If you were in Oman, you would like to have a school accredited at a high standard so that the graduates could compete for residency programs in the United States. In reality, that's a very complex issue.

I was asked to go over to Oman to lend my expertise in curriculum and to help them develop the courses that they needed to start the premedical-education program. In other words, I was to consult on what was needed in their "undergraduate" curriculum to prepare them for a US style of medical education. One of the great opportunities that I had, being flown over to Oman to spend ten to fourteen days consulting, was the amount of travel I got to do in the country. You have to realize that Oman is a very different country in the Gulf region, especially compared to its northern neighbor, Iraq.

The other countries surrounding Oman are the United Arab Emirates to the north and Saudi Arabia to the west. To the southwest is Yemen, a country that is less developed and politically unstable. It's a very interesting region of the world, yet Oman's history was very different from those countries that are close to it. Oman always had a history of being a stopping place for east-west trading systems. Marco Polo made travels through this region. Thus, Oman had always been influenced by these travels and survived on commerce. So its view of

Western and other influences is much different than other Arab nations. In fact, this particular Muslim population and their predominant sect of Islam is very different from what we hear about and read about in our newspapers today. It is much more advanced, and they appreciate the interaction with people from the West. Oman has always been a supporter of Western militaries, as well as trade and commerce.

One of Oman's greatest assets is the amount of oil that it has. Its leader, the Sultan of Oman, is very progressive and realizes that the oil in Oman will not last forever. The sultan took Oman from a backward, tribal country to the modern, westernized country it is today with the proceeds from oil discovered in the early 1950s. Yet he realizes that oil revenues and reserves and wealth, so to speak, will only be available for the next twenty-five years or so, until they're depleted. Thus, it's been his mission, since he took over the country from his father in a bloody revolution, to make Oman independent. The sultan is a very forward-looking leader, even though he had to kill his dad to start this revolution.

However, when I went over to Oman in 2003, I did not know all this history. I just went to consult in an Arab nation that I didn't know much about. Our university was consulting with them to build the facilities, offices, labs, classrooms, and everything else they would need. WVU health professionals played a big role in developing Oman Medical College. From early 2003, I visited every year or every other year, until my last visit in 2008. I brought many of our people over to Oman to help us establish what they needed to be successful. The association with WVU happened because of relationships. One of our former associate deans, Dr. Tony DiBartolomeo, had a relationship with a businessman who had a relationship with Oman. He found out that they were interested in talking to Tony. He was the Associate Dean for Medical Affairs at WVU until his early, unfortunate death a number of years back.

One of the things I got to do, in addition to consulting and helping them set up the educational programs, was to tour and visit various parts of Oman. It was very hot, 120 degrees Fahrenheit or more in the summer, but it was beautiful and in the seventies in the winter. I tried to time my trips for December, February, and March. By April, it was getting hot again. That heat would last through October.

It certainly worked to the advantage of West Virginia University's School of Medicine that the school in Oman hired a faculty member from our college. He was a friend of mine, and had been appointed the dean of Oman Medical College. I always had a strong relationship with him. There was a personal and professional connection between us. Like any new school, this one needed a moderate amount of work to be successful. Since I was an accreditation professional in the United States, and since I worked for the Liaison Committee on Medical Education and was part of teams that accredited twenty medical schools over my career, I was in a good position to help them meet the standards and the criteria of excellence that were expected. Today, I suspect that the Ministry of Health has developed an accreditation system for all of the schools in higher education. You have to realize that Oman Medical College was the second medical school in Oman. There was also the more traditional, older school in Oman that was part of the government-run system.

I took advantage of the opportunity to travel and see as much as I could, in addition to working the long hours. These were day trips. On several occasions, I got to see some areas of Oman that were not necessarily on the tourist list. Of course, most people want to go to Muscat, which is the capital of Oman. Our new medical school was a few miles outside of Muscat. I went on a trip where we got dropped off at one of the palaces just a little bit north of Muscat. One of the faculty members that we were working with was Middle Eastern, and we got into an extended conversation. He was from Iraq. We talked about the turbulent times in Iraq under dictatorial leadership. It was an interesting conversation because he was an Iraqi citizen, and I was a US citizen. Not too many years before that, we had been at war with each other. These were the types of fascinating conversations I could have in Oman without worrying about the political implications of what was said.

Even though the Middle East is considered dangerous, there was no question in my mind that I felt safe all the time in Oman. I didn't feel threatened. Oman is a very different country than Saudi Arabia, where I spent a couple of months during the winters of 1983 and 1984.

One of the opportunities I had on a later visit to Oman was that I got to travel independently. In other words, I borrowed a car. I had another colleague with me, one a little younger than I am, Scott Cottrell, who took over my role at the university after I retired. Either Scott or I would drive from Muscat to Sohar, which was where the medical school was, a two-hour drive north, up the coast. When you're driving in Oman, people really don't know how to drive on these big freeways. They really don't know how to design them, either. One of the things that they designed were roundabouts on freeways. You had to slow down to get into the roundabout to go where you wanted to go, if you were making a turn into a little village or something.

One time, as we approached a roundabout, we were going sixty or seventy miles an hour on the straight part. We slowed down to take the roundabout to turn onto another road. We got in the roundabout and started going to our west. All of a sudden, a car zoomed by us and almost hit us without slowing down in the roundabout. We were to their right, and we were going to be crossing left in the roundabout, but the other car cut the corners of the roundabout so that it could keep going straight. We considered ourselves lucky for not getting hit. Car accident injuries were the majority of accidents seen in the trauma center at the Sohar Hospital. We were lucky that day that we didn't get clobbered, because people, in my opinion, really don't know how to drive on these big, Westernized highways. It was dangerous to drive in Oman.

Overall, I found Oman to be a very dynamic and intellectually active country. All of the people I talked with, many of whom were Omani people, were well-versed in Western culture. I think this is significantly different than people from some of the other Middle Eastern countries in that region. I was impressed, and I was very taken by their lifestyles and the beauty of their country. It is so unlike parts of Saudi Arabia and the United Arab Emirates that I had had the opportunity to visit in earlier years. Oman is clean and prosperous.

CHAPTER 82

In 2007, before I knew that I had ALS, I could walk, and my arms worked. I really had no clue that something was wrong with me. Also, I had taken up fly-fishing about ten years prior, in the mid-1990s. Ever since Betsy and I had Wesley, since we had become a family, I couldn't always do the extreme stuff I did when I was young. I was looking for something that would keep me connected with the outdoors, knowing that I wasn't going to go backpacking or on extended river trips like the early days. I still wanted to spend time outside, near rivers. Plus, I wanted to develop a skill that I could live with into old age, and fly-fishing seemed the natural thing for me, because it had a technical nature to it. This skill required me to gently put a fly on the river to fool a trout. I learned to make my own flies, and having a trout hit a fly that I made was a special experience.

As a fly-fisherman, one of the things I always wanted to do, on my bucket list, was to go and fish on the Yellowstone River, out west, in Yellowstone National Park. It's really the pinnacle of the fly-fishing experience. I wanted to go because of its beauty, because of the number of fish in the Yellowstone River, because of the quality and the size of the trout, but mostly because it is such an unspoiled wilderness area that is very accessible, because it is a national park. Yellowstone River was considered the mecca for fly-fishing for trout in the United States.

In 2007, Jim McGraw invited another friend and me on a trip to Yellowstone to go fishing with him. I knew Jim through his wife, Ann

325

Chester. For many years, Ann and I went kayaking together. We would go just about every other weekend for the day to the Youghiogheny River and run the Lower Youghiogheny, and then we would come back home at the end of the day. Over time, Betsy and I got to know Ann and Jim as a couple, and we did things together. I met Ann because she worked at the Health Sciences Center, where I was working, and she was the first equal opportunity officer of the Health Sciences Center. She dealt with employment equality and other issues that would arise in that area. She had gotten her PhD at Duke University but moved into administrative positions rather than traditional biology faculty positions. Jim had also earned his PhD at Duke and had taken his first professional job at WVU in the biology department in 1982. They've been here ever since.

Jim knew I was into fly-fishing, and he had just started. We flew out; I rented a car. The easiest but longest way is to fly into Salt Lake City, rent a car, then make the six hour or so drive to Yellowstone, located in the northwest corner of Wyoming.

As I entered the park, what was striking to me were the bison, also called buffalo, which roam freely. In fact, they're right around the roads. You get views of these large animals up close and personally. So many of the pictures I've taken are of the bison in Yellowstone National Park.

It's important to understand that I didn't fish for food; I fished for sport. I de-barbed my hooks, and I returned the trout to the river after I brought them in, looked at them, and measured them. I returned each fish to the stream to be caught on another day by another person.

Jim and his wife had a place nearby, not too far from Big Sky ski resort in Montana. They have a condominium there that Jim shares with his brother's family, so we had a place to stay and call our home base. The main trip, however, was to go into Yellowstone National Park, about forty-five minutes from Big Sky, to fish.

We fished several different streams coming into the Yellowstone River, as well as the big river itself. Perhaps one of the most dramatic places we fished was a bend in the Yellowstone River, where bison grazed right next to us as we were fishing. Of course, we needed to be careful not to upset the bison, because they were a lot bigger and a lot faster than we were. We fished in peace and harmony, coexisting with the bison and fish and nature all around us.

We didn't have to do that much hiking, only a mile or two, but when we were out all day and fishing a particular stream, we were tired at the end of the day. We camped out at the campgrounds, which we had reserved ahead of time, for a couple of nights. We would usually go out for dinner at one of the lodges in the area, so we didn't really have to prepare much food. In the mornings, we usually ate some cereal and dried fruit, and then during the day, while fishing, we would eat nuts and camping food. Out on the streams and the big river, it wasn't really crowded with other fly-fishermen. It was mid-July, and there was a huge area with lots of water. Whether we were fishing at the hot fishing spots or not, we didn't know, but it was never a problem. At certain places in the Yellowstone River, you could walk out a fair distance and put your line into the main current to catch fish, such as cutthroat trout.

One place I remember in particular was a little stream coming into the Yellowstone River. We hiked up a cliff, then got to a different bench, and right before the stream tumbled over the cliff into its next section, there was a wonderful place to fish. I remember putting my fly into a rocky area of the stream, about one hundred yards before it tumbled down the cliff. A huge trout looked at my line, and a smaller trout took my fly. Then, the big trout went for the smaller trout that was fighting on my line. I had no expectation of catching the big trout, but I do remember fighting with the small trout. The big guy was probably two feet long. The small guy was probably nine inches to one foot long. It was all very magical, because I could see what was happening; the water was so clear. Going to Yellowstone was like going to nirvana land. It's a spectacular treasure that all of us who have had the opportunity to visit really appreciate. One of the things we saw was tremendous variation in the types of landscapes. There were valleys and mountains and rivers that cut deep, deep gorges. Then, there were meadows and ponds. Yellowstone National Park offers such a variety of geography, and it's all very accessible if one is willing to walk and take in the surrounding beauty. There are also the geyser basins, warm water coming from geysers or hot springs that eventually dump into the river.

As a side note, I was the slowest hiker among my group. Normally, that would not have been the case. I really didn't know what was going on with my body. I wondered why I was a little slower hiking, but it wasn't until a year later that I was diagnosed with ALS.

You Never Know What the Future Brings

CHAPTER 83

THE FIRST TIME I REALIZED that something was different, or was happening to me, was years ago, probably in the early 2000s. I was playing tennis, which I did every week in the winter with Jim McGraw and a couple of other faculty members from WVU. We had a foursome, so we would play doubles for a couple of hours. One evening, when I was running sideways at the net to hit the ball, I tripped, and I stepped on my big toe. While I felt I was okay, that instance was probably one of the first times that something like this had happened. Whether that was an early, early precursor to my motor neurons dying, I have no idea.

Of course, there was the fishing trip with Jim McGraw, where I was always the slowest hiker. Now, I was nearly ten years older than everybody else on the trip, but hiking and walking were slower for me. I don't recall any difference in how I walked—my gait—or anything. I was just a little bit slower, but I could keep up, and I got through the hiking in river beds and falling streams, too.

It really wasn't until later in the 2000s that I noticed some subtle changes in the movement of my right leg. I was an Alpine downhill skier, and I used skis with free heels, part of the Telemark style of skiing. I was a fairly confident skier, so I could use the Telemark method, which was more of an Alpine method. I could unweight my skis even if my heels weren't attached. Over my last couple of years of skiing, what I noticed was that I could turn to the right very well. I put my weight on my left ski, and because of the design of the ski, I would go to the right.

So my left leg was normal. But I noticed that when I put my weight on my right leg to turn left, it was weaker. I couldn't put as much weight and force on it as I could my left ski. Of course, I didn't have any idea that my motor neurons were getting weaker and dying on my right side. I just thought that, because I was sixty years old, it was a normal sign of aging.

Around 2008, I found that when I walked, my foot would sort of drop on my right side. First, I thought I was just being clumsy or lazy. I even told a physician colleague about this, and he agreed that I was just being clumsy or lazy. So I thought, *Okay, things happen when you're sixty years old, and you're getting older.* Eventually, when my foot was seriously dropping, and I couldn't maintain a normal, healthy gait, I decided to go see a specialist. I had no idea why my musculature and nerve stimuli were different in my right foot than my left foot.

At this time, I didn't feel unstable. I still had strength in both legs, but the right leg wasn't keeping the same pace as my left leg. I saw a neurologist, and he did tests, but he didn't want to say anything or make a diagnosis for a year. He just wanted to follow me and see what was going on. I had all sorts of tests for biological or chemical imbalances, as well as infectious diseases. Everything had to be ruled out. It was the right approach for me, because I was relatively young, healthy, and active. I wasn't overweight, and I ate right, so they couldn't really come up with an external or environmental factor for my illness. I wasn't told about ALS until about a year after I initially started having the symptoms. In the meantime, over that year, I had every test there was to figure out what was going on with me.

So it wasn't until around 2008 or 2009 that my neurologist made the definitive diagnosis of amyotrophic lateral sclerosis, or ALS. I was informed very matter-of-factly by my neurologist, who was very good physician, but his sensitivity skills were not his strongest attribute. It's not that he was mean or dishonest, but he was too brutally and painfully honest. He spoke without any kind of windup and didn't know how to help his patients deal with difficult things. If I were to describe how I felt after hearing this diagnosis for the first time, I must admit that I was very upset. It's not like I'd never heard of this disease. It has quite a history, and all sorts of documentaries about the disease have been made. I knew the story of Lou Gehrig, the famous baseball player. People have written about it, and I had read the book *Tuesdays with Morrie* a long time ago.

The diagnosis stunned me. Then, there were tears. And then came the denial questions: could it be something else? I didn't want to believe that it was going to happen to me.

After that time, the progression of the disease in my right leg, including its weakness and spasticity, became much more evident. At first, I spent about six months walking with a cane, just to give me a little support. And then, when my right leg became weaker, I had two canes so that I could have at least three points on the ground as I walked. That worked fine for about six months, until I needed a walker, which I could hold onto with both hands and push in front of me. At that point, I was still able to get around with the physical support of a walker. Because my right leg was still strong enough to bend and to push on the accelerator, I could still drive. I changed my driving style, braking with my left foot, which is not recommended. Someone who drives with the right foot on the accelerator and his or her left foot on the brake can be dangerous, because one can speed up while the brake light is still on. It means that the person is resting the left foot on the brake. So, for a while, I still drove. I could hop out of the vehicle and reach across and pull out the walker. Thus, I was still working. Eventually, I borrowed a power chair that I kept at the office because I didn't yet have a vehicle that could transport a power chair. Kim Helmick, my administrative assistant, would meet me at the curb with the power chair when Betsy dropped me off at the Health Sciences Center. Kim was always supportive of me and tried to be helpful.

People don't always know how to react to someone with ALS. In one of my visits, during the early stages, my doctor wanted me to have a series of MRI scans to look at my brain and spinal column to rule out other reasons why I could be having neurological problems. So I went. It was late afternoon or early evening, and I went to the lab where the MRI scans were to take place. There was a receptionist who was trying to be friendly. She must have looked at my chart and saw that I had been diagnosed with ALS. Without any sort of introduction to me, she told me that her mother was diagnosed with ALS. She started telling me stories. When this receptionist had a baby, she would take the baby over to see her mother, but her mother's foot went into spasm. It was not that dissimilar from my experience; it was a normal muscle reaction for ALS, because the nerves are confused. She continued to tell the story about her mother putting the baby on her lap and then bouncing it off her lap because her leg went into a vibrating spasm. And while this woman was trying to be friendly, she really didn't know anything about me. I was sensitive, and while her comments to me probably were inappropriate, she already knew that in real life, stuff happens.

The physical changes were subtle. It's not like an accident, where one day you're healthy, and the next day you have a broken leg. The changes are very slow. There's no question that I'm weaker now than I was a month ago. There's no question that my ability to take in oxygen is decreased. My breathing is weaker, so my talking is weaker, too, because I don't have as much air running across my vocal cords to vibrate them to produce speech.

I think the mind is a powerful ally, but it can also be a damaging enemy if you let it run amok. I realize that I'm going to think all sorts of things, but I don't have to believe everything I think, nor do I have to act on all of my thoughts. So I try to live day-by-day, minimizing my thoughts about the future, while realizing that it's impossible to totally eliminate negative thoughts.

I get angry for having this disease. I ask, "Why me? What did I do to deserve this?" But I'm the one who has it, and I'm the one who has to manage it with help from others. I understand that my mind and my thoughts are going to be all over the place. But why dwell on thoughts of the future, which is, to a large extent, a fantasy, because the future hasn't happened? I stay in the present and make modifications as best I can. So that's been my approach. Is it perfect? No. Is it scary? Sometimes, yes. Do I get angry? Yes. Do I say mean and hateful things to others? I hope not, but it's possible that I do occasionally. It's difficult to always be upbeat, but I remember I have a family who loves me. They have to deal with this, too. So if I want to help them deal with it, I don't make it more difficult for them by being negative and pissed off all the time. They love me, and they're going to be there with me.

CHAPTER 84

THERE HAVE ALSO BEEN FRIENDS around to help me. I have one who is a big guy, six-feet-something, and strong. Strat Douglas is a professor of economics at WVU. He and I were both white-water boaters. So my friend Strat took me out on rivers when I still had the ability to paddle with my arms, but my legs were so weak that I couldn't walk. He helped me get out on the Lower Youghiogheny in a small raft once. Another time, Strat actually had to pick me up, and he put me in the canoe, up front so I could paddle.

We were on a section of the Blackwater River, where it starts in Canaan Valley. Jorge Flores paddled his kayak along with us to help us. The interesting thing about it was that it wasn't a matter of just putting me in the canoe at the beginning and taking me out at the end. There was a gas line that crossed the river, six or seven different times. The river went to the right, went to the left, and went to the right again. The gas company ran their line straight, and the water level was high enough that we couldn't get under the pipeline. The only way to get around it was for Strat to lift me out of the boat onto the shore, take the boat over the pipeline, then go to the shore, pick me up, and put me back into the canoe. Basically, he had to portage me several times. We got back from this trip in the evening, as it was turning to dusk on us. So that's an indication of what a friend would do to let me try to continue to enjoy what I've done for the past twenty years. Strat also took me to the Cheat River Festival and pushed me around in a manual wheelchair several times because my powerchair was too heavy and low for the rough ground.

I regularly see friends, a very close group of people that we met when we first came to Morgantown, usually every month, when we have pot luck suppers in different homes. Some friends, like Mary Wimmer, are here more often. She has even stayed for a few days to help care for me if Betsy needed to go out of town. I've had people coming in to visit me from many of the East Coast states. I also regularly see my Chapel Hill friends, so that's been good, too. Some of them also have stayed for a few days to help me when Betsy traveled. My life is one where seeing friends, and being with people, is a daily process. It's an important part of what I'm doing and how I want to live my life with others. My family and I are doing a good job of opening our home. It helps me to stay positive and upbeat, and it lets me keep focusing on what's important.

CHAPTER 85

I WANT TO TELL MY story, so to speak, and I've given multiple presentations to residents, medical student groups, and others who will listen. So I've been on the speech circuit. I've talked to undergraduate classes and graduate-level classes. I have my "dog and pony show." I try to tell people about who I was, what I did, and all the outdoor adventures that I've written about, but (of course) not all of them. I give them the sense of the outdoor life that I've led. Some who have listened knew me professionally as one of the deans in the School of Medicine or in Pharmacy. I can offer them a different perspective of who I am and what I'm now dealing with. Following are my notes from the most recent presentation I gave, in July of 2014, to a WVU class on personal wellness. The story I tell goes something like this, although the important parts of any presentation often come from the questions that others ask me:

> This presentation is about my past, present, and future. I am sixty-six years old with a disabling disease, but thirty-five years ago, I was a rock climber and did some mountaineering out in the West. Twenty-six years ago, my wife, Betsy, and I canoed in a tandem, open boat down the Colorado River through the Grand Canyon. Six years ago, I was a Telemark downhill skier, a cross-country skier, a winter camper. I kayaked and canoed rivers and streams through the Southeast, in Kentucky, Tennessee,

338

North Carolina, South Carolina, Georgia, and, of course, West Virginia. I was also a soccer dad, tennis player, fly-fisherman, fly-tier, and piano player.

Six years ago, I was diagnosed with ALS, a progressive disease that ends in death, usually by lung failure. Amyotrophic lateral sclerosis, or ALS, is a disease of the nerve cells in the brain and spinal cord that control voluntary muscle movement. ALS is also known as Lou Gehrig's disease. There is typically a three- to five-year survival rate, but this varies among individuals. A notable exception is Stephen Hawking.

My symptoms started with tripping and, later, right-leg weakness while skiing. First I needed one cane, then two, and then a walker. Now, I have a powered wheelchair that I can control with my chin, because my hands no longer work.

In 2011, on my birthday, December 16, I suffered a serious setback: I had a cerebral stroke within the left occipital lobe and at the splenium of the corpus callosum. It affected my ability to read, and it caused visual loss in the upper right quadrant. The stroke also affected my temporal lobe. I temporarily suffered alexia without agraphia, which means that I could not read, but I could write. It's a less common stroke outcome. As a consequence, I had been on medical leave from the university. I resigned on June 30, 2012, as a faculty member and associate dean in the School of Medicine. I am now an emeritus professor of medicine. I am medically and legally disabled, and I am receiving social security disability and disability insurance benefits.

I participated in a phase-three clinical trial of an experimental ALS drug therapy called dexpramipexole. This drug is in the family of dopamine antagonists. Unfortunately, I had to withdraw because of a severe drug reaction. Eventually, the doctor running the trial at the University of Pittsburgh contacted me to say that it was discontinued because it did not cause improvement.

ALS affects approximately five out of every one hundred thousand people worldwide. With ALS, nerve cells, called neurons, waste away or die and can no longer send messages to muscles. This eventually leads to muscle weakening, twitching, and an inability to move the arms, legs, and body. The condition slowly gets worse. When the muscles in the chest area stop working, it becomes hard or impossible to breathe on one's own.

There are no known risk factors except for having a family member who has a hereditary form of the disease, which is rare. Less than three percent of all cases are hereditary. The triggering cause remains unknown.

There is no known cure for ALS. The first and only drug treatment approved for the disease is a medicine called riluzole. Riluzole slows disease progression and prolongs life but only for a few months. Treatments to control symptoms are primarily baclofen or diazepam, which may be used to control spasticity that interferes with daily activities.

Symptoms usually do not develop until after age fifty, but they can start in younger people. ALS does not affect the senses—sight, smell, taste, hearing, or touch. It only rarely affects bladder or bowel function. Eventually, it may affect a person's ability to think or reason. The symptoms include: difficulty breathing, difficulty swallowing, choking easily, drooling, gagging, weight loss, head dropping due to weakness of the neck muscles, muscle cramps, and muscle contractions called fasciculations. This muscle weakness slowly gets worse, and the disease commonly involves one part of the body first, such as the arms or legs. It eventually leads to difficulty lifting, climbing stairs, and walking, as well as speech problems, such as a slow or abnormal speech pattern or slurring of words. There are also voice changes and hoarseness.

Physical therapy, rehabilitation, the use of braces or a wheelchair, or other orthotic measures may be needed to maximize muscle function and general health.

Proper nutrition is important because patients with ALS tend to lose weight. The illness itself increases the need for food and calories, but at the same time, problems with swallowing make it hard to eat. I used to weigh 160 pounds; now, I weigh about 125.

Let me tell you what is important to me. These have been the things I've emphasized with my son. My list includes family and profession, and, now that I have resigned, writing a book of my adventures, musical and creative pursuits (including my piano lessons and piano playing), athletic and sports abilities, and my understanding of the "spiritual" or unexplained nature of things.

My uniqueness, or the something special I can contribute, is important to me. It is important enough that I differentiate what is physiological or biological, and what comes from the mind or thoughts. The role of each and their interactions in health are important. My way of thinking comes from something I learned in my sociology classes as an undergraduate, and that is that we are born with a biological and an environmental cultural heritage. The brain is biological, and, in my case, the motor neurons are dying. The mind is environmental and is the harbor of thoughts.

The nature and role of thought includes awareness that we have thoughts as an important insight. Thoughts come and go, like a stream or river carrying "things." A common assumption is: problems and external influences cause people to think and feel the way they do. The common paradigm for most thought models is: external factors influence what we think and feel, and our perceptions influence our behaviors or actions. The common interventions used for our unproductive thinking are to employ methods that fix external factors and deal with the content of people's thinking.

There is an alternative way to view this common paradigm, which I subscribe to and believe. Stress is the internal experience of life seen through insecure thinking. It is innate for people to experience dynamic, responsive flows of thoughts, which can be productive, nonproductive, good, or bad. When people understand the innate and dynamic qualities of thought, what they think becomes malleable, and they can recognize when to leave their thinking alone to get insights about what to do.

This view of thinking is an inside-out paradigm. Another way of saying it is this: understand that we *do* think (and we generate our own thoughts), instead of just acknowledging *what* we think. So this is what I recognize: we are constantly thinking. We are like a stream or river containing thoughts that pass by and return. Our perceived experiences and our states of mind change as our thinking changes. The awareness of how thinking connects to experience allows us to know when to leave our thinking alone. In other words, you don't have to believe everything you think.

So, how do I help myself with understanding the nature of my thoughts? By staying in the present; by relating to my disease but not reading ahead or imagining and thinking about the future; by understanding and listening to the wellness inside of me; by remaining in a present "state of mind" that encourages me to be courageous, humble, respectful, joyful, creative, loving, and compassionate; and by helping others understand how I am approaching my life.

As I mentioned, I gave versions of this speech at various places. I also ultimately had to resign my position at the university. I did so in the following letter:

May 30, 2012

Arthur Ross, MD
Dean, West Virginia University School of Medicine
Morgantown, WV 26505

Dear Art:
I am writing this letter to inform you that as of June 30, 2012, I resign my administrative and faculty positions in the WVU School of Medicine. I am deeply saddened that my medical problems have forced me to make the difficult decision to leave my employment with the university sooner than I had intended to finish my career.

Because you may not be familiar with my history at WVU, I offer you a brief summary of my faculty and administrative roles. I have been a faculty member since my arrival at WVU in January 1985, received tenure in 1990, and became a full professor of Internal Medicine and Pediatrics in 1996. In 1991, I was appointed as the Associate Dean for Medical Education and Director of the Office of Medical Education, positions which I have held continuously. For the 1994–95 academic year, I was appointed the Interim Dean of the WVU School of Pharmacy. I am also an adjunct professor of Clinical Pharmacy.

I also believe a summary of my local, national, and international contributions is appropriate. I regularly facilitated problem-based learning groups of first-year, as well as ethics case-based groups of second-year medical students. I have been a Liaison Committee for Medical Education (LCME) team member for the accreditation of medical schools in North

America and Canada since 1989. In 1996–97 AY, I was chair of the Southern Group on Educational Affairs (SGEA) of the Association of American Medical Colleges (AAMC). In 1998, I served as chair of the WVU Faculty Senate. I am former chair of the University Visiting Committee of the WVU Extension Service. In 2000, I was on sabbatical at the University of Dundee, Scotland, studying outcomes-based education and the assessment of student competence. Based on that experience, I have written articles and have spoken about the topic at a number of medical schools. I collaborated with an international consortium, the International Virtual Medical School (IVIMEDS), to increase access to medical education worldwide through the development of virtual medical education curriculum blending evidence-based e-learning and face-to-face educational activities. In 2002–04, I served as the national chair of the AAMC's Group on Educational Affairs' (GEA) section on undergraduate medical education. I conducted internal reviews of Oman Medical College as part of their accreditation process, starting in 2004. I have been an active member of the Society of Directors of Research in Medical Education (SDRME) and currently serve as its communications committee chair. I am the recent past-chair (2009) of the Generalists in Medical Education, a national organization whose mission is to "promote innovation and collaboration in medical education." In 2010, I received the Servant Leadership Award from the Generalists. In 2011, I received the Career Educator Award from the SGEA of the AAMC.

I feel fortunate to have selected a profession that I truly enjoyed, and to have had colleagues with whom it was a pleasure to work. I feel a deep sense of commitment to WVU and especially to the School of Medicine. I am very grateful for the opportunities for professional growth that I have had during my medical education career here. I ask that I be permitted to remain affiliated with the university and School of Medicine as an emeritus professor so that I can continue teaching and taking on special projects as needed. I look forward to an opportunity to make future contributions, and wish you continued success with the School of Medicine.

Sincerely,

James M. Shumway, PhD
Associate Dean for Medical Education
Professor of Medicine and Pediatrics

NOTE: In November of 2014, following Jamie's death, the Generalists in Medical Education decided that the Servant Leadership Award would be renamed the Jamie Shumway Servant Leadership Award. He was one of the organizing members of this professional association.

Epilogue

Being "off belay" means being in a place of relative safety, but when it comes to writing, I'm still uncomfortable. I look at it as a new dimension for me to tell my stories. These stories take reflection, and reflection is a good thing that many of us don't slow down enough to do. I've been lucky to have the ability to reflect on my life, even if it is because of my physical condition and my disease. I see luck as something that a random event gives you, but you have to have awareness to know you've been lucky. I can't say I wanted or was blessed with this disease, but life creates unexpected opportunities.

This book has been over three years in the making. I wanted you to understand why and how I chose to write this tome. It first started when I created a forty-page outline of things I wanted to write about. It continued with recorded interviews that were turned into transcripts. I would talk to friends and family, telling them my stories, and answering questions about them. Many people helped me create these transcripts. Many friends were involved, including Greg Good, Rob Klein, Candice Elliott, Kim Shultz-Park, Mary Wimmer, and Paul Turner. My family—Betsy; Wesley; my mother, Berte; and my brother, Ralph—were all part of it, too. Kim Helmick, my administrative assistant at work, helped by retyping the two previously published articles that are included in this book. Together, we created about five hundred pages of transcripts and text. All of these people contributed during the earlier stages of my final product.

Another strategy that helped me recall some of my stories came from the thousands of photographs I'd taken. Before 2000, I used Kodachrome slide film. Now, everything is digital. I got help from friends and family to scan slides into digital files when I could no longer do this. Ann Chester and Jim McGraw came after work for a while to visit, and they scanned slides while we talked. Wesley and his friend Sean Marique scanned some of them, and so did Kim Shultz-Park and Betsy. While I worked on different sections of the book, I could look at the pictures to relive my adventures.

I was surprised by what I remembered and what I did not remember. As I worked on this project, it was like my memory would come and go, drop in and out. It surprises me what I can recall vividly, which are often the earlier memories, while recent memory is fleeting. I see past memories in my mind with clarity, as if they'd just happened. They are familiar and full of comfort. There are also my dreams, and when I'm dreaming, it's as if I'm still physical and active, not limited by my disease.

There are many stories I have not told in this book. Some stories just stand out. My short-term memory is suspect, but I have faith in my long-term memory. When I think about what I wanted the stories to do, I think about my trip to Nepal. In telling the stories of that trip, it strikes me as being the most complete in terms of who I am, the most representative of me. There are the impressions of the culture, so different from what we experience in America. There is the connection to my outdoor activities and climbing by being so close to Everest and Annapurna, two of the world's classic climbs, ones I'd read about. The connection to my position at the university was included as the instigation for the trip. Traveling in a third-world area allowed me to share some of the ways we had to think quickly on our feet in order to get where we needed to go. And, most importantly, I was involved with saving a life. There was such variety and adventure in this one trip that made it the kind of story I yearned to share.

So I got to the point where I had captured the essence of my stories in the transcripts my friends and family helped me to assemble. The problem was that transcripts aren't as interesting to read as crafted stories. I wanted to create a narrative, in first person, from my point of view, something that other people would enjoy.

I told one of my physicians, Josh Dower, about my interest in writing a memoir. He, in turn, looked for a writer to work with me and met a person he thought might be able to help. Josh suggested that it would be a good idea to talk with her about my memoir project. That's how I came to meet and work with Renée Nicholson. It was a freezing January evening, with snow thick on the ground, when we all assembled in my living room to see if she could help me. Renée shared with me that, although she'd written and published her own writings, she'd never worked in collaboration with someone to help write his book. However, she was willing to look at my outline and transcripts to see how she might help me.

Together, Renée and I started to shape the transcripts into stories, the ones included in this book. She would take the raw material and create a draft, and we would read together, so I could make additions and changes. She taught me different writing techniques and how to connect various aspects of my life through the stories. She helped draw out my thoughts and feelings. I think that all writing has educational value, and I have also explored its deeper level. I may have ended my professional career prematurely; however, this book gave me something important and meaningful to do, and that's why I chose to write it.

Now that I'm at the end of the book, it's like a double-edged sword. The first edge is that the completion of the book is what I wanted to do before I die. And I accomplished that. But the other edge is a bit of sadness, because so much more will happen, but I won't be here to experience it. But books are also experiences of their own. Writing a book helps create an infinite number of experiences for readers, and they can go with the stories to places they may not be able to go themselves. The relationship each reader has with my book will be unique, so I will, in a sense, still get to experience more of life through them. It's one of the hopeful aspects of writing.

Even after having written in professional contexts, and having created the forty-page outline of what I wanted to write about, and having sat with friends and family to record the stories, and having those turned into nearly five hundred pages of transcripts, and after months of working with Renée on crafting the raw material into the many pages that it takes to create a book, I will tell you this: *I don't have much confidence in my writing skills.* When I was in grammar school, I was put in a lower reading level, and from that point on, I had a dislike of reading and writing and no confidence in those skills. But I was cut short in my career, and writing this book gave me a productive alternative to working in the more traditional sense. So I'm not surprised to be writing.

Amazed? Yes. I am amazed that writing would be so important to me, given my current circumstances, since I can't actually execute the physical writing part.

Writing this book has given me a strong sense of purpose. Twice a week for many months, Renée and I sat in my kitchen, working on this book; and as we did, the long, cold winter melted into spring, and then into the humid, hot summer. It allowed me to access my memories, and it now allows me to share them with you. I struggle to stay in the present and not imagine the future with my disease. Being with my family and seeing friends helps me to stay in the present. Writing this book gives me a reason to stay alive.

REFERENCES CITED

Burmeister, Walter F. 1978. *Appalachian Waters V: The Upper Ohio & Its Tributaries*. Oakton, Virginia: Appalachian Books.

Burrell, Bob, and Paul Davidson. 1982. *Wild Water West Virginia*. Hillsborough, North Carolina: Menasha Ridge Press.

Longfellow, Henry Wadsworth. 1858. "The Courtship of Miles Standish," in Henry Wadsworth Longfellow: A Maine Historical Society Website. http://www.hwlongfellow.org/poems_poem.php?pid=186

Pyle, Betsy. 1989. "Tandem in the Canyon: A double dose of BIG WATER," in *American Whitewater: Journal of the American Whitewater Affiliation*. Vol. 34, No. 2, March/April.

Shumway, Asahel Adams. 1909. *Genealogy of the Shumway Family in the United States of America*. New York: Tobias A. Wright.

Shumway, Jamie. 1988. "An Adventure: Dark Waters of Laurel Fork, Part 1," in *Mountain State Sierran*. Vol. 14, No. 3, May/June.

Shumway, Jamie. 1988. "An Adventure: Dark Waters of Laurel Fork, Part 2," in *Mountain State Sierran*. Vol. 14, No. 4, July/August.

Stevens, Larry. 1983. *The Colorado River in Grand Canyon: A Guide*. Flagstaff, Arizona: Red Lake Books.

ABOUT THE AUTHOR, HIS WRITING COACH, AND THE BOOK'S WEBSITE

JAMIE SHUMWAY GREW UP AND attended college as an undergraduate in Northern California. In high school, he learned to ski in the Sierras. During his first year at the University of the Pacific, a backpacking trip in Yosemite National Park ignited his passion for the outdoors. He moved to North Carolina in the early 1970s, chasing a failed relationship, but he pursued graduate studies at the University of North Carolina at Chapel Hill. During his studies, he expanded his outdoor pursuits to include rock climbing. Jamie earned his MEd and PhD degrees at the University of North Carolina and then took his first professional job at the University of Kentucky. While working as an educator in the health professions in Lexington, he developed skills

Renée Nicholson (L) held a microphone for Jamie during their presentation to a WVU wellness class in July 2014

in white-water boating with a local club. Jamie eventually moved to Morgantown, West Virginia, where he enjoyed a long career in medical education. Once in West Virginia, he continued to pursue outdoor interests and traveled internationally, frequently as part of his work. He retired earlier than planned because he faced a serious neurological disease: ALS, also known as Lou Gehrig's disease. While declining from ALS, he took on the new, important challenge of writing this book. In his memoir, he shares stories of his life and adventures as well as his strategy for dealing with a debilitating disease. He died at home in October of 2014, where he had been living with his wife and their son, who cared for him along with the support of their friends and family.

Renée Nicholson was Jamie's writing coach. Renée is an assistant professor in the multidisciplinary studies program at West Virginia University (WVU) and the author of the poetry collection *Roundabout Directions to Lincoln Center* and coeditor of *Bodies of Truth: Narratives of Illness, Disability, and Medicine*. Renée's performing career as a ballet dancer was cut short by the onset of rheumatoid arthritis, and now she helps patients with cancer write their life stories at WVU's Cancer Institute. She has served as assistant to the director of the West Virginia Writers' Workshop since 2007; she was named the 2011 Emerging Writer-in-Residence at Penn State Altoona; and she is a member of both the National Book Critics Circle and the Dance Critics Association. Renée's writing has appeared in *Midwestern Gothic*, *Poets & Writers*, *Paste*, *The Gettysburg Review*, and elsewhere, and she is the recipient of grants from the West Virginia Commission on the Arts, West Virginia Clinical and Translational Science Institute, and the Claude Worthington Benedum Foundation.

Website for *Off Belay: A Last Great Adventure* To learn more about Jamie Shumway and see more photographs from his life and adventures (including his travels in Nepal and Oman, and his canoe trips on the Colorado River in the Grand Canyon and on the Missinaibi River in northern Canada), go to **www.jamieshumway.com**. This companion website to *Off Belay: A Last Great Adventure* also includes more information about ALS, narrative medicine, and legacy projects.